NATURE
CONSERVANCY
COUNCIL

The Flow Country

The peatlands of
Caithness and Sutherland

D1438611

R A Lindsay, D J Charman, F Everingham, R M O'Reilly,
M A Palmer, T A Rowell and D A Stroud

Edited by D A Ratcliffe and P H Oswald

Contents

Acknowledgements

This report describes a large area of Scotland and a programme of survey which has extended over several years. The survey is the result of the efforts of a considerable number of people, whilst the report itself, during the 18 months of its production, has involved an even larger number of people, to all of whom we owe grateful thanks.

The Peatland Survey of Northern Scotland was funded by the Nature Conservancy Council's Chief Scientist Directorate, supplemented by the Scottish Field Survey Unit in 1984/85. We are most grateful to all the owners and occupiers for permission to survey their land and for the great kindness and interest shown by many of them during the course of our discussions with them. We thank the estate gamekeepers and agents who gave generously of their time and local knowledge. We are also indebted to the Forestry Commission and Fountain Forestry for permission to survey areas within forest industry holdings.

We thank Dr David Goode for initiating the project, Dr Derek Langslow for continued support in later years, and Dr Peter Pitkin for organising the Scottish Field Survey Unit's work on the peatlands.

The principal fieldwork was undertaken by Richard Lindsay, John Riggall, Fiona Burd, John Ratcliffe, Fiona Everingham, Sarah Garnett, Bob Missin, Sara Oldfield, Dr Jane Smart, David Stroud, Sylvia White, Dr Elizabeth Charter and Naomi Duxfield. Dr Chris Ferreira kindly offered much valuable information and advice during the course of the work, which we gratefully acknowledge.

We owe a great debt to the staff of the NCC's North-West Scotland Region, in particular to Dr Peter Tilbrook, Regional Officer, for his constant support and sound advice, Sandy MacLennan, Deputy Regional Officer, who was instrumental in setting up the original survey, and the Assistant Regional Officers for Caithness and Sutherland, Dr Stewart Angus, Lesley Cranna, Dr Terry Keatinge and Kristin Scott. Ian Mitchell also provided valuable information. Their help over the years has done much to ensure the smooth running of the survey programme.

The main stages of data analysis would not have been possible without the considerable efforts of John Riggall and Fiona Burd, who went to great lengths to tailor existing computer packages into a unified system which could accept the various types of data obtained from the survey. They were assisted by Carol Fox, Ian Cheesman and Sara Oldfield, to whom we are also grateful. Dr Stuart Ball provided a most valuable computerised mapping programme,

whilst Dr Chris Goody, Head of Data and Information Division, and his team, Brian Marsh, Bob Beattie and Valentine Francis, gave much help and support from central computing services.

Much of the map analysis has been carried out with the assistance of Doric Computer Systems Ltd, using the Arc/Info Geographic Information System. Indeed the majority of maps and associated area calculations which appear in the later chapters of this report could not have been produced in the time available but for the Arc/Info system and the efforts of Doric staff. Colin Willers in particular has spent a great deal of time on this work, for which we are especially grateful.

Several people gave valuable advice on particular aspects, notably Rob Soutar on forestry matters, Dr Ian McLean and Edward Milner on invertebrates, Dr Sarah Woodin on acid deposition, and Dr Martin Holdgate on the mires of southern Patagonia.

A number of people read and commented on the first draft of this report. The final version owes a substantial amount to the generous efforts of six people – Professor Hugo Sjörs, Emeritus Professor of the University of Uppsala, Sweden; Professor R S Clymo of Queen Mary College, London; Dr D A Ratcliffe, the NCC's Chief Scientist; Dr Stewart Angus; Dr Terry Keatinge; and Lesley Cranna. Professor Sjörs provided an enormous amount of information based on his lifetime's experience of bog systems around the world. Professor Clymo provided a critical review of, and much valuable detail for, the early chapters on peatland ecology. Dr Ratcliffe kindly took on the job of general editing, making a substantial contribution to the overall structure of the report and providing, in addition, the final chapter, which draws together all the threads in the conservation argument. Stewart Angus, Terry Keatinge and Lesley Cranna provided detailed, critical reviews based on the local perspective. We extend our deepest gratitude to all six for their efforts.

Other people who read the report and provided valuable advice and comments were Professor John Allen, Dr Martin Ball, Professor John Birks, Dr John Cross, David Duncan, Dr Tony Fox, Dr Martin Holdgate, Dr Peter Hulme, Dr Derek Langslow, Sandy MacLennan, Dr John Miles, Dr Michael Pienkowski and Dr Peter Tilbrook.

We are very grateful to Stuart Wallace for preparing many of the diagrams and to Fiona Burd, Lynda Davis and Alison Rothwell for several other illustrations. We also thank Janet Southey for her helpful advice and supervision of the illustrative material. Sandra Lackie and Sylvia White typed several sections of text, whilst David Dyer assisted with the collation of the list of references. Sylvia White also typed and formatted some of the larger tables.

Finally we record our warmest thanks to Philip Oswald for checking the bibliographical references and editing the text for publication.

Introduction

The north-west Highlands and Islands of Scotland contain some of the most spectacular scenery in Britain. They are celebrated as a region of high mountains and rugged moorland, where steepness of slope and abundance of bare rock prevail. These dramatic landscapes occupy much of Wester Ross and west Sutherland. In sharp contrast, however, the far north-eastern corner, in Caithness and east Sutherland, is a district of low-lying, gently undulating or even flat moorlands, more akin to the desolate rolling tundras of the Arctic regions.

The high mountains of the west have long invited exploration by naturalists, and their importance for plants and animals has become fairly well known. The importance of this western district was recognised in *Nature Reserves in Scotland* (Cmd 7814) with the proposal for a Special Conservation Area here, though this recommendation was not followed through in practice. The undramatic moorlands to the east remained largely unknown, though they had been described in 1911 by C B Crampton, a remarkable geologist whose interests included botany and plant ecology. By the late 1950s, Nature Conservancy surveyors had penetrated the east in places and described it as "the flow country" from the huge expanse of almost level bogland, "flow" being a northern term for any flat, deep and wet bog. This was clearly the largest continuous expanse in Britain of the type of peat moorland known to ecologists as "blanket bog". When more scattered areas in west Sutherland were included, the total extent of blanket bog in these two Districts (Caithness and Sutherland) proved to be 4000 km^2.

Priorities for survey nevertheless lay elsewhere and, after the identification of a number of outstandingly important areas of bog in apparently near-pristine condition, the Caithness and Sutherland flows were left to await fuller study in future. There was then nothing to indicate that they were under immediate threat from land-use change. A concerted effort at exploration and survey was finally mounted in the late 1970s, by which time the great scientific interest of these peatlands and their conservation importance internationally were clear.

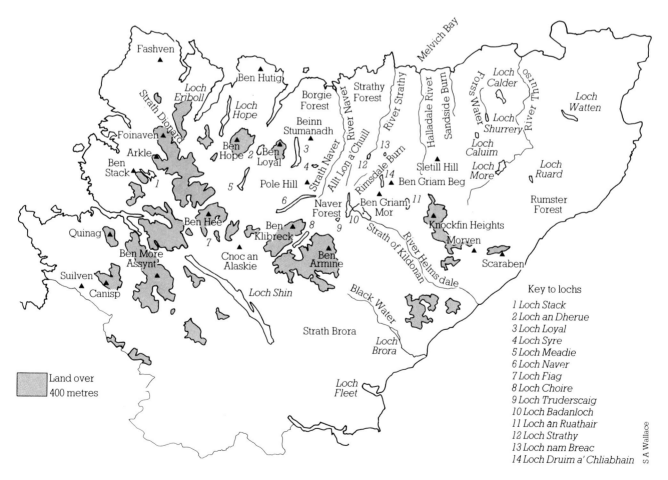

Figure 1a Caithness and Sutherland, indicating geophysical features referred to in the text. Land above the 400 m contour is also delineated.

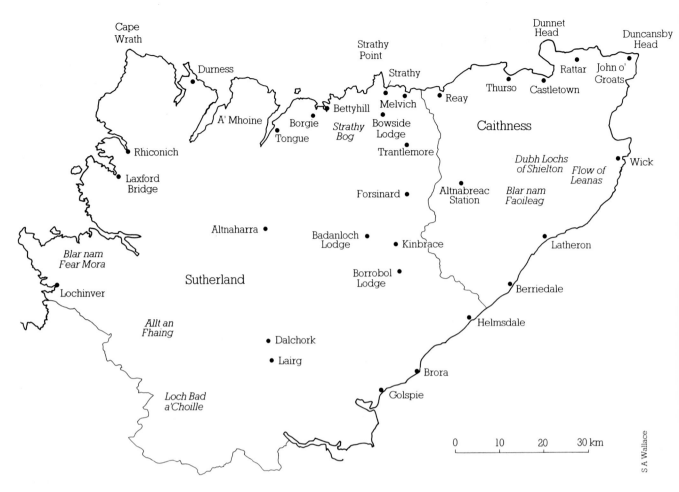

Figure 1b Caithness and Sutherland, indicating place names referred to in the text.

The Flow Country represents a complex ecosystem. It is covered with a deep mantle of peat containing, in its preserved pollen grains and other plant remains, a record of its development and controlling environment, beginning several thousand years ago. The surface is mostly a spongy, living layer of *Sphagnum* bog-moss which continually builds its level higher by upward growth but is in many places thrown into strange and distinctive patterns by swarms of small peaty pools. There are numerous larger lochs, some mainly peaty but some with firmer, stony or sandy margins, and many streams of varying size and character drain the moorlands. The whole is the summer breeding haunt of a fascinating bird fauna, which has much in common with that of the true Arctic tundras and represents a group of mainly northern and boreal species here inhabiting a southern and oceanic region. Spread over this large area, the numbers of several local moorland birds represent a substantial proportion of their total European populations south of the Baltic.

An account of this bird fauna, its nature conservation value and the threats to its future has already been presented in the Nature Conservancy Council's report *Birds, Bogs and Forestry* (Stroud, Reed, Pienkowski & Lindsay 1987), which contains a summary description of the peatlands as habitat. The present report deals in detail with the peatlands –

their development, structure, relations to environment, vegetation and flora. It is prefaced by an account of peatlands in general and blanket bog in particular, to provide a context for assessment of the scientific and nature conservation value of the Caithness and Sutherland examples. The main part of the report gives the results of the NCC's Peatlands Survey in characterising the field of ecological variation in these blanket bogs as the basis for a conservation strategy and programme. The impact of afforestation, as the main threat to the continued existence of these blanket bogs, is discussed briefly. The nature conservation requirements are then defined, in terms of peatland areas requiring protection.

In addition, the NCC has conducted surveys of lochs and of rivers in Caithness and Sutherland as separate studies. Although the river survey is incomplete, enough information has been gained to make parallel assessments and recommendations for conservation of these freshwater habitats. This analysis is presented in a separate section. For completeness, a summary of the bird surveys and recommendations is also given, and there is a final composite statement of the total nature conservation requirement, in terms of protected areas, when all three sets of interests are combined.

1   The development and hydrology of mire systems

Mires (bogs) are natural 'museums', where objects which have elsewhere vanished long ago are sometimes kept in a remarkable state of preservation. Celebrated examples are Lindow Man, now on display at the British Museum, and Tollund Man in Copenhagen Museum. This ability to preserve material is derived from a particular combination of environmental conditions. Wherever the ground surface is waterlogged and deoxygenated, decomposition of accumulated dead plant material is slowed down relative to areas of better oxygenation. Where this reduction in the rate of breakdown causes at least some dead plant material to be retained and carried over into the next season, the deposit resulting from this steady accumulation of organic matter is known as peat. The Scandinavian term *myr*, anglicised from Old Norse to "mire", refers to any ecosystem which accumulates peat (Goode & Ratcliffe 1977) and is therefore used here as the general term for peatlands, whatever the nutrient status or water flux.

Fraser (1948) discussed the range of conditions which lead to peat formation. Various factors promote waterlogging of the ground. Both the amount and distribution of precipitation, and factors which affect evapo-transpiration (water loss from the vegetation–ground surface) such as atmospheric humidity and air temperature, are important. Topography (slope and ground-form) and permeability of soil are also crucial factors. Then there are the factors which independently affect the rate of microbial decomposition of dead organic remains, notably pH, nature of plant material, degree of aeration (related to stagnation of waterlogging) and soil temperature.

Table 1 shows the interaction of the various factors which result in the formation of peat. Broadly, conditions for peat development are optimal in basins or on flat ground, underlain by clay or impermeable bedrock, in areas of acidic catchment, covered with especially fibrous vegetation, and under a climate with high, evenly distributed rainfall and relatively low temperatures. Fraser (1948) points out that soil temperature is affected by cloud cover, the interception of sunlight being an important factor in maintaining relatively low soil temperatures. The proximity of mountain masses helps in this,

particularly as the lowered temperatures affect the decomposer bacteria more than plant growth. Stach *et al.* (1975) – quoted by Hobbs (1986) – describe the ideal temperature for decomposition of organic material as between 35°C and 40°C, so that many wet areas in the tropics do not develop peat because the rate of decomposition outstrips that of accumulation. Under such conditions, peat accumulation is dependent on the acidity of the system rather than simply on waterlogging, because active bacteria generally prefer a neutral or alkaline pH. In contrast, fungi are more acid-tolerant, but generally demand oxygen (with the exception of yeasts) and are much slower at breaking down plant material. Thompson & Hamilton (1983) state that pH values of less than 5.5 are necessary in Africa for peat accumulation. In cooler climates, peat accumulates under conditions of high pH, but it is then often more highly humified and may itself be neutral or alkaline and base-rich: it is then usually known as fen peat.

Ivanov (1981), Clymo (1983) and Hobbs (1986) all give excellent summaries of the development and properties of bog systems, while Sjörs (1983) summarises the ideas of numerous previous workers concerning the origin of peat development. He identifies three primary pathways.

Pathways of peat development

1 Terrestrialisation of water bodies

Bodies of stagnant or near-stagnant open water develop anoxic layers in their bottom sediments. When dead aquatic or fen vegetation collapses into these layers at the end of the growing season, the remains cannot be attacked efficiently by the decomposer fauna and flora, so these accumulate year by year. Decomposition occurs even under the most anaerobic conditions, probably involving sulphur-metabolising bacteria (Clymo 1983) and perhaps also those which metabolise methane (Professor H Sjörs pers. comm.), but the process is much slower than under aerobic conditions.

With continued accumulation, the former water body eventually becomes completely filled with peat, but the general ground water table maintains anaerobic

	Inhospitable Extreme	Character	Hospitable Extreme
1	Low	Precipitation	High
2	Low	Number of days on which rain falls	High
3	Low	Atmospheric humidity	High
4	Low	Cloud cover	High
5	High	Temperature range	Low
6	High	Mean temperature	Low
7	High (90°)	Angle of slope	Low (0°)
8	Convex	Topography	Basin
9	High	Substrate permeability	Low
10	High	Substrate water pH and base-content	Low
11	High	Substrate-water aeration	Low
12	High	Nutrient status of vegetation	Low

Table 1

Factors affecting peat formation. These are the factors which are generally considered to play a significant part in determining the rate of peat accumulation in any locality. An extreme tendency to 'inhospitable' in 6, 7 and 11 will prevent peat formation however suitable the other factors may be. Blanket bog formation requires a marked or extreme tendency to 'hospitable' in 2,3,5,6,7,10 and 11.

conditions. At this point, however, if the climate is sufficiently wet, the central part of the peat expanse continues to accumulate material, whilst the margins, where the water table falls or becomes influenced by the mineral-enriched catchment, are subject to more rapid decomposition. The result is a steady elevation of the central part of the peat mass relative to the margins, forming the classic dome of a "raised bog". See Ivanov (1981, pp. 16–18) for a detailed account of this process.

2 Primary mire formation

Sjörs (1983) regards this as an under-recognised means of peat formation, whereby wet ground freshly exposed by processes such as crustal uplift forms peat directly on previously unvegetated mineral ground. Examples of this can be seen around the Isle of Hailuoto, in the Gulf of Bothnia, where isostatic recoil exposes many hundreds of hectares from beneath the Baltic every century.

3 Paludification of dry ground

Where ground which was once dry subsequently becomes wet and then covered by peat, the process is known as paludification. Examples of this are many and various, though perhaps the most frequently quoted are areas paludified by wetness of climate. Godwin (1981) gives a striking photograph of a paludified rock capped by a significant thickness of peat. In sufficiently cool, wet climates even quite steeply sloping ground can become paludified; under such conditions terrestrialisation may not necessarily occur, but the two processes are often juxtaposed, so that basins become peat-filled by terrestrialisation, whilst the surrounding slopes become peat-clad by the more direct process of paludification. The total peat mass then usually becomes continuous at the surface, so that stratigraphic study is necessary to elucidate the range of developmental processes involved.

The two major processes of acidic bog formation in Britain have been terrestrialisation and paludification. Together they have produced more than 1,300,000 ha of commercially exploitable peat reserves (Robertson & Jowsey 1968) and an even greater total area of peat soils, a large proportion of which is located in northern and western parts of Scotland (see Figure 2). The total area of peat-covered ground is, however, not accurately documented because of problems in definition and survey. Most quantitative reviews (e.g. Robertson & Jowsey 1968) are therefore restricted to peat deposits which have some potential for exploitation.

Peat and blanket bog development

In cool, continuously wet regions with predominantly gentle relief, conditions are suitable for the paludification of entire landscapes. Constant precipitation with low evaporation tends to leach porous terrain such as glacial till, leading to the production of an iron pan. This podsolisation further helps to waterlog the base-deficient leached soil and create conditions in which the acidophilous members of the genus *Sphagnum* can begin to carpet the ground in a process of paludification (Fraser 1948; Pearsall 1950; Hobbs 1986). *Sphagnum* species are chemically poor in nitrogen and phosphorus and are therefore not easily broken down by soil micro-organisms (Gorham 1966; Coulson & Butterfield 1978; Dickinson 1983, Figure 5.3). In addition, although all living tissues produce H^+ ions, *Sphagnum* has such a high cation exchange ability (CEA) that it easily binds metal ions to its surface at the expense of H^+ ions, which are released from the plant into the external solution, thereby making the surrounding soil water increasingly acidic (Clymo 1967).

Much the same process of acidification occurs in the central parts of basins which are in an advanced state of terrestrialisation. Where basins are surrounded by a zone of substantial water

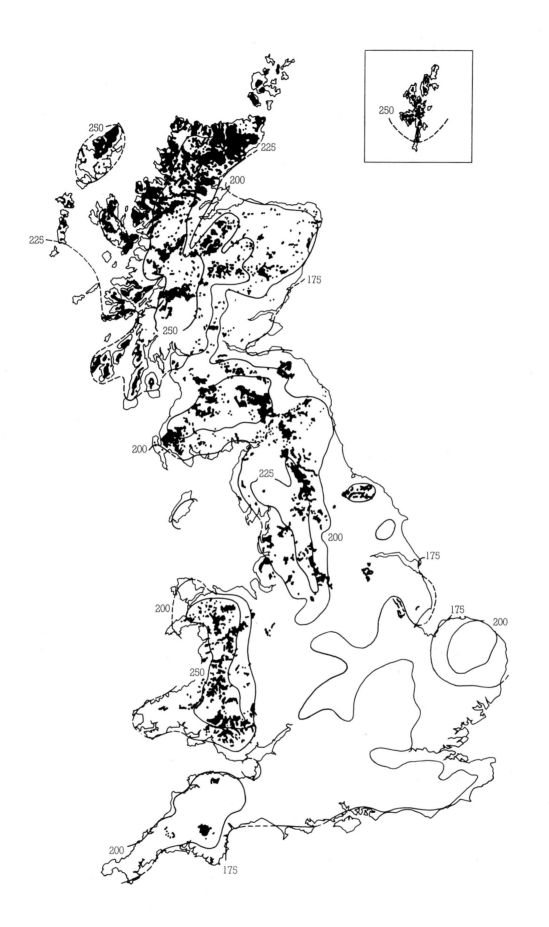

Figure 2 Major deep peat (bog) deposits in Britain (based on Taylor 1983, LANDSAT imagery and unpublished NCC survey data). This does not show the total extent of peat soils, which would cover a much wider area. Isopleths for annual average number of "rain days" (1901-1930) are shown. The close correlation between the isopleth for 200 "rain days" and the limit of extensive peat formation is evident, although the warmer conditions of East Anglia cause this relationship to break down. A "rain day" is defined by the Meteorological Office as a 24-hour period during which at least 0.25 mm precipitation is recorded.

movement, the mound of peat is confined by that seepage (Ivanov 1981; Ingram 1982). However, where the basin is not delimited by such a feature, the mound of peat encourages swamping around its marginal slopes by water flow from the dome and general impedance of the surrounding ground water table. Mire development may thus extend outwards from the original basin quite rapidly if the surrounding relief is gentle, to form massifs with shallow gradients and wide marginal fens of up to 2 km (Ivanov 1981). This is an intermediate state of development, which may continue its lateral expansion if the topography is suitable.

If the climate is sufficiently cool and wet, therefore, basins, plateaux and gentle slopes come to be swamped by peat, formed from acidic vegetation composed largely of *Sphagnum* bog-mosses. Slopes of up to 20° are commonly cloaked in this way, and in extreme conditions even 30° slopes may be thus affected (Ratcliffe 1964; Ingram 1967; Goode & Ratcliffe 1977). Where both terrestrialisation of basins and paludification of plateaux and gentle slopes occur at different places in the same landscape, the individual mire units may eventually begin to coalesce to form what Ivanov (1981) calls *mire macrotopes* (see Chapter 2). These are equivalent to Sjörs' (1948) mire complexes, which combine several congruent and hydrologically interrelated mire sites into a continuous peatland system. Even the influence of base-rich rock (including limestone) may be overridden by paludification, except on steep slopes, and the tendency to an enveloping mantle of peat led H Godwin to describe it as "blanket bog" in preference to Osvald's "cover moss" (Osvald 1949; Pearsall 1950). Within any one area of such bog, the underlying peat varies considerably in depth and humification, according especially to the angle of slope and degree of waterlogging.

Atmospheric flushing and rate of peat formation

High rainfall, however, creates contrasting effects – waterlogging, which tends to encourage peat accumulation, and flushing, which tends to increase peat breakdown. The total annual rainfall and number of wet days can combine to produce optimal conditions for vigorous blanket bog development, but Bellamy & Bellamy (1966) have suggested that, if the annual volume of precipitation exceeds the limits of this optimum, the mire surface may become subject to marked "atmospheric flushing", resulting in reduced rates of peat accumulation. Evidence for flushing is visible to a certain extent in all examples of ombrotrophic mire in Britain. For example, *Sphagnum papillosum* is regarded as a species of minerotrophic mires in Finland but is the dominant species on many of Britain's ombrotrophic bogs.

The effect arises because larger volumes of precipitation entering a site produce an increase in the flux of oxygen and electrolytes through the surface layers of peat, particularly in oceanic areas where spray can contribute significant quantities to precipitation. The greater the flux, the greater the rate of humification of freshly-dead plant material before this can reach the anoxic lower layer or *catotelm* (see below). Ingram (1967) discusses the role of increased water flow and nutrient flux associated with water-tracks, or flushes, on mire expanses and emphasises the important role played by the *rate* of electrolyte supply, as opposed to the *concentration* of dissolved solids, which is normally measured when oligotrophic vegetation is being investigated. He also points out that the species composition of such areas is often *Molinia*-dominated. His field measurements at Inverpolly, however, suggest that the dominance of *Molinia* is not necessarily always linked to high oxygen flux in the peat as proposed by Jefferies (1915). He suggests instead that high concentrations of toxins such as hydrogen sulphide in relatively stagnant areas of the mire surface might be more of a limiting factor. The presence of *Molinia* in mire systems can therefore be used as an indication of low concentrations of hydrogen sulphide.

Armstrong & Boatman (1966) provide evidence which supports Ingram's (1967) suggestion of hydrogen sulphide toxicity, by demonstrating that living *Molinia* roots are only found where hydrogen sulphide is absent. They show that such conditions occur in flushed peats, which have high oxygen levels to depths of 16–18 cm, whereas in stagnant conditions oxygen penetrates to less than 6 cm.

Coulson & Butterfield (1978) have demonstrated that the decomposition rate of peat is limited by the "palatability" of the dead plant material. Where this has grown under conditions of high nutrient supply, the decomposers in the peat are able to break the material down more rapidly than plant material grown under normal oligotrophic conditions. N was found to be a limiting factor in this process. Increased rainfall amounts can thus be expected to generate vegetation richer in nutrients and so increase the rate of peat decomposition. However, the increased input of dissolved solids to oceanic areas is generally high in cations such as Na, K and Mg but low in particulate matter rich in N and P (Groenendael, Hochstenbach, Mansfeld & Roozen 1975).

Under conditions of maximum stagnation and waterlogging, therefore, the peat is composed largely of *Sphagnum* in an unhumified condition; in better-drained or in flushed situations, the remains of vascular plants make a much larger contribution and occur in a more humified condition. The climatic and biotic "peat template" (Bellamy & Pritchard 1973) produced in blanket bog is nevertheless too severe an environment for most plants, and a highly specialised range of species comes to characterise the peat surface.

Characteristics of peat soils

There are at least three ways in which the hydrology of peat systems differs fundamentally from that of mineral soils.

First, the great mass of peat which forms a bog is not simply a superficial deposit interposed between bedrock and surface vegetation to a thickness determined largely by geomorphological processes. The peat depth and shape are both products of biological processes directly comparable with organic growth. The factors which determine this growth are climate, the nature of the immediate terrain, and the rate of peat accumulation. A peat body is thus not only of a biologically determined shape, but is generally a continually growing feature. Such characteristics are in marked contrast to most mineral soil deposits.

The same arguments apply to the shape of the undulations on a bog surface. In a mineral soil, such undulations and irregularities are largely a product of physical processes, whereas the patterns of pools, hummocks and ridges on a mire surface are a direct result of organic growth and surface hydrology.

Finally, because the components of peat soil are organic rather than inorganic, drying such material tends to produce physical changes resulting from aeration, shrinkage and decomposition of the organic matter (98% of the soil – see below). Such changes are irreversible, and a peat soil thus affected can only recover from such effects by fresh growth of vegetation and subsequent accumulation of peat. In mineral soils, the process of 'dewatering' is reversible (except in some clays). The ability of bog peat to hold water is quite remarkable. Individual *Sphagnum* plants can absorb many times their own weight of water, and Hobbs (1986) gives figures of 6% (by volume) of solids to 94% water in a 5 metre sample core of peat. In other words, as Goodwillie (1987) observes, there are fewer solids in peat than there are in the same volume of milk.

Three types of water are generally recognised as forming part of the peat matrix, though the boundaries between these three states are not sharp – the intracellular water, tightly-bound intraparticle water, and loosely-bound interparticle (interstitial) water, which is the only source of mobile water under most natural conditions. Despite their high water content, bogs have a significant shear strength because peat has a fibrous nature even when highly decomposed. The great physical stability of the peat mass is derived from the immense cation exchange ability (CEA) of *Sphagnum* peat (Hobbs 1986). The low rate of cation input from rainfall means that up to 80–90% of exchange sites may still retain the weakly bound H^+ ion instead of a metallic ion. The proportion of H^+ ions still attached to exchange sites is lower than this in blanket peat and fenland peat and is also lower in coastal areas, where rain and spray contribute considerable amounts of magnesium ions which bind strongly to the exchange sites. The ash (i.e. non-organic) content of

peat can be as low as 2%, though Iceland's volcanic activity gives some blanket peats there an ash content of 20% (Clymo 1983, and see Chapter 3). Higher rates of solute uptake, associated with water flow through the peat, can also increase the ash content. Lefebvre, Langlois, Lupien and Lavallée (1984) give values of 30% for flushed muskeg. Blanket bog peat, though not flushed to this extent, typically has a higher ash concentration than raised bog peat.

The high CEA gives peat a very high liquid limit – i.e. the limit at which the peat, under pressure, begins to flow. The mound of peat is not therefore generally in danger of collapsing, despite its essentially liquid state. Increased humification, which increases the concentration of metal ions in the peat matrix, lowers this liquid limit.

With these characteristics, the dynamics of peat masses are evidently more complex than is generally the case for mineral soils, and their hydrology far more sensitive to interference. The fundamental differences between peat and mineral soils are perhaps most clearly revealed by examining the way in which the character and shape of a peat body, or "mire unit", are controlled.

Morphology of the peat body ("diplotelm" dynamics)

Granlund (1932) and Wickman (1951), in some of the earliest studies of mire hydromorphology, generated a model which identified a link between climate, bog diameter and maximum height of the dome. This tentative model has since been developed by Ingram (1982) into the Ground Water Mound Theory. This theory is based on the original concept of ground water mounds as defined by Childs (1969), as well as work carried out at Dun Moss and a substantial body of Russian research now available through Ivanov (1981). Whilst Clymo (1984) has shown in general terms that bog growth is limited by the quotient of input to decay in the lower layer of a bog, Ingram's model permits the calculation of the outer limit of stable shapes for a site under a given set of conditions.

The model demonstrates that, under a given climatic regime, a hemi-ellipse is generally the maximum upper limit to the domed profile for the bog to remain stable. This maximum profile can be described with the use of the Dupuit–Forchheimer Approximation. It is determined by a function of bog diameter, the amount of precipitation, and is related to the duration of the severest drought period. The bog retains its stability through dry summers and wet winters by swelling and contracting in what Prytz (1932) described as *mooratmung* (mire-breathing). Fox (1984) has demonstrated this process for Cors Fochno in Wales, where an annual surface rise and fall of 15 cm was recorded.

Essentially, the Ground Water Mound theory is concerned with the lower layer of peat, often many metres thick, which gives the mire its overall shape.

This is termed the "catotelm" and represents the body of compressed peat, which slows down water flow from the bog to such an extent that the mound of peat remains fully saturated simply through precipitation (Ingram 1982; Ingram & Bragg 1984).

The upper, surface layer, or "acrotelm", is extremely shallow (only 10–50 cm) and includes the living surface of vegetation. This thin but tough layer covers the deep mound of dead but saturated peat of the catotelm. The acrotelm is the layer of most active water movement, with water flowing many times faster through its structure than through the more amorphous, and often more humified, peat of the catotelm. It is also the layer in which the vegetation, root mat and, more strikingly, most of the small-scale surface patterns so typical of bog systems occur (see Figure 3).

Ivanov (1981) summarises the character of the two layers as follows –

Catotelm

(Ivanov's "inert layer")

- a constant or little changing water content;
- a very slow exchange of water with the subadjacent mineral strata and the area surrounding it;
- very slow hydraulic conductivity in comparison with the acrotelm (a difference of 3–5 orders of magnitude);
- no access of atmospheric oxygen to the pores of the peat soil;
- no aerobic micro-organisms and a reduced quantity of other kinds in comparison with the acrotelm.

The thin surface layer, which sits upon the catotelm, cloaking it from external influences, has the following properties –

Acrotelm

(Ivanov's "active layer")

- an intensive exchange of moisture with the atmosphere and the surrounding area;
- frequent fluctuations in the level of the water table and a changing content of moisture;
- high hydraulic conductivity and water yield and a rapid decline of these with depth;
- periodic access of air to interstitial spaces during periods of lowered water table;
- a relatively large quantity of aerobic bacteria and micro-organisms facilitating the rapid decomposition and transformation into peat of each year's dying vegetation;
- the presence of a living plant cover, which constitutes the top layer of the acrotelm, and which binds the whole surface together into a 'skin', preventing the water-saturated catotelm from starting to flow, even under heavy rains.

Acrotelm dynamics and surface patterns

Crampton (1911) was one of the first authors to describe the maze of peat lochans (*dubh lochain*) which occupy the higher, flatter parts of the Caithness flows. Since then a wide range of explanations has been proposed for the striking surface patterns which are found on so many boreal mires, from the early accounts of Osvald (1923), Aario (1932) and Tansley (1939), through the papers by Sjörs (1948), Ratcliffe & Walker (1958), Ruuhijärvi

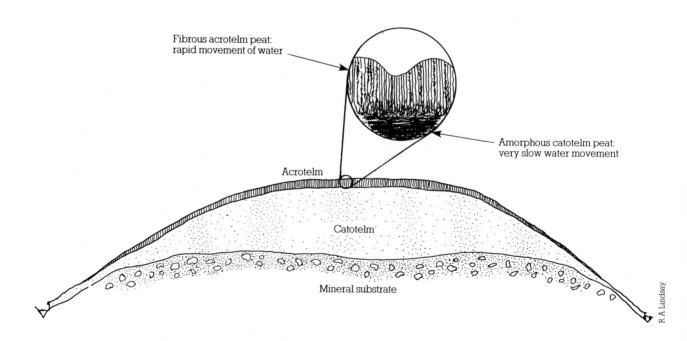

Figure 3 The "diplotelmic" profile (Ingram 1982) of a watershed blanket bog, illustrating (inset) the change in detailed structure from the surface layer ("acrotelm") to the underlying peat ("catotelm"). The vertical scale, particularly of the acrotelm, has been greatly exaggerated.

(1960) and Eurola (1962), to the detailed studies carried out on British patterned mires by Boatman & Tomlinson (1973), Goode (1973), Boatman, Goode & Hulme (1981), Barber (1981) and Hulme (1986). Indeed the use of surface pattern classifications is now becoming widespread in national peatland inventories (e.g. Moen 1985; Wells & Zoltai 1985; Eurola & Holappa 1985; Lindsay, Riggall & Burd 1985). The origin and dynamics of these patterns have been, and continue to be, the subject of much conjecture and debate.

The well-documented patterned landscapes of the tundra, where ice-action plays such an important part in generating the surface pattern, offer little in the way of mechanisms to explain patterns in the most oceanic regions of the boreal. The majority of such oceanic fringes remain relatively free from ice throughout the year and therefore some mechanism other than freezing is required to explain the origin of their patterning. Even in less oceanic parts of the boreal, patterns may not be generated by freezing, but could be accentuated by its effects.

Osvald (1923) suggested the term *regenerations-komplex* in relation to the hummocks and hollows of the Swedish raised bog Komosse, and this term was adopted by Tansley (1939), Godwin & Conway (1939) and Pearsall (1950) as "regeneration complex" to mean cyclic replacement of hummocks by hollows and *vice versa*, through differential upward growth of these contrasting surface features.

Troll (1944) proposed that the patterns might result from some form of soil creep. Pearsall (1956) subsequently theorised that open pool formation, as found at Strathy and Druimbasbie Bogs in Sutherland, was not necessarily part of the cyclic system, but might instead result either from peat splitting owing to surface tensions resulting from downslope movement, like crevasses in glaciers, or from furrowing due to shrinkage of the peat body since the onset of what he considered to be the contemporary dry climatic regime.

Pearson (1954) and Moore & Bellamy (1974) present evidence from Muckle Moss, in Northumberland, which clearly demonstrates that mass movement can occur, because a fence line has twice been bent, then broken, in a downslope direction. A series of crescentic pools is taken as further evidence of surface splitting and peat movement. There is no doubt in this case that the peat body has moved, and it is therefore interesting to note the difference between this site and normal patterned mires. First, the site lies in a climatic region within which open pools are not recorded on ombrotrophic mire surfaces (see Figure 4). The nearest example, apparently itself on the limit of such patterning, is Butterburn Flow, on the Cheviot divide, within a slightly wetter climatic region than Muckle Moss. Secondly, the pools are not orientated in the same way as typically crescentic or circular boreal patterns, but are clearly of a type and orientation consistent with mass downward movement and surface splitting. Thirdly, the mire is actually a valley

mire which is only barely, if at all, ombrotrophic and therefore has a significantly different pattern of water movement from that of entirely ombrotrophic peatlands. Finally, the moving fence was erected by the Forestry Commission when it drained and planted the lower end of the valley mire. Such drainage and consequent shrinkage could be expected to have a marked effect on such a wet, deep peat deposit, including the mass movement of the peat body by gravity slide, particularly in view of Hobbs' (1986) observations on the liquid limit of peat.

Sjörs (1961) discusses the phenomenon of patterning throughout the boreal zone, particularly in relation to the so-called "string fens" or *aapa* mires. Here he points out that the patterns of ridges and pools (or "flarks") are not correlated with downslope movement of the peat because extensive patterns develop on very shallow gradients. He also points to the historical stability of these patterns, stating that there is little evidence for infilling of flarks. He identifies two general forms of patterning, namely those which are derived purely from peat growth, and those which are influenced by, or are a product of, permafrost. Most importantly, Sjörs regards the tundra ecosystem, with flooded frost polygons overlying permafrost, as being quite different from the patterns of boreal peatlands where permafrost is absent.

The generalised diagram of ombrotrophic mire surface patterns in Britain provided by Lindsay *et al.* (1985) is modified in Figure 4 on the basis of interpretation from more detailed aerial photographs. Overall trends in surface patterning are apparent, with increasing proportions of hollows and pools making up the pattern as the climate becomes progressively cooler and wetter to the north and west.

Goode (1973), using Darcy's Law of water flow through a porous medium, has constructed a model which defines a relationship between the scale of surface microtopography and the overall gradient of the mire surface (see Figure 5), and he re-emphasises the relative stability of such patterns on the Silver Flowe (Boatman, Goode & Hulme 1981). Hulme (1986) has also shown the stability of these patterns. Smart (1982) confirms both the relative persistence of such patterns and the early genesis of pools, from a site in Caithness, suggesting that Pearsall's ideas of surface movement due to the build-up of peat (Pearsall 1956) were incorrect. Korchunov, Kusmin & Ivanov (1980) demonstrate the genesis and relational stability of both hollows and pools throughout the development sequence of a raised mire system.

The link between slope, surface pattern and vegetation is described in detail by Ivanov (1981), confirming the general relationship between surface pattern and slope identified by Goode (1973). Ivanov's synthesis of Russian research shows that the stability of the surface layer determines the stability or otherwise of the massif's major water exchanges.

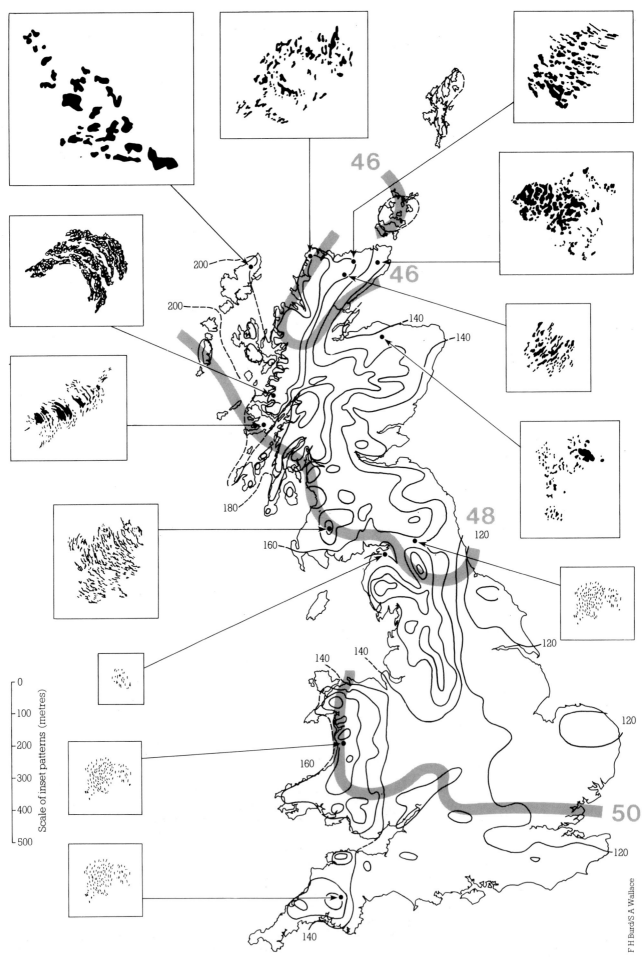

Figure 4 Distribution and general structure, seen from above, of bog surface patterns recorded from a range of sites throughout Britain. Patterns have been mapped directly from aerial photographs standardised to the same scale. Pools and hollows are shaded black, ridges and hummocks white. Isopleths for annual average number of "wet days" are also indicated, as compiled by Ratcliffe (1968) from data published in *British Rainfall* (1951-1960) (see Figure 12b). Superimposed are the isotherms for three average means of daily mean temperatures over the period 1901-1930 – 46°F (7.8°C), 48°F (8.9°C) and 50°F (10°C).

Overall mire gradient

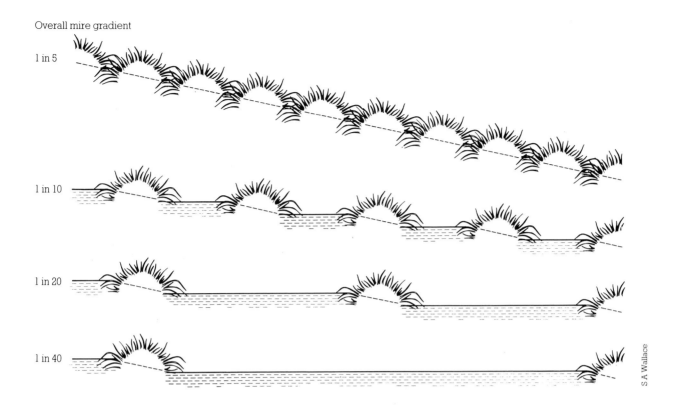

Figure 5 Generalised model indicating the relationship between ridge microtopes and pool microtopes on sites possessing differing overall hydrological gradients. If the gradient of the water table within ridges is maintained at 1:5, for example, bogs with overall shallow gradients support wider pools than areas with steeper hydrological gradients. (Based on Goode 1973.)

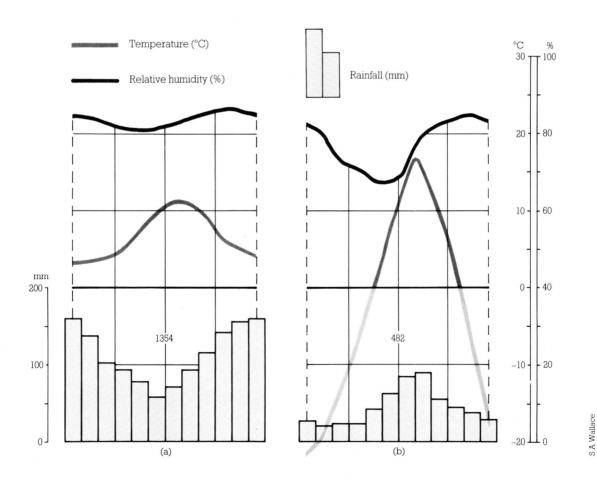

Figure 6 Climate diagrams for (a) Fort William in Highland Region and (b) central Siberia. (Taken from *Physico-geographical Atlas of the World* (Academy of Sciences of the U.S.S.R. 1964).)

The stability of this surface layer is ensured by the surface "strip-ridge" pattern or microtopography (Ivanov's "microtope"; see Chapter 2 and Figure 5). The vegetation both generates and is then controlled by the surface pattern. Ivanov subsequently gives a wide range of mathematical solutions for the arrangement of surface patterns (microtopes), demonstrating that these patterns are in fact the major source of hydrological stability within the mire system rather than, as is so frequently suggested, being products of instability.

The patterned ground of the tundra

Vast tracts of organic terrain characterise certain regions of the Arctic, such as the enormous expanse of the Hudson Bay lowlands in Ontario and Manitoba or the drainage basin of the Ob and Yenisey in western Siberia. Here, the landscapes take on a superficial resemblance to the Caithness and Sutherland plain, with vast numbers of shallow lakes lying in a peat matrix and forming what Ivanov (1981) terms a "bog-lake complex". The relatively dry climate, the prolonged freezing in winter and the short but warm summers in these regions are, however, in marked contrast to the permanently cool, but never really cold, and extremely humid conditions described above and also in Chapters 3

and 4 for blanket bogs in northern Scotland. Farther south, within the *taiga* zone, the juxtaposition of forest or the presence of an open or depauperate tree growth on or around the organic deposits also contrasts with the treeless character of British and Irish blanket bogs.

The great flows of Caithness and Sutherland have a quite striking resemblance, at first sight (see Sage 1986, Plates 2.2 and 5.5), to some of the tundras of the Arctic region – a correspondence often remarked on by overseas visitors. This analogy with Arctic tundra should not be taken too literally because the similarity is ecologically superficial. However, Pruitt (1978) notes that the word "tundra" originates from the Finnish word *tunturi*, a region in northern Finland which is simply "beyond the poleward limit of trees" and which consists of many vegetation types. Arctic tundra also includes dry types, but the wet types most resembling blanket bog are especially developed on areas where permafrost maintains permanently waterlogged ground during the period of summer thaw, but most often under conditions of low annual precipitation and atmospheric humidity (see Figure 6). The organic layer is usually much shallower than in blanket bog. Patterning, including pool and hollow development in the tundra also gives superficial similarities to many of our blanket bog pool and hummock systems.

2 Classification of mire systems

The vernacular terminology for peatlands in Britain is far too loose to be of value in classification. "Peat moss" (or, in place names, "Moss") and 'flow' are applied in northern England and Scotland to areas of flat, deep peat bog in both lowland and upland situations, while "mire" is a term used widely for a variety of bogs, but especially lowland fens. The taxonomy of peatland systems in Britain and Ireland has, in fact, lagged behind that in continental Europe, and a brief review of different approaches is relevant. While this report follows the Scandinavian use of "mire" as a general term for peatlands, it deals with types which in Britain are usually known as "bogs", and we have preferred to use "blanket bog" because it is so well established a name in the literature.

The taxonomy of peatlands is complex, and blanket bogs give special problems. Moore (1984) has observed that "one group of mires in Europe, the blanket mires . . . has been neglected in the development of classificatory work". This chapter will examine the wider application of these concepts, the range of categories and the relevant terminology developed by peatland ecologists around the world. It is intended as context to the treatment of the Caithness and Sutherland mires.

General criteria for peatland classification

Dierssen (1982), following Grosse-Brauckmann (1962), summarises a wide range of criteria which have been used in mire classification. The main attributes used for distinguishing between mire systems include –

1 Morphology – whether the site is domed, producing raised mire, or undulating, with blanket bog.

2 Ecological development (ontogeny) – based on what the peat record indicates of the site's development, including the ideas of primary, secondary and tertiary peat development (Moore & Bellamy 1974). It also includes the concepts of topogenous, soligenous and ombrogenous (von Post and Granlund 1926), as well as Du Rietz's (1954) concepts of ombrotrophy and minerotrophy (rain- and groundwater-fed).

3 Geographic or topographic relationships – i.e. plateau, saddle, basin, valley. These have been commonly employed in broad classifications of British and Irish accounts of minerotrophic (fen) systems (e.g. Goode & Ratcliffe 1977; Wheeler 1984) but they are also one of the commonest systems for

distinguishing separate units within blanket mire landscapes (Osvald 1949; Ratcliffe & Walker 1958; Goode & Ratcliffe 1977).

The geomorphology of a site is given some prominence by the Austrian Mire Conservation Catalogue (Steiner 1984) on the grounds that geomorphology influences the pattern of water flow through, across or round a site. This source of variation is also used extensively in the USSR, where mire systems are defined on the basis of geo- and hydromorphology (Ivanov 1981).

Steiner (1984) describes 14 geomorphological classes, whilst the hydromorphological system used in the USSR (Ivanov 1981; Botch & Masing 1983) employs nine classes, which are divided into 20 sub-classes.

4 Vegetational and floristic features – perhaps the most constant feature of any mire description. Two major techniques have become established – that of the northern European school, quantitative ordination, and that of the southern and central European school, phytosociology. In Britain, phytosociology is commonly perceived as an inflexible system unable to cater for geographical variation in either vegetation composition or ecological amplitude of species. It is also prone to nomenclatural absurdities. Thus the major Class for bog hollows is Scheuchzerio-Caricetea nigrae (Nordh. 36) Tx. 37, yet *Scheuchzeria palustris* is almost completely absent from the bog hollows of Britain and Ireland. The various attempts to bring about a unified system of classification have concentrated on bridging this major divide, but as recently as 1985 the unresolved differences have led to suggestions that a unified system is neither practicable nor desirable (Sjörs 1985b). Nevertheless, the wider application of phytosociology by those formally trained in the method (e.g. Dierssen 1982; Rybniček 1985; Malmer 1985) has given a clearer insight into the usefulness of the system in north-west Europe and has led to a number of published accounts for Britain and Ireland employing the concepts, or the formal structure, of phytosociology (e.g. McVean & Ratcliffe 1962; Moore, J.J. 1968; Birks 1973; Wheeler 1980a,b,c; Birse 1980, 1984; O'Connell, Ryan & MacGowran 1984; Proctor & Rodwell 1986).

At the same time, development of computer-based ordination and classification techniques has stimulated the use of more 'objective' techniques typically favoured by British workers. Many recent analyses of mire vegetation, notably those of Daniels (1978), Ratcliffe & Hattey (1982) and Proctor & Rodwell (1986), have used M O Hill's TWINSPAN package (Hill 1979) or modified versions or precursors of this.

The advantage of phytosociology is that it provides a single standardised classification system to which subsequent workers can relate their results, whereas 'objective' ordination and classification techniques allow more flexibility for the infinite variety of nature but rarely produce the same vegetation type from two separate analyses; indeed the same analysis processed and interpreted by different people will often give different results.

To some extent the two methods appear to be drawing closer together through TWINSPAN, because some of the more formal schools of phytosociology in central Europe (e.g. the Botanical Institute at the University of Vienna) have begun to use TWINSPAN for the initial ordering of raw relevé tables.

5 Palaeobotanical features – Some systems make use of the sequence of mire development displayed within the peat profile to classify mire types (e.g. that of Tolpa, Jasnowski & Dalczynski 1967; Moore 1973b). However, this is not a practicable method for large-scale surveys and classification systems covering a wide geographical region. *A Nature Conservation Review* (Ratcliffe 1977), however, does recognise the importance of sites which have contributed significantly to our knowledge of peat development, vegetational (or sometimes human) history or climatic change through the record revealed in their profiles.

6 Soil chemistry and water relations – Initial ideas relating to the simple distinction between base-poor bog and base-rich fen have since been found merely to describe the two ends of a continuum (Sjörs 1950a; Malmer & Sjörs 1955; Wheeler 1984). Five general categories of base status are suggested by Succow

(1974, 1980) and Succow & Lange (1984) and are used extensively in Central Europe. For Britain, Goode & Ratcliffe (1977) restrict the classification of mires in terms of base status to oligotrophic, mesotrophic and eutrophic systems.

7 Chemical and physical variables for exploitation – A number of classifications have considered mires in terms of their workability and potential for exploitation, particularly in Scotland for forestry or peat extraction (Fraser 1948; Tolonen, Pairanen & Kurki 1982; DAFS 1965, 1968). These give useful data about the depth and condition of the mires investigated, but they cannot be used to produce a classification for general application in their present form. Recent initiatives sponsored by the EEC will produce a review of exploitable peat resources within the next four or five years.

Levels of functional hydrology: the classification system of the USSR

Four levels of functional hydrology are listed by Ivanov (1981) and are equivalent to the structural features described in western literature, but they are defined as active features which both control, and are themselves controlled by, the underlying hydrology. The synthesis of Russian work provided by Ivanov (1981) clearly demonstrates that the shape of such features is a key factor in controlling hydrological stability. Figure 7 illustrates many of the concepts embodied in the Russian classification system.

Mire macrotope

Where mires escape their immediate hydrological confines to coalesce into larger composite units, the resulting complex is termed a mire macrotope. Thus a "ridge-raised" (Moore & Bellamy 1974) or "partly-

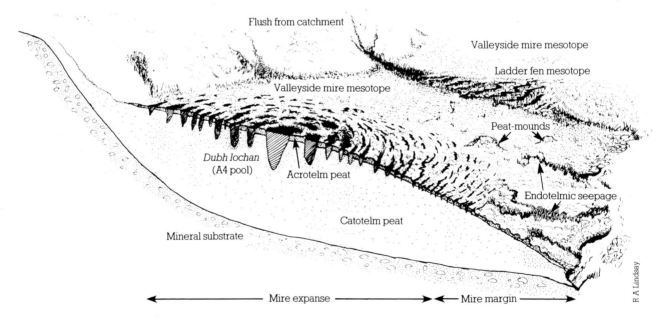

Figure 7 Two valleyside mire mesotopes linked by a ladder fen mesotope. Surface microtopes of pools and ridges are indicated, as are peat-mound microforms. The entire complex, including the hill slope catchment, forms a blanket mire macrotope. The vertical scale has been exaggerated. For explanation of terms see Chapters 1 and 2.

confined" (Hulme 1980) mire, where two raised mires coalesce, is one of the simplest types of macrotope. The Silver Flowe, in Galloway, is a more complex example, where parts are clearly mesotopes of blanket bog, others of raised bog, and others intermediate between the two. Ultimate expressions of macrotopes are the extensive blanket bogs of Britain and Ireland, the Red Lake Peatland and James Bay, the muskegs of central Canada, and the *taiga* mires of western and eastern Siberia.

The macrotope is a complex hydrological entity combining the hydraulics of the component mesotopes including their microtopes. Each level of hydrological interaction is dependent upon the other levels for stability (see Chapters 1 and 5), and it is generally impossible to affect one part of a macrotope without affecting the functioning of at least one or two other elements within that macrotope. In Siberia some of these macrotopes are "many thousands of square kilometres" in extent (Ivanov 1981), whereas the macrotopes identified for Caithness and Sutherland are more modest features (see Chapter 8).

Mire mesotope

The mesotope is equivalent to the mire massif or mire unit, being a body of peat which has developed as a single hydrological entity. Thus a single raised mire or a valleyside mire would represent a mire mesotope, the surface of which may contain a range of microtopes.

Mire microtope

This term relates to the arrangement and combination of surface features (microforms) which particularly characterise ombrotrophic mires, for example the regular organisation of ridges and pools across a mire expanse.

Mire microform

This term relates to the individual surface features within the patterning of a mire, for example a single hummock or pool.

Classification of mire complexes (macrotopes)

Moore & Bellamy (1974) emphasise through a diagram that blanket bogs are complexes possessing primary, secondary and tertiary peats in the one overall system. Moore, Merryfield & Price (1984) describe the habitat as a "complex unity" combining flushed and ombrotrophic mire types which occupy a variety of geomorphological positions and which "become inextricably linked in an interdependent, but floristically and hydrologically diverse, series".

Russian peatland specialists have, for many years, employed the concept of a mire complex for a wide range of peatland types. The method of classification which they have developed embodies many of the principles required also for the classification of blanket bog habitats. Faced with the problem of classifying extensive tracts of organic terrain, they have employed aerial stereo-photography as a rapid and resource-effective means of mapping and classifying mire systems. It has proved possible to identify four major levels of information from the air photographs, and a combination of these is used in classification. The information consists of geomorphology of the catchment, the shape of individual mire units (massifs), the surface patterns (microtopes) within the massifs, and the "flow-net" of water movement within and between these massifs and microtopes (Ivanov 1981).

When this technique is used, the definition of whole mire complexes forms a simple and logical step in the classification process, because the hydrological links between individual mire massifs are clearly revealed, thereby emphasising the need to define a boundary which does not traverse or truncate these functional connections.

The concept of a mire macrotope or mire complex, as described by Ivanov (1981), is not new. Cajander (1913) described whole *aapa* moor complexes in Finland as single functional units, whilst Sjörs (1948), Ruuhijärvi (1960) and Eurola (1962) further developed this approach within Fennoscandian classification systems.

The Norwegian mire conservation programme embodies the concept of a mire complex (*sensu* Ruuhijärvi 1960; Sjörs 1948), employing a classification based on hydromorphology, surface pattern and vegetation for the process of site selection (Moen 1985). The emphasis on hydromorphology is also adopted in the Austrian Mire Conservation Catalogue, although a more extensive classification of geomorphological location is employed than that described for the Canadian system (Steiner 1984). The system is similar to that described by Wells & Zoltai (1985) for Canada (see below).

Moen (1985) also highlights the important distinction between units for classification and the definition of site boundaries for conservation purposes. The conservation unit, often a complex, is defined as "the entire extent of a mire as bounded by the dry mineral ground". Within such complexes are what are termed "synsites", which correspond generally with Sjörs' (1983) concept of an extended mire unit, being the entire area of ground and range of features naturally associated with a particular mire unit or mesotope.

In practice it is difficult to adopt the concept of mire mesotopes as a means of defining boundaries in blanket bog landscapes because such continuous expanses of peat do not permit the identification of discrete units, other than at a very large scale. Ivanov (1981) acknowledges this problem when discussing the hydrology of similar types of organic terrain, as found, for example, in the Ob–Irtysh water divide, where a mire complex can occupy many thousands of square kilometres.

In Fennoscandia problems are encountered with the delineation of the appropriate limits for mire complexes for conservation management purposes, because many fen (aapa) systems extend and interlink over wide areas of gentle terrain. Indeed the word aapa simply means vast. The delimitation of boundaries of ecologically coherent and self-supporting units is therefore not an easy task. In Britain similar problems are encountered in such fenland areas as Broadland, but there can also be an acute problem in some extensive blanket bog landscapes, where the arbitrary limits to this peatland category make site definition a difficult process.

In terrain normally characteristic of blanket bog, peat development within a basin is often defined by the surrounding slopes, whereas on a plateau the maximum extent of deep peat is limited by the point at which the ground slopes too steeply from the plateau for significant peat formation (e.g. a rock face). These steeper slopes often support flush systems associated with seepage from the plateau above, or, where the ground slopes steeply before levelling out into a further area of peat, flushes may contribute to the margins of this lower-lying area of peat. In such cases, the boundary of the mire mosaic includes these flushed slopes.

The mire complex, or macrotope, is adopted by Moen (1985) and Wells & Zoltai (1985) for the practical definition of boundaries around areas requiring protection. In terms of classification, however, both use the smaller mire unit, or synsite (Ivanov's mesotope), as the classification unit.

Classification of mire units (mesotopes)

The most familiar classifications of peatland deal with this level of organisation. Goode & Ratcliffe (1977) followed established British practice, in using a broad classification according to topographic–hydrological (hydromorphological) features, giving six main categories – raised mire, blanket mire, open water transitions and flood-plain mire, basin mire, valley mire and soligenous mire. Within each category, futher subdivision according to vegetation was recognised. Raised and blanket mires, belonging to the ombrotrophic (rain-fed) class, have only acidophilous vegetation, but the others have vegetation varying from calcicolous to acidophilous according to the base-status of the ground-water supply.

Blanket bogs are a widely recognised but highly localised global type (see Chapter 3). Raised bogs belong to a broad zone within the boreal and cool temperate regions, with only moderate rainfall and fairly cold winters – a relatively continental climate. They are the principal class of ombrotrophic bog in Sweden, Finland, much of central Canada, the USSR and the main expanse of central Patagonia. Palsa mires occur in sub-arctic conditions, where frozen blocks of ice are cloaked with a mound of peat which insulates the ice sufficiently to prevent its thawing in the summer. Typically the vegetation of these palsa

mires is somewhat minerotrophic, through the influence of snow-melt. Palsa mires are found throughout northern Norway, Finland and Sweden, and also in northern Canada. Aapa mires are essentially minerotrophic and soligenous, receiving the bulk of their water inputs during summer snow-melt. Narrow ridges form across the line of water flow in the appearance of a ladder, with wide pools between the 'rungs', leading to their common name of "string fens". Such patterned fens are characteristic of central and northern Fennoscandia, as well as central parts of Canada, USA and USSR.

As well as the classification of overall bog type, a further level of mesotope classification relates to the topographical location within the overall mire macrotope. This is particularly relevant with blanket bogs, as the differing patterns and vegetation are closely related to gradients determined by the hydromorphology. Thus a site may be a saddle mire or a valleyside mire. The range of hydromorphological types is discussed in more detail in Chapter 8.

Classification of microtopes within mire units (mesotopes)

Sjörs (1948) identifies three main sources of variation *within* the mire unit for Swedish mires –

* the mire margin–mire expanse gradient;
* the rich–poor nutrient gradient;
* the gradient of wet to dry within the hummock–hollow pattern.

In Sweden, the transition from forest to open mire highlights a series of quite clear zones from the edge of the peat onto the central open mire. The mire margin is often characterised by growth of small trees and shrubs which increase in height towards the edge of the mire, whilst the mire expanse is generally characterised by an open vegetation dominated by Sphagnum mosses and dwarf shrubs. The conditions of nutrient supply and hydrology on the mire margin are very different from those of the mire expanse, and this is reflected in the marked vegetation differences.

While British raised mires show a transition from mire margin to central expanse, such a distinction is necessarily less clear on extensive blanket bogs. Variations in peat depth and surface wetness have more complex relationships to topography, but they exert an important influence on the distribution of breeding waders, the pattern of invertebrate populations and the distribution of plant species that require higher fluxes of oxygen or dissolved solids.

Another approach not often employed in accounts of British mires is the use of surface pattern to characterise mire types, as demonstrated by Ruuhijärvi (1960) for Finland and more recently by Moen (1985), Zoltai & Pollett (1983), Eurola, Hicks & Kaakinen (1984) and Dierssen (1982) for Norway,

Canada, Finland and north-west Europe respectively. The British tradition is centred more on straightforward vegetation classification (e.g. McVean & Ratcliffe 1962; Ratcliffe 1964; Birks 1973; Daniels 1978), although a number of accounts examine the relationship between vegetation and Sjörs' (1948) wet–dry gradient (Ratcliffe & Walker 1958; Goode 1970; Goode & Lindsay 1979; Lindsay, Riggall & Bignal 1983; Boatman 1983; Lindsay *et al.* 1985).

Vegetation pattern and mire unit (or hydromorphological type) have both commonly been used either singly or together in British classification systems (McVean & Ratcliffe 1962; Ratcliffe 1964; Moore 1968; Bellamy 1968; Birks 1973; Goode & Ratcliffe 1977; Daniels 1978; Birse 1980; Hulme & Blyth 1984; Proctor & Rodwell 1986). However, the smaller- and larger-scale variation provided by surface patterning and mire complexes respectively have tended to be ignored as a basis for classification. The presence of surface patterns has been used by many of the above authors to characterise certain classes of vegetation, but the classification of surface patterns themselves, in the manner adopted by Ruuhijärvi (1960) or Eurola & Holappa (1985) for Finland, is used only rarely in Britain (e.g. Bellamy & Pritchard, 1973; Lindsay *et al.* 1985).

Dierssen (1982) summarises the range of surface features found on mire systems throughout north-west Europe and gives a general account of the overall configuration adopted by these microforms on mire types.

Classification of microforms within a patterned microtope

Lindsay *et al.* (1985) examine the range of microforms found on British ombrotrophic mires and compare these with features described by Sjörs (1948), Ratcliffe & Walker (1958), Eurola (1962), Goode (1970) and Goode & Lindsay (1979). The generalised regime of niche zonation identified from their work is shown in Figure 8.

The total range of features identified by the various authors comprises a wide list, a high proportion of the features being found in Caithness and Sutherland. Descriptions below are taken from Dierssen (1982) or Lindsay *et al.*(1985).

1 Hummocks (T3)

These are defined as mounds of (generally) *Sphagnum* which can be up to 1 m high and 1–2 m in diameter, with a variable cover of vascular plants. Some are crowned by *Racomitrium lanuginosum*, hypnaceous mosses or lichens. Ordinarily, they are somewhat lower than 1 m, and the vegetation forming the hummock therefore lies approximately 30–75 cm above the average water table.

2 High ridge (T2)

This is characterised by a dominance of dwarf shrubs, particularly *Calluna vulgaris* in Britain, often growing in a senescent *Sphagnum* carpet, and lies

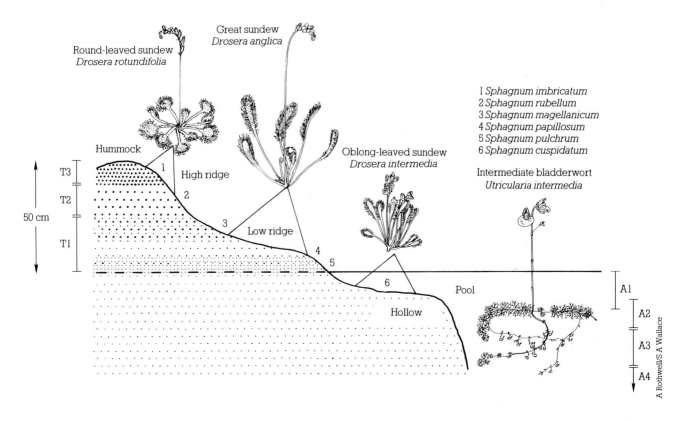

Figure 8 Distribution within the pattern of surface microforms, indicating niche zonation. (Zones based on Lindsay, Riggall & Burd 1985.)

23

between 10 and 20 cm above the water table. This microform appears not only as narrow ridges between pools but also as wide expanses of drier vegetation within pool systems.

3 Low ridge (T1)

This is distinguished from high ridge because it tends to be far less dominated by dwarf shrubs. It is characteristic of soft, undamaged mire systems, in which it is the major ridge component. On most sites it forms a *Sphagnum*-rich fringe to the expanses of high ridge and hummocks. The *Sphagna* are especially *S. tenellum*, *S. magellanicum* and *S. papillosum*. It occupies the first 10 cm of the mire surface above the water table and is characterised by a reduced cover of *Calluna* and increased cover of *Erica tetralix*, or it may have few dwarf shrubs at all.

4 *Sphagnum* hollows (A1)

Sjörs (1948) terms this zone "carpet" and distinguishes it from the "lawn" (T1 low ridge) because this is essentially an aquatic zone. Although free water is often not visible, the dense carpet of *Sphagnum* sits in an aqueous matrix and cannot support any great weight. In Britain this level is defined particularly by *Sphagnum cuspidatum* on areas of patterned bog, with *S. auriculatum* and *S. pulchrum* locally. In slightly enriched conditions these are replaced by *S. recurvum*. In northern Europe species such as *S. balticum* and *S. majus* may instead predominate (Sjörs 1983), usually with *S. balticum* above *S. cuspidatum* or *S. majus*.

5 Mud-bottom hollows (A2)

This occurs at the same level as *Sphagnum* hollows, but may also extend to 20 cm below the water table, and it is distinguished from the "carpet" by being relatively limited in its moss cover, but with a significant occurrence of higher plants. The zone is characterised by a fairly firm peat base to the hollow, above which is a depth of up to 20 cm of free water. These areas often dry out during the summer months, though characteristic species such as *Drosera intermedia* can continue to trap food even if submerged all year.

6 Drought-sensitive pools (A3)

These are not specifically defined by Lindsay *et al.* (1985), being combined with permanent (A4) pools. They have since been recognised as distinct from permanent deep pools as a result of further observations of systems in severe drought conditions, where the deepest pools remained water-filled but many others exposed a soft, highly humified peat matrix.

7 Permanent pools (A4)

These are found only on watersheds and may be several metres deep in extreme cases. There is no evidence that they are "fen windows" extending down to the mineral ground, but some examples are clearly almost as deep as the peat deposit itself. The only vegetation normally recorded in these pools comprises floating columns of *Sphagnum cuspidatum* bound together by rhizomes and roots of *Menyanthes trifoliata*.

8 Erosion channels (TA2)

These also were not formally defined by Lindsay *et al.* (1985), but Dierssen (1982) describes them as a distinct feature (*Erosionrinne*) and Goode & Lindsay (1979) give vegetation data for erosion channels in the Outer Hebrides. They are coded as TA2 because they are similar to mud-bottom hollows, but spend most of the year exposed as dry peat.

9 Erosion hags (T4)

When bogs become eroded their surface microtopography usually becomes accentuated because the range of water table fluctuations becomes very much greater. Deep erosion gullies trace a network of water channels around dissected ridges and isolated hummocks which occur as steep-sided upstanding blocks of peat. Water tables are often more than 50 cm lower in these blocks of peat, or erosion hags, than in the ridges or hummocks of non-eroding bogs. Erosion hags are a small-scale version of the summits which form a dissected-plateau landscape. The hag tops lie at the original level of the undamaged bog surface, but, in cutting deeply into the bog plain, erosion leaves the surviving ridges as dry hags dominated by dwarf shrubs and *Racomitrium lanuginosum*, with little *Sphagnum*.

10 Peat-mounds (T5)

These are tall structures (for a bog), which can attain heights of 1–2 m above the general surface and are 5–15 m in diameter. They look like small *palsa* mounds, but the latter are formed around a permanent ice core (see above) and no such cores have been found in peat-mounds. Their existence has only recently been recognised, and their status is therefore still somewhat uncertain. However, they are discussed in more detail in Chapter 9.

Composite classification systems

The Canadian and United States wetland inventories both use a hierarchical approach to wetland classification which incorporates many of the factors discussed above (Wells & Zoltai 1985; Cowardin, Carter, Golet & LaRoe 1979). Although the systems are not identical, together they provide a basis for classification of wetlands throughout the North American continent.

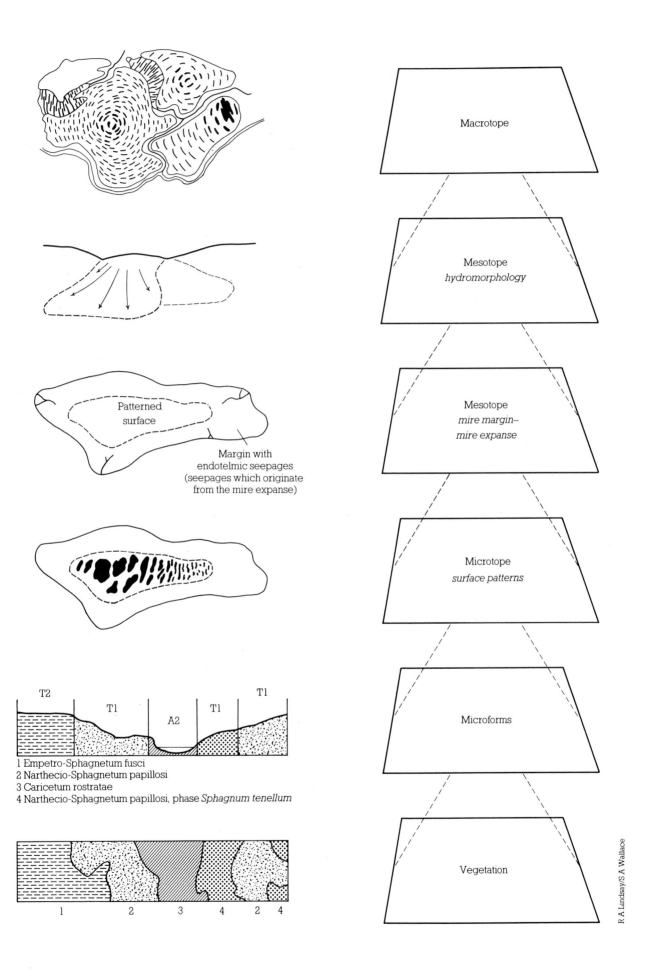

1 Empetro-Sphagnetum fusci
2 Narthecio-Sphagnetum papillosi
3 Caricetum rostratae
4 Narthecio-Sphagnetum papillosi, phase *Sphagnum tenellum*

R A Lindsay/S A Wallace

Figure 9 Classification system used by the NCC for bog systems, particularly blanket bogs, incorporating the four levels of functional hydrology – macrotope, mesotope, microtope and microform – described by Ivanov (1981). (Vegetation maps taken from Dierssen 1982.)

The United States system is perhaps the simpler of the two, intended for rapid assessment by relatively unskilled workers. It is designed to be used in hierarchical steps, the first step being a division into five gross types of wetland "systems" – estuarine, palustrine, riverine, lacustrine and marine. Subsequent divisions are made on the basis of vegetation physiognomy and substrate type.

The Canadian system uses certain ecosystem attributes for wetland classification which are of particular relevance in mire habitats. It uses four levels of information (Wells & Zoltai 1985). The first level identifies major wetland classes such as bog, fen and swamp. Each of these is then subdivided into what are termed "wetland forms", recognised on the basis of morphology, topography and overall surface physiognomy. These "forms" are subdivided at the third level into "wetland types" based on the broad categorisation of the surface physiognomy, for example the presence of wet *Sphagnum* lawns or dry lichen–*Sphagnum* hummocks. The final level of division depends on the application to which the classification is being put and recognises such "specialisms" as engineering, vegetation, forestry and energy. Each has its own range of sub-classes at this final level which are tailored to enable the classification to be applied to the specific problem in hand. Both the Canadian and the United States systems recognise as a further selection step that biogeographical gradients play an important part in the distribution of plant and animal species and that the "regionality" of systems must therefore be considered if the full range of site conditions is to be represented. This is echoed in Ivanov's (1981) observation that mire systems are essentially zonal in terms of their climatic responses.

The NCC's system of classification for blanket bog

The classification adopted by the NCC is derived from the Canadian hierarchical approach and incorporates several levels of classification based on many of the attributes discussed above (see Figure 9). For a detailed account of the methodology employed for each level in the Caithness and Sutherland survey, see Chapter 8.

1 At the highest level, areas assessed for conservation value and possible protection are described at the scale of the *macrotope* or mire complex. This definition ensures that as many of the ecosystem links as possible are incorporated into the site boundary. While this approach cannot prevent widespread impacts such as acid deposition from affecting the site, it attempts to define an area as isolated as possible from the effect of land-use changes which may occur on land immediately adjacent to the site. As far as possible, therefore, a site defined at the macrotope scale is a self-contained unit in terms of vegetation and hydrology, though clearly the protection of the more mobile birds and other animals cannot be wholly catered for in this approach.

2 Making up the macrotope are one or more *mesotopes* or mire units. Each mesotope is classified initially in terms of *hydromorphological type* (e.g. saddle mire, watershed mire, ladder fen).

3 The mesotope is then divided into the broad categories of *mire margin* and *mire expanse*. In general, but by no means always, this division is based on the distinction between patterned and non-patterned ground.

4 Within the area of mire expanse, the overall pattern of surface features, or the *microtope pattern*, is recorded. On mires with little or no surface water the pattern may be very simple or homogeneous. However, with increasing numbers of hollows and pools, the range of patterns adopted by these features becomes increasingly significant. The general orientation and shape of pattern adopted by the microtope therefore form the basis of this level of classification.

5 The relative frequency of the individual surface features within the microtope pattern (e.g. hummocks, low ridges and pools) is used to classify sites according to *microform*. This can be one of the more difficult parts of the classification process, as measurements of the area of these features are not usually feasible without a considerable period of painstaking work. However, at its simplest, this level can be based instead on subjective estimates after field survey, or even on the simple presence or absence of particular microforms.

6 Finally, it is possible to locate different classes of *vegetation type* within these various structural levels. At the finest level of detail, *vegetation associations*, or, more usually, *variants* can be identified within the range of microforms present on the bog (see e.g. Dierssen 1982, p. 249; Lindsay *et al.* 1983). The difficulties of providing accurate, measured figures of microform abundance also apply to the vegetation within microform patterns. Sampling within the various levels of microform ensures that the range of variation in vegetation within and between these structural elements can be recognised. However, to obtain an estimate of abundance for each community would generally require a sampling frequency which is not feasible within the resource constraints of most survey programmes. Consequently it is often necessary to use a simple, subjective system such as the DAFOR scale, or merely to note the presence or absence of communities.

At a broader scale *National Vegetation Classification (NVC) communities* and phytosociological *associations* or even *Orders* are more appropriate for descriptions of the mire margin–mire expanse or that of microtope pattern. The NVC recognises the phytosociological distinction between pools and ridges within areas of patterning and therefore generally describes a mosaic of two or even three communities for the mire expanse and one or more from the mire margin.

3 Climate and world blanket bog distribution

Blanket bog development requires a climate which is continuously both wet and cool (Chapter 1). An annual mean precipitation of 1000 mm is probably a necessary minimum, but above this level the total amount becomes much less important than its distribution, especially as measured by length of drought periods. Since it is difficult to measure the rate of bog growth (i.e. peat formation) directly, ecologists have looked for parameters of climate which appear to coincide most closely with the geographical limits of blanket bog occurrence.

Tansley (1939) pointed to the general correspondence between the distribution of blanket bog in Britain and Ireland and the map of mean annual number of "rain days". (A "rain day" is the meteorological category of a period of 24 hours with precipitation of at least 0.25 mm.) Goode & Ratcliffe (1977) considered that an even better correlation is found between blanket bog distribution and "wet days" (a "wet day" being a period of 24 hours with precipitation of at least 1 mm). The geographical limits of blanket bog correspond well with the isoline of 160 wet days, though this takes no account of possible climatic changes over the whole Post-glacial period of blanket bog development and is only a crude present-day correlation. Pearsall (1956) deduced that blanket bogs in northern Scotland were in a senescent state under a drier climate than hitherto, because the present annual precipitation appeared to be too low to allow active growth. This highly questionable interpretation appeared to result from an insufficient appreciation of the importance of distribution of rainfall rather than its total amount.

Both rain days and wet days tend to be closely correlated with length and frequency of drought periods, but the wet day appears to be a better index of effective wetness for vegetation than the rain day. The point at which evapo-transpiration changes from an annual water deficit to a water surplus may also be significant for peat development. Stroud et al. (1987) have shown that another close correlation exists in Britain between extensive occurrence of blanket bog and evapo-transpiration surplus of over 200 mm during the six months April–September.

The other important element of climate is temperature regime. Absolute temperatures must not be so low as to limit the growing season unduly through a prolonged winter, nor so high during summer that they promote too rapid decomposition of plant remains. An equable temperature regime with annual means for the warmest month in the range 9–15°C appears to be necessary and occurs mainly in the oceanic regions of the cool temperate zones.

These climatic considerations explain why blanket bog is limited to fairly high elevations in south-west England but occurs widely almost down to sea level in northern and western Scotland and in western Ireland. The relatively dry climate of the North York Moors appears to be close to the limits for blanket bog development and contrasts with the similar moorland plateau of Dartmoor, where it is well represented under a wetter climate.

As climate diverges from these rather narrowly defined parameters, so does blanket bog become replaced by other types of mire with similar peat characteristics but different structural and hydromorphological features. There are transitional types, even in Britain, and in districts such as Cumbria and Galloway there are extensive bogs which might be best regarded as an intermediate category between blanket and raised bogs. It becomes a matter of opinion where the limits of blanket bog are drawn in practice.

There are thus problems in specifying accurately the distribution and extent of blanket bogs in other parts of the world. For some of these there is little published description of blanket bog vegetation or survey information on distribution and area. With increasing distance between locations, the floristics of blanket bog become ever more divergent. The British and Irish blanket bogs are most similar to each other, and both have much in common with those of Fennoscandia. There is far less similarity between European and North American types, while those of the southern hemisphere are almost completely different from all of these northern blanket bogs. The common features are peat characteristics, bog structure and relationships to topography.

The following assessment is thus compiled from direct field experience of European blanket bogs, published work and verbal information, and prediction based on occurrence of suitable climate.

The combination of conditions generally regarded as necessary for blanket bog formation can be summarised as –
- a minimum annual rainfall of 1000 mm;
- a minimum of 160 wet days;
- a cool climate (mean temperature less than 15°C for the warmest month) with relatively minor seasonal fluctuation.

Examination of climatic patterns from around the globe, using either the range provided by Walters & Leith (1960) or *Physico-geographical Atlas of the World* (Academy of Sciences of the U.S.S.R. 1964), reveals relatively few stations where these conditions are met. Although the number of wet days

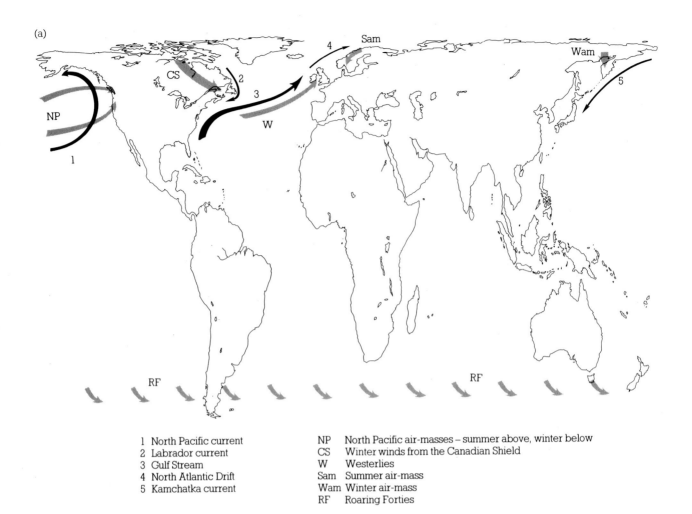

(a)

1 North Pacific current
2 Labrador current
3 Gulf Stream
4 North Atlantic Drift
5 Kamchatka current

NP   North Pacific air-masses – summer above, winter below
CS   Winter winds from the Canadian Shield
W   Westerlies
Sam Summer air-mass
Wam Winter air-mass
RF   Roaring Forties

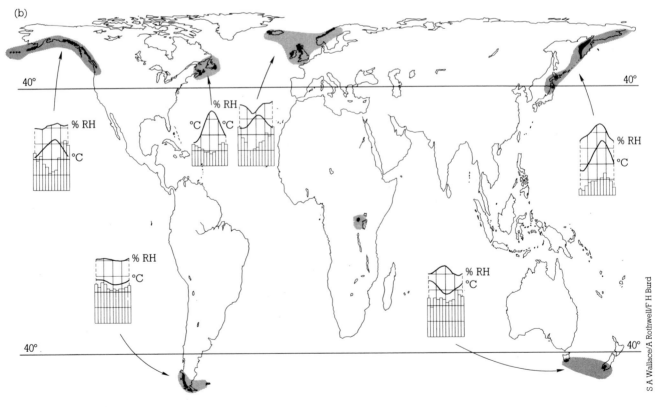

Figure 10 World distribution of blanket bog –
(a) General pattern of air and water masses. (Based on *Physico-geographical Atlas of the World* (Academy of Sciences of the U.S.S.R. 1964).)
(b) Identified localities. Shaded areas indicate areas of the globe with climate suitable for blanket bog formation, based on climate diagrams from *Physico-geographical Atlas of the World* (1964). Dark shading indicates regions where blanket bog is recorded, rather than the actual extent of the resource.

is not available from these sources, relative humidity is an integral part of the climate diagram, and this is therefore taken as a broad indication of their frequency.

Figure 10 indicates those parts of the globe where the climate appears suitable for blanket bog development on the basis of these climate diagrams. As can be seen, nearly all examples are situated on the fringes of the great oceans and, because of the temperature restriction, are also limited to latitudes between 45° and 60°. This distribution accords well with that given by Goodwillie (1980) for Europe and the accounts given by various authors in Gore (1983b) for the distributions of peat types in a range of countries. The combined information obtained from Sjörs (1950b, 1985a), Roivainen (1954), Wace (1960), Katz (1971), Neiland (1971), Goodwillie (1980), Dierssen (1982), Gore (1983b), Ryan & Cross (1984), Banner, Pojar & Trowbridge (1986) and Dr Martin Holdgate, Dr Richard Weyl, Dr Antti Huttenen, Dr Stephen Talbot and Professor Hugo Sjörs, (pers. comm.) has been used to draw up the provisional map of world blanket bog shown in Figure 10. The Peters Projection has been used in this map because the projection shows correctly proportioned land areas.

Regions of the world potentially able to support blanket bog can be identified quite clearly by their climate diagrams, the pattern exemplified in Figure 6 being characteristic of such areas (see Figure 10b) and easy to pick out amidst the range of other climatic zones mainly by the relationship between temperature and humidity shown in Figure 6.

Professor H Sjörs (pers. comm.) has observed that attempts to assess the global distribution of blanket bog should not be unduly influenced by treelessness as a criterion for blanket bog. In some areas of the globe there are trees better adapted to hyperoceanic conditions or wet peat substrates than in Europe. Thus trees grow on blanket bogs along the Pacific seaboard, although they are dwarfed and scattered on the large mire expanses. Tall trees only occur on blanket peats where ground is better-draining, on shallower peats, in marginal areas or on very small deposits.

Ireland

Plateau blanket bog occurs widely in most of the mountain massifs of Ireland where topography is suitable, including those in the east (e.g. Wicklow). The largest areas are, however, at fairly low levels in the extreme west, especially in Counties Mayo, Galway, Sligo and Donegal. The mountains of Kerry and Cork are climatically suitable but too rugged to have more than highly dissected occurrences of blanket bog. The largest single area was the Bog of Erris in north Mayo, which closely resembled parts of the Caithness and Sutherland flows. Since 1945 extensive commercial working of the larger areas of blanket bog (and of the once extensive raised bogs of the central lowlands) for fuel peat has greatly reduced the total original area of about 700,000 ha.

The Irish blanket bogs are botanically quite similar to those of northern Scotland. The *Sphagna* and abundant vascular plants are mostly shared in common, but the distinguishing feature of the western Irish bogs is the constancy and local codominance of black bog-rush *Schoenus nigricans* in the T1 and T2 communities. Dwarf shrubs are more poorly represented, though in a few areas the Lusitanian species *Erica mackaiana* is represented. Patterned surfaces are much less well developed than in Scotland, but occur in Mayo and Donegal.

The rest of Europe

Goodwillie (1980) states that blanket bog occurs in Iceland, the Pyrenees, western Norway, Britain and Ireland. However, he states that "blanket mire is better developed in Ireland and Scotland than elsewhere in Europe". Although Goodwillie shows Iceland with a fringe of blanket bog, he also states that much of this is actually fen vegetation because volcanic ash regularly enriches the peat surface. Only the western fringe of Iceland supports true oligotrophic blanket bog (D A Stroud pers. comm.). Norway has a large belt of blanket bog country running west of the central highlands between Rogaland and Nordland and onto the Lofoten Islands and Andöya (Dierssen 1982), but the extent of any one mire system is apparently quite limited because of the rugged terrain. Whilst examples of Norwegian blanket bog are perhaps closer in floristics to British and Irish types than anywhere else in the world, the climatic pattern of Norway is different in two important respects. First, it lies at a higher latitude than mainland Britain. Secondly, whilst Britain and Ireland are subject to westerly winds all year round, during winter months Norway has a high prevalence of northerly winds blowing down from cyclones in the Barents Sea (*Physico-geographical Atlas of the World* 1964). The effects combine to give the majority of blanket bog areas in Norway less equable temperatures than those experienced by such areas in Britain and Ireland.

An interesting type of mire which is orogenic (mountain-generated) rather than oceanic occurs in Austria and might be classed as a very special form of blanket bog. It is more accurately described by Steiner (1984) as "condensation mire" and occurs on steep, rocky avalanche debris on mountain slopes. Cold air is funnelled down through this blocky scree from glacial regions high in the Austrian Alps. When this cold air eventually emerges in the warmer valleys it causes water vapour to condense around the scree slopes, providing enough constant moisture for deposits of 1–2 m of peat to develop on slopes of 45°.

East coast of Canada

Zoltai & Pollett (1983) state that the Atlantic Oceanic Wetland Region (which is the only one of their regions stated to contain blanket bogs) occurs around the northern coast of New Brunswick, on

Cape Breton Island and along both west and east coasts of Newfoundland. However, the recently published map of Canada's Wetland Regions (*Department of Energy, Mines and Resources, Canada* 1986) indicates that the Atlantic Oceanic Wetland Region, typified by blanket bog, is restricted to part of the south-easternmost tip of Newfoundland (Avalon Peninsula).

Zoltai & Pollet (1983) present some striking air photographs to illustrate the wetland types of Canada, from which it is possible to see the close similarity between the patterning of the plateau raised bogs from the Atlantic Oceanic Wetland Region and the patterns of raised bogs in western Ireland. However, the clearly "confined" (Hulme 1980) nature of this type is evident (p. 262), when compared with the "unconfined" blanket bog also illustrated.

The climate of the region is of interest because it has a markedly continental temperature range, with mean summer temperatures of +15°C and −7°C in winter (*Physico-geographical Atlas of the World* 1964). It seems likely that this continentality results from a combination of winter winds which often blow from the north-west, coupled with the effect of the cold Labrador Current, which flows throughout the year down from Baffin Bay through the Davis Strait and past Newfoundland's Atlantic coast, further insulating the area from the moderating influence of the Gulf Stream (*Physico-geographical Atlas of the World* 1964). However, the Avalon Peninsula has a fairly mild winter.

The vegetation of Newfoundland blanket bogs differs from its relative this side of the Atlantic in lacking *Calluna*, which was originally absent from the North American continent. Its place is taken by *Chamaedaphne calyculata* (leatherleaf) and *Kalmia angustifolia*.

North American Pacific coast

The distribution of blanket bog in this region is still the subject of some debate. Wells & Zoltai (1983) describe the Pacific Oceanic Wetland Region as being dominated by slope bogs, raised bogs and flat fens, a description confirmed by the map of Canada's Wetland Regions (1986). Neiland (1971) and Banner *et al.* (1986) give detailed accounts of the mires of, respectively, the Alaskan 'panhandle' and British Columbia's Pacific coast, of which a high proportion are considered to be blanket bog (Banner *et al.* 1986; Dr J Pojar pers. comm.). Both publications also give photographs of the types. From these and the descriptions it is clear that blanket bogs of the Pacific seaboard are not treeless, scattered small pines (*Pinus contorta* subsp. *contorta*) usually being found across the mire expanse. These mires have a general character more akin to boreal mire regions of Fennoscandia, e.g. the open forest-mire landscape around the summit of Finland's Riisitunturi, a gently contoured mountain with just the beginnings of open blanket bog development.

The deep ombrotrophic bog defined by Banner *et al.* (1986) is dominated by *Pinus contorta* and species of *Chamaecyparis*, *Trichophorum* and *Sphagnum*. The *Pinus contorta* is extremely stunted ("bonsai"), whilst dwarf shrubs such as *Empetrum nigrum*, *Ledum groenlandicum*, *Juniperus communis* subsp. *nana*, *Kalmia polifolia*, *Vaccinium uliginosum* and *V. vitis-idaea* form a dominant shrub layer. Terraced pools occur, characterised by either *Rhynchospora alba*, *Eriophorum angustifolium*, *Menyanthes trifoliata* or *Nuphar lutea* subsp. *polysepala*. Banner *et al.* also describe a sloping *Trichophorum*-dominated bog which occurs at high altitude and which sounds remarkably similar to the ladder fen type discussed in Chapter 8.

The Aleutian Islands are likened by Dr Stephen Talbot of the United States Fish and Wildlife Service (pers. comm.) to the peat-draped landscapes of the ancient foreland of western Sutherland, with thin, saturated and treeless peat cloaking steep rocky outcrops and peat-filled hollows showing varying degrees of standing water and patterning.

Sjörs (1984) recognises the vegetational and occasionally topographical similarity to west European blanket bog, but points out various differences, such as the often extreme topography and the growth of trees, sometimes abundantly, sometimes only scattered. He concludes that he is unwilling to classify the Alaskan 'panhandle' fully as blanket bogs in European terms. Floristically, the blanket bogs of the North American Pacific coast are of a type unique to that area with regard to their much richer vascular flora, but their cryptogamic flora is strikingly similar to that of hyperoceanic western Europe.

The "Magellanic Tundra Complex" of South America

The overriding feature of the climate in the southern tip of America is the constant westerly airflow. Pisano (1983) describes how the interaction of the South Pacific and South Atlantic Polar Fronts produces summers of high humidity, high winds and low temperature and winters of similar humidity but somewhat lower temperatures and windspeed. He also points to the extreme west–east divide across the area caused by the Andean spine which runs down the west coast, causing extreme climatic differences. Rainfall can be 5000 mm in the west and only 220 mm in the trans-Andean Patagonian region. Similar, but less extreme, differences occur in Norway and on South Island in New Zealand, and to a lesser extent in Britain.

Auer (1933, 1965) and Roivainen (1954) give detailed accounts of the mires of the main island of Tierra del Fuego, whilst Pisano (1983) provides a classification for the whole "Magellanic Tundra Complex". The blanket bog systems of this complex are different from those of the northern hemisphere in being formed largely of 'cushion plants', rather than bryophytes. In a fine example of convergent evolution, species such as *Donatia fascicularis* and *Astelia pumila* can form raised lenses of ombrotrophic peat very similar to the classic raised mires of the north. Indeed, mixed within these areas of cushion mire are true *Sphagnum* raised mires dominated by *Sphagnum magellanicum* in its *locus classicus*.

Roivainen (1954) produces 19 types and sub-types of vegetation, five of which he regards as rain-dependent – ombrogenous meadow bogs with *Marsippospermum grandiflora*, flat cushion bogs dominated by *Donatia fascicularis* and *Astelia pumila*, raised cushion bogs with *Racomitrium lanuginosum* and *Chorisodontium magellanicum*, ombrogenous "white" moors with *Tetroncium magellanicum*, and ombrogenous heath with *Empetrum rubrum*. This accords fairly well with Pisano's (1983) classification, but Pisano defines only the cushion bogs as blanket bog, assigning the remainder of Roivainen's types to raised bog, dwarf heath or "Magellanic Tundra".

Godley (1960) and Dr M W Holdgate (unpublished notes) give accounts of the blanket bogs of Isla Wellington, at the northern limit of Pisano's Magellanic Tundra Complex, and of blanket bog systems on the southern (wetter) side of Isla Navarino, at the southern tip of the complex. Neither area was visited by Roivainen, but Pisano classes both regions as low-altitude cushion bogs. Holdgate confirms this classification, listing *Astelia, Donatia* and *Oreobolus* as the dominant blanket bog genera.

The Falkland Islands are covered with blanket bog, although, lying in the rain shadow of the Chilean Andes, they are quite dry, with only 340–635 mm of rain a year (Roper undated). Apart from the influence of the sea, conditions are remarkably similar to those of the Caithness and Sutherland plain. It is well known in the Falklands that "all the water sits on top of the hills" (M Felton pers. comm.), which suggests that the majority of blanket bogs are either watershed or saddle mires. However, the depth of peat and extent of patterning are considerably more restricted than in Caithness and Sutherland. Both cushion- and *Sphagnum*-bogs occur, the former characterised by *Oreobolus obtusangulus* and *Astelia pumila* (Holdgate unpublished notes).

New Zealand and other Southern Ocean islands

The island groups which lie within the appropriate latitudes of the Southern Ocean (40° to 60°) may support some form of blanket bog where they are not too steep. Schwaar (1977), for example, describes the blanket peat of Gough Island, which lies at 40° S in the South Atlantic. It receives 3250 mm annual rainfall, and the average temperature is 11.7°C, making it rather warm for a blanket bog region. Peat depths of 1 m are given, the vegetation consisting of ferns and the shrub *Phylica arborea* below about 300 m, with peat-forming herbaceous

vegetation dominated by grasses above and bryophyte communities covering upland valley and plateau mires. Gore (1983a), quoting Schwaar's (1977) account, likens the peat composition to that of Moor House in the Pennines, but Wace (1961) describes nothing immediately recognisable as ombrotrophic blanket bog and Holdgate (pers. comm.) considers that only certain of the upland plateau mires are truly ombrogenous. Islands like Heard Island, which rise steeply to 3000 m, are unlikely to encourage blanket bog development, but Kerguelen Island, Marion Island (Bakker, Winterbottom & Dyer 1971), the Crozet Islands and Macquarie Island are possible locations, and South Georgia seems to have quite extensive peat deposits. However, the total area of blanket bog in the Southern Ocean islands is likely to be minute.

Thompson (1980) states that blanket bogs occur in the Otago Mountains of New Zealand's South Island but gives little information about their nature. Campbell (1983) describes cushion mires in the mist-shrouded uplands of South Island but regards these as isolated mire units rather than part of a blanket bog complex. He also describes a widespread type from the humid west coast (where Hokitika has year-round monthly rainfall in excess of 200 mm and temperatures from +5° to +15°C) known as *pakihi*. This is a gley podsol with variable peat cover extending in many small units over an area of some 300,000 ha, but it should perhaps be regarded as incipient rather than true blanket bog.

North-east Asia

Few climate diagrams are known for north-east Asia, *Physico-geographical Atlas of the World* (1964) giving records for the south-west tip of Kamchatka and eastern Hokkaido. Both diagrams suggest climates within which blanket bog could occur, though both have distinctly low winter temperatures owing mainly to the winter cyclonic pattern, which subjects both areas to prevailing winds from central Asia, whilst summer conditions ensure prevailing winds from the southern Pacific. Both areas are, however, subject to the cooling effects of the Oya Shio current flowing south from the Bering Sea.

Botch & Masing (1983) describe the Western Kamchatka Province as "one of the most paludified territories in the USSR", with 80% of the province covered by blanket bog types. Quoting Neishtadt (1935, 1936), they divide the mires into wet *Sphagnum* bogs and dry *Cladonia* bogs, both of which are treeless. The hollows are dominated by *Sphagnum lindbergii, S. papillosum* or mud bottoms, whilst the ridges and hummocks consist largely of *S. fuscum*. The true charcter of this type is not clear, however, because the Western Kamchatka mires are also classed as a special raised mire type (Lyubimova 1940), whilst Nikonov (1955) classes the province as dominated by peat basins and Katz (1971) describes the mires of Kamchatka as domed mires. The problems of access into this area make confirmation of the mire type difficult.

Japan lies at the southern latitudinal limit for true blanket bog in the northern hemisphere, but Gore (1983a) states that simple, unpatterned blanket bog occurs on the slopes of Mount Taisetsu in Hokkaido and several mountains on Honshu. Gimingham (1984) describes the Oze mire complex on Honshu as a series of patterned raised mires lying in an upland valley. The hydromorphological similarity between this complex and that of the Silver Flowe in Galloway, described by Ratcliffe & Walker (1958), is noteworthy.

Africa

Finally, in complete contrast to the oceanic conditions discussed so far, Thompson & Hamilton (1983) describe blanket peats from central equatorial Africa. These are peats of purely orogenic origin, being formed on the higher slopes of the Ruwenzori Mountains in Uganda and fed by a bimodal rainfall pattern resulting from adiabatic cooling of first northerly, then southerly airstreams as they pass over the Ruwenzori range through the year. These are described as "sedge mires" and are therefore yet another distinct variant in the range of blanket bog forms. However, these mires, the less extensive, very strongly sloping and very shallow ones on Mount Kenya and the mountain mires of Lesotho in southern Africa could as well be regarded as sloping fen.

Global resource of blanket bog

Total estimates for the global blanket bog resource are difficult, partly because definition of the type is itself sometimes difficult, defeating even the most experienced worker (see Sjörs 1984), partly because it is not clear whether all areas defined as blanket bog truly fall into this category (see comments about Kamchatka above) and partly because the habitat is typical of some of the least accessible and least visited parts of the globe. The basic climatic requirements for the habitat limit its total possible distribution to something around 100 million ha, of which it appears that only 10% or so actually supports blanket bog, because of unsuitable terrain, vulcanism and other factors.

With 1,300,000 ha of mire, the larger part originally blanket bog, it appears that Britain supported something like 13% of the total world resource. Clearly, this is a very rough estimate, but the fact remains that Britain and Ireland are regarded throughout the world as the 'type' regions for blanket bog. Hugo Sjörs, Professor Emeritus at the University of Uppsala, Sweden, and one of the most experienced and widely travelled mire ecologists in the world today, has commented that "nowhere occurs the blanket bog in more impressive expanses than in Ireland and Scotland. This is especially true of the lowland type found in northernmost Scotland and in Mayo and Connemara in western Ireland."

Part II   The peatlands of Caithness and Sutherland

4   The physical environment

The extreme development of blanket bog in Caithness and Sutherland results from the combination of two essential conditions – suitable climate and suitable topography. Because topography results in local modifications of the regional climate it will be considered first.

Topography and geology

A key feature of the eastern half of the region is the large extent of low, gently contoured or almost flat upland. East Sutherland has a considerable expanse of such ground, and in Caithness these uplands descend north-eastwards to merge imperceptibly into lowland plain. To the west the softly undulating moorlands become increasingly interrupted by high mountain peaks and ranges, but these finally give way to an Atlantic coastal zone of low but rugged, ancient foreland. The simplified map (Figure 11) shows that, although geological changes tend also to run in an east-west direction, the topography most suitable for blanket bog development is not confined to any one main rock formation. The largest continuous areas of blanket bog are spread over the Old Red Sandstone of Caithness, the large granitic intrusion along the Caithness–Sutherland boundary and roughly half of the area of Moine granulites and schists in Sutherland.

Old Red Sandstone ("Caithness Flags") forms most of the north-eastern expanse of low moorland and coastal plain, covering much of Caithness. The drift deposits of this area contain calcareous shell material, brought in from the east at the last glaciation. Further west the boulder clay is more sandy and free from lime (Crampton 1911). This geological combination and the low elevation produce the only good-quality agricultural land of the region, graded as Class 3 (Soil and Land Capability for Agriculture: Futty & Towers 1982). This tract of fertile land is interrupted only by an outcrop of granite at Helmsdale on the coast. Much of this land was previously peat-covered but has been cut and reclaimed during more than a millenium of human habitation. Apart from this north-eastern and coastal agricultural zone, most of Caithness is covered by a vast, almost continuous expanse of peat, and there are still outliers behind the coastal

headlands of Dunnet and Duncansby. In the south, the peatlands are interrupted by the abrupt peaks of the Morven range, the most conspicuous landmarks in Caithness.

Crampton (1911) suggests that the present surface vegetation of the Caithness peat is largely insulated from the effects of underlying geology, but identifies two processes whereby the hydrogeology of the basal deposits has a bearing on the present vegetation. First, areas of springs and seepage in the central plain are rarely capable of supporting more than base-poor fen vegetation of the Caricion lasiocarpae or the Caricion curto-nigrae type because the underlying deposits of granite, schists or drift are themselves base-poor. However, the shelly drift and calcareous flags of north-eastern Caithness have in places afforded the opportunity for extremely base-rich fen communities to develop.

Secondly, and by contrast, the ice-sheet which moved over the western parts of Caithness and most of central Sutherland brought with it a mixed type of drift which varies from stiff clay to loose sands and gravels (DAFS 1965). Crampton suggests that this looser drift at the base of the peat encourages water flow at the peat-drift interface, leading to sub-surface water scouring and tunnelling beneath the peat. The final effect of this is the appearance of "sink-holes" and associated erosion complexes within bog-pool systems. These features are discussed in more detail in Chapter 5.

By far the largest of the rock formations is the central expanse of Moine granulites and schists. The landform of this section is, for the most part but especially in the eastern half, a series of low summits, mainly below 650 m. Between the hills is gently sloping ground covered with a maze of water bodies ranging in size from tiny pools to large lakes, most of them lying within a vast expanse of peat, which cloaks much of this landscape. As in Caithness, it is the relatively gentle gradients of this terrain which allow such large areas of peat to form. Westwards, several high upland massifs rise above the general level of the plain, notably Ben Hope, Ben Hee, Ben Loyal, Ben Armine and Ben Klibreck. However, these peaks occur as isolated landmarks within an otherwise almost level and waterlogged

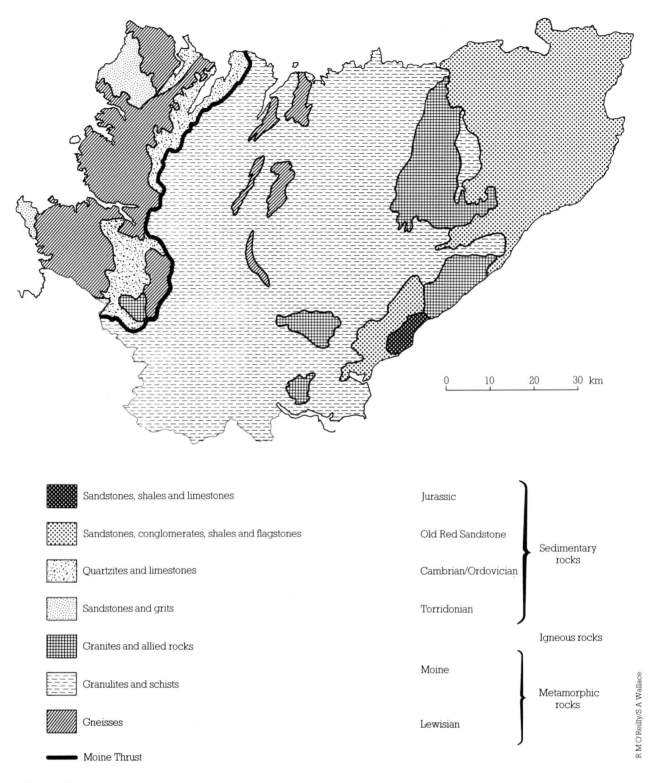

Figure 11 Simplified map of the solid geology of Caithness and Sutherland.

Legend:

- Sandstones, shales and limestones — Jurassic
- Sandstones, conglomerates, shales and flagstones — Old Red Sandstone
- Quartzites and limestones — Cambrian/Ordovician
- Sandstones and grits — Torridonian

(Sedimentary rocks)

- Granites and allied rocks — Igneous rocks

- Granulites and schists — Moine
- Gneisses — Lewisian

(Metamorphic rocks)

— Moine Thrust

landscape. All the rocks of the Moine Series and its intrusions are hard and resistant to weathering: they are mostly non-calcareous and acidic and so give rise to mainly infertile, base-deficient soils. Agriculture is largely confined to coastal strips and the bottom lands of the main straths.

To the west, high ranges become more continuous along the line of the Moine Thrust, which runs from Loch Eriboll to Ben More Assynt and beyond. Variably composed of Moine rocks, Cambrian quartzites and Lewisian Gneiss, these steep and rugged massifs create an extensive break in the peatland topography, though all of them have small areas of bog. These dramatic landforms give way to a much lower coastal zone running parallel to the Minch, composed mainly of Lewisian Gneiss and Torridonian Sandstone. The gneiss forms a complex, irregularly undulating tract of low moorland, with a large number of mostly small lochs, much bare rock exposed as slabs and bosses, and a variable cover of glacial drift. The sandstone produces the striking peaks of Suilven and Quinag, but also forms part of the low hills of the Parphe behind Cape Wrath. Apart from the Durness Limestone, which gives a few small areas of fertile land, the rocks west of the Moine Thrust are mainly hard and acidic. While they favour acid peat formation, the irregular topography gives an extremely variable and patchy development of blanket bog. The Parphe has some fairly large areas, but farther south it is much dissected and mostly shallow.

Climate

Climate is of overriding importance in the development of blanket bog (see Chapter 3). The widespread occurrence of this vegetation and its associated deep peat across Caithness and Sutherland suggests that the climate of the whole region is, or has been, suitable for its development. The combination of high and regular precipitation, high atmospheric humidity, relatively cool mean temperatures and small annual temperature range required for the growth of ombrotrophic bog is eminently well satisfied across the region. There are, nevertheless, various gradients of climate which need to be considered.

The prevailing westerly airstreams from the Atlantic impose an underlying gradient of climatic wetness from west to east. The moisture-laden air gives high

rainfall and atmospheric humidity in western, coastal areas, and there is a decrease in both conditions with distance eastwards, so that the eastern coastal areas are drier. As in other parts of Britain, the presence of a high range of mountains close to and parallel with the west coast greatly amplifies this broad geographical gradient. The western mountains of Sutherland produce extremely high orographic rainfall (up to 2500 mm) and then a marked rain shadow effect eastwards, so that precipitation rapidly declines to 1200 mm in central Sutherland and is only 700 mm at the north-east tip of Caithness (see Figure 12a).

There is an anomaly, in that the high mountain topography which produces the heaviest rainfall is also the least conducive to extensive waterlogging and development of blanket bog. Although also very wet and humid, the lower western zone of coastal moorlands is also mostly too rugged and irregular to allow extensive growth of bog. In both these zones of Sutherland there is a general prevalence of heavily leached and acidic soils, with surface horizons of 'mor' humus or shallow peat with frequent occurrence of deeper peat wherever topography allows.

Extensive development of blanket bog occurs in east Sutherland and Caithness under conditions of lower rainfall but optimal topography and geology. On the other hand, under conditions of extreme rainfall,

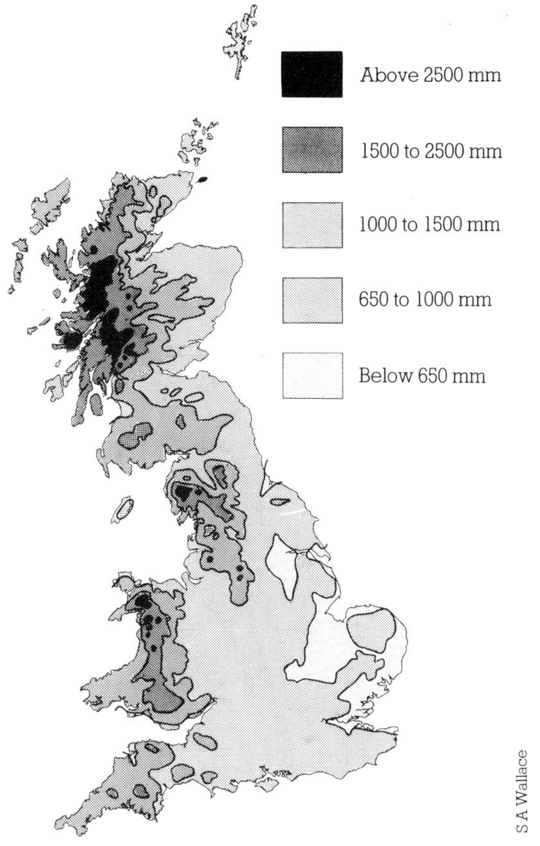

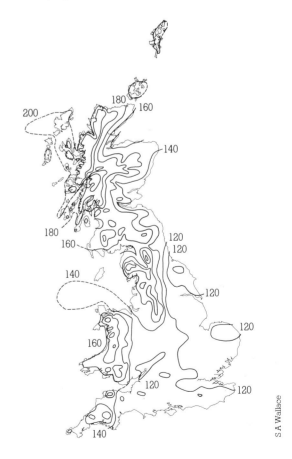

Above 2500 mm

1500 to 2500 mm

1000 to 1500 mm

650 to 1000 mm

Below 650 mm

S A Wallace

S A Wallace

Figure 12a Average annual rainfall, after *Climatological Atlas of the British Isles* (Meteorological Office 1952).

Figure 12b Distribution of "wet days". A "wet day" is a period of 24 hours during which 1 mm of precipitation is recorded. (Compiled by Ratcliffe (1968) from data published in *British Rainfall* (1951-60).)

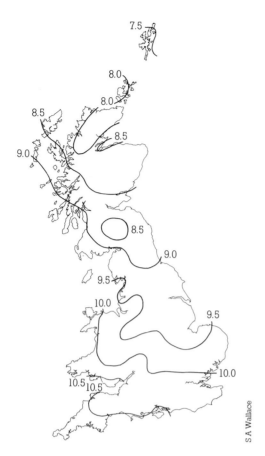

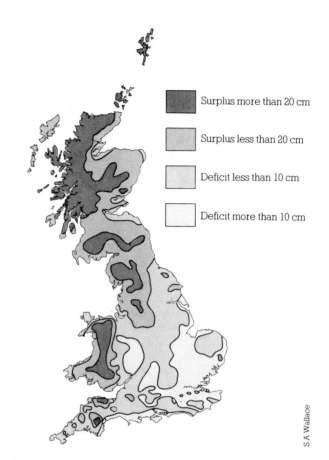

Figure 12c Average means of daily mean temperature, after *Climatological Atlas of the British Isles* (Meteorological Office 1952).

Figure 12d West to east gradients of oceanicity across Britain. This index of climatic wetness is the difference between precipitation and evapo-transpiration for the six months April to September. (Redrawn from Macdonald, Wood, Edwards & Aldhous 1957.)

shallow peat occurs on slopes of up to 20°, or even steeper angles on shady north aspects.

The relatively low rainfall in the east of the region has led some ecologists (Crampton 1911; Pearsall 1956) to wonder whether it was sufficient to allow active bog growth at the present day. Their doubt appears to have resulted from an insufficient appreciation of the importance of rainfall frequency and low mean temperature in maintaining constancy of ground moisture. Boatman & Armstrong (1968), in describing a patterned blanket bog in the far west of Sutherland, point out that the rainfall recorded close to the site is, at 1400 mm, barely half that on the Silver Flowe, a series of similar patterned bogs in Galloway. While the rainfall of Caithness is similar to that of, say, Dorset, this gives no idea of the large number of days with drizzle and dampness or simply complete cloud-cover and of the general coolness of the summers. Figure 13 shows both the even distribution of rainfall, measured as frequency rather than amount, and the consistent differences between two Sutherland locations, both of them in the Flow Country. Figure 14 shows even more clearly the lack of correlation between amount and frequency of rainfall over a larger area of the northern Highlands and Islands.

Crampton (1911) gives rainfall and temperature records for Caithness which indicate a range of 50-100 mm of rainfall each month and a temperature

range from 3°C on the high plateau in winter to 14°C on the lowland plain in summer. He points out that the warmest months (though even these are relatively cool) have a consistently high rainfall. Wilson & Womersley (1975) state that, although the mean January temperature is similar to that of Kew (4.4°C), the mean July temperature in Wick is 12.7°C whereas that of Kew is 17.7°C. They note that Caithness has a relatively low rainfall but that this is spread over a total of 225 rain days. This regular precipitation is reflected in the fact that between May and September the average daily insolation is only about 4.6 hours and the relative humidity averages 85% throughout the year. Wilson & Womersley also comment on the small number of days with no wind. Records for the north coast give annual average windspeeds of 30 km per hour, with north-easterly gales in spring and north-westerly gales in autumn.

The map of mean annual numbers of wet days (Figure 12b) – regarded as the best ecological index of precipitation (see Chapter 3) – shows that virtually the whole region has more than 160 wet days, which appear to be around the critical limit for development of blanket bog in Britain and Ireland. When this is compared with the map for mean annual temperature (Figure 12c), the favourable combination of general wetness and coolness of climate in this far northern region of Scotland is made clear.

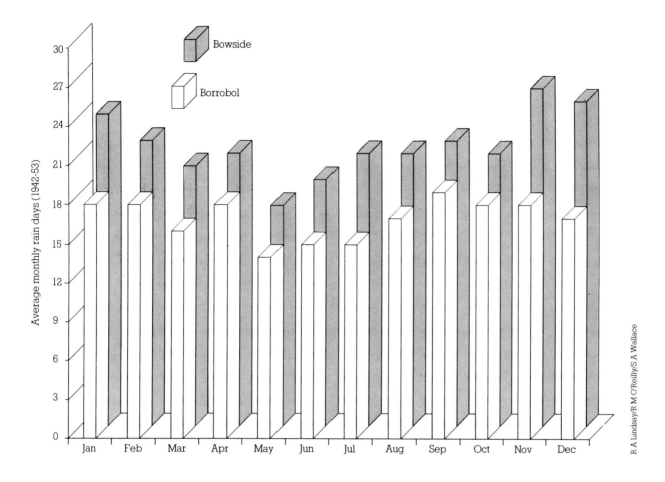

Figure 13 Average monthly distribution of "rain days" (see Figure 2) for Bowside in northern Sutherland and Borrobol in central Sutherland. (Figures taken from *Scottish Peat Surveys*, Vol. 2 (DAFS 1965), provided by courtesy of the Meteorological Office.)

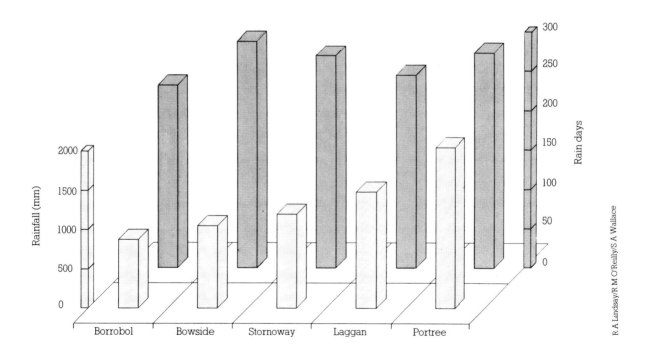

Figure 14 Average annual "rain days" and total rainfall (mm) for Borrobol in central Sutherland, Bowside in north Sutherland, Stornoway in Lewis, Laggan on Islay and Portree on Skye (1942-1953). (Figures taken from *Scottish Peat Surveys*, Vol. 2 (DAFS 1965), provided by courtesy of the Meteorological Office.)

The modern concept of evapo-transpiration has been valuable in integrating various aspects of climate into an ecologically meaningful index of effective wetness (Green 1964). The map in Figure 12d suggests that a water surplus (excess of rainfall over evapo-transpiration) during the six months April to September favours the development of blanket bog. The whole of Caithness and Sutherland experiences such a water surplus, and indeed over all but the eastern coastal zone the excess is 200 mm or more.

Precipitation, humidity and cloud cover increase with altitude, while temperature and evapo-transpiration decrease. Other factors being equal, there is thus a tendency for increasing altitude to favour blanket bog development, and this is especially noticeable in more southern and climatically marginal districts for this formation, such as Dartmoor. The altitudinal effect thus produces local, orographic gradients relevant to the understanding of blanket bog distribution and characteristics within Caithness and Sutherland. The reduction in temperature with increasing altitude also affects plant growth directly. Birse (1971) uses accumulated temperature in day-degrees (see below) as a measure of temperature for plant growth. In Caithness and Sutherland an accumulated temperature of 275-550 day°C is estimated for the highest ground (e.g. Ben Klibreck, Ben More Assynt). On the coasts and in north-east Caithness, the figure is 1100-1375 day°C. Most of the peatland area occurs well within these two extremes at 825-1100 day°C (Birse & Dry 1970).

Birse & Robertson (1970) also consider exposure and accumulated frost. Both factors attain moderate values for the majority of the peatland area. Exposure increases towards the west coast, and winters are very mild on all coasts, especially the west. Altitude increases both exposure and frost throughout the two districts. The winters, then, are mild in comparison with the rest of Scotland, especially the Grampian Highlands, but exposure is generally quite severe and little different from that in other northern Scottish regions.

The two maps of Birse & Dry (1970) and Birse & Robertson (1970) are combined by Birse (1971) to construct a map of bioclimatic sub-regions in order to relate climatic conditions in Scotland to climate categories employed in Europe (e.g. Tuhkamen 1987). Thermal zonation (south to north, low- to high-altitude), oceanicity and moisture status are the determinants of bioclimatic zones. These categories are used as ecologically relevant subdivisions of climate for blanket bog development and differentiation.

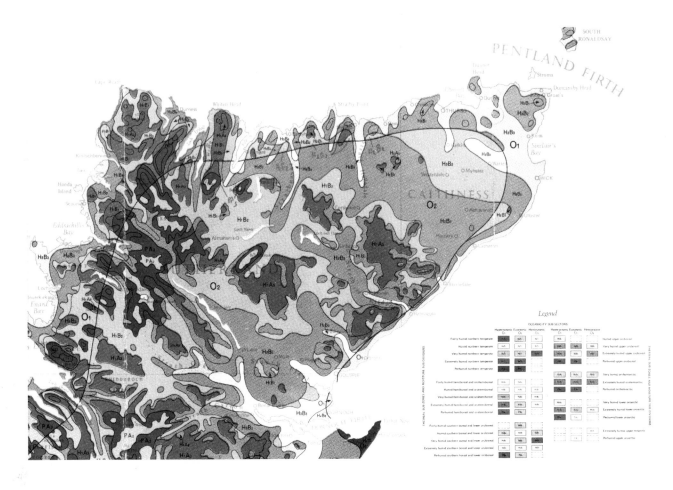

Figure 15 Bioclimatic sub-regions for Caithness and Sutherland, derived by Birse (1971). For explanation of categories, see text. (Copyright Macaulay Land Use Research Institute.)

Bioclimatic zones of Caithness and Sutherland

Birse (1971) derives a total of 62 bioclimatic sub-regions for Scotland, which are grouped into three categories of oceanicity and seven thermal/moisture subdivisions (Figure 15). The primary separation in Caithness and Sutherland is into a coastal hyperoceanic zone (O1) and an inland euoceanic zone (O2), on the basis of length and intensity of growing season, relative humidity and degree of windiness. Within each oceanicity zone, O1 and O2, there are seven thermal sub-zones and two moisture divisions, the wetter of the two (Humid) divided into four subdivisions of annual potential water deficit.

Of the 62 sub-regions identified, 27 occur in Caithness and Sutherland, from the hyperoceanic perhumid lower oroarctic (O1.PA2) on the summit of Foinaven to the euoceanic fairly humid hemiboreal (O2.H4/B3) around Dornoch (see Figure 15).

The main peatland areas are subject to a somewhat more moderate range of conditions. Of the 27 bioclimatic zones which occur in Caithness and Sutherland, half are associated with the peatlands, the remainder being concentrated amongst the complex landforms of the Moine Thrust zone. The conditions which characterise each bioclimatic zone can be seen in Figure 16.

The entire coastal strip is distinguished from more central parts by the moderating influence of the sea, with some parts experiencing less than 20 day-degrees of frost a year. This is in contrast to inland high-level ground such as Knockfin Heights (altitude 450 m) which may experience up to 230 day-degrees of frost. However, the price of such mild winters is high incidence of gales, so that the coastal belt shares with Knockfin Heights mean wind speeds of 6.2-8.0 m/s, whilst the more sheltered central plain experiences speeds of 4.4-6.2m/s and the straths have wind speeds only half those of the coastal and high-level zones.

The bulk of the peatlands area is divided into five main lowland climatic zones and two high-altitude zones, together with one or two others which are of particular note.

O1.H3/B3 Hyperoceanic humid hemiboreal

The zone occurs at its most extensive in Scotland across the wide agricultural belt of north-east Caithness. Its other main occrrence is along the west coast of the Uists, but it also affects a narrow coastal fringe around Lewis and the westernmost strip of Sutherland and Wester Ross. The extreme exposure of these other areas is in contrast to the apparently sheltered nature of the Caithness agricultural interior.

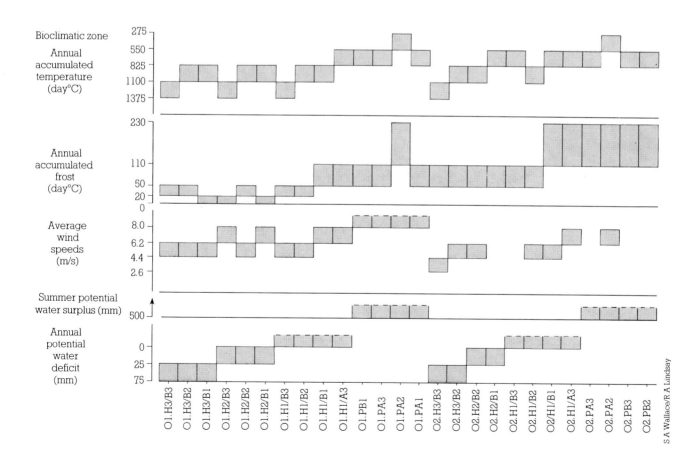

Figure 16 Climatic regime for the bioclimatic sub-regions which occur in Caithness and Sutherland, based on Birse & Dry (1970), Birse & Robertson (1970) and Birse (1971).

O1.H3/B2 Hyperoceanic humid southern boreal

The centre of distribution is Shetland, where a high proportion of the lower-lying ground dominated by thin peat and organic soils falls within this category. In Caithness, which is its other major occurrence in Scotland, it prevails over low-lying coastal ground which has not yet been subject to intensive agricultural development and is therefore still largely peat-covered.

O1.H3/B1 Hyperoceanic humid upper oroboreal

In contrast to H3/B3, this zone is largely restricted to the Orkneys, with only a few small localities in Caithness and Sutherland, which support peat of a thin, maritime heath type rather than deep ombrotrophic peat.

O1.H1/B1 Hyperoceanic extremely humid upper oroboreal

This is an extremely localised zone, restricted to the far west coast and associated with high-level ground. It is characteristic of central Barvas Moor and the great sweep of peat to the north of Achmore in the Outer Hebrides, as well as of the lower slopes of the Trotternish Ridge on Skye. In Sutherland it occurs mainly in the north-west corner, where the peninsulas of A'Mhoine and Cape Wrath represent its major centre of occurrence in Scotland.

O2.H3/B2 Euoceanic humid southern boreal

This coincides with the other major zone of agricultural reclamation, where a number of substantial mire systems remain. Effectively the zone occurs nowhere else in Scotland, and it contains one of the 'classic' Caithness mire sites in the Dubh Lochs of Shielton.

O2.H2/B2 Euoceanic very humid southern boreal and lower oroboreal

Although forming the major climatic zone of the Caithness and Sutherland lowland plain, this zone is also represented – perhaps rather surprisingly – on the northern slopes of the Moorfoot, Lammermuir and Pentland Hills. The difference between the two regions appears to be that the more southerly occurrence is essentially oroboreal and therefore has the potential for a more extended growing season than the true southern boreal zone of Caithness and Sutherland. The contrast in altitude (300-500 m for the Southern Uplands as opposed to 150 m for the Flow Country) and latitude (less than 56°N for the Southern Uplands and more than 58°N for the Flow Country) throws the difference between the two areas into sharp relief.

This zone corresponds to the major area of peat formation throughout the low-lying areas of the Flow Country. It is also the bioclimatic zone within which the majority of recent afforestation has taken place.

O2.H1/B2 Euoceanic extremely humid southern boreal and lower oroboreal

Like the previous zone, this has a discontinuous distribution across Scotland, though with a major occurrence in Caithness and Sutherland. The different areas where this zone is found display some of the same contrasts as described for H2/B2, although the zone is clearly somewhat orogenic even in the Flow Country. It occupies the higher flat ground in the west of the region, rising in places to 330 m, in contrast to a limit of 700 m in the Southern Uplands. However, its general distribution in Caithness and Sutherland also demonstrates the phenomenon of "north-west oceanicity" alluded to by Pearsall (1956). This arises because Ben Klibreck, Ben Armine, the Ben Griams and Knockfin Heights generate markedly higher rainfall over ground lying to the north-west of their summits during the frequent north-westerly gales. Rannoch Moor, lying in a high-level basin within the Grampian Mountains, is also characterised by this climatic zone.

O2.H1/B1 Euoceanic extremely humid upper oroboreal

This occurs widely throughout Scotland as the zone associated with the lower slopes of upland massifs within the central climatic belt. It thus occurs locally in the Southern Uplands, as a central band through the Grampian Mountains, and fringing all the highest plateaux in Caithness and Sutherland.

O2.H1/A3 Euoceanic extremely humid orohemiarctic

Characterising all high ground above 330 m, apart from mountain summits such as Ben Klibreck and Ben Hope, this zone characterises the altitudinal upper limit of blanket bog formation in Caithness and Sutherland, mainly because any higher land tends to be too steep rather than because of any climatic limit. It combines the high precipitation levels typical of an oceanic climate with a temperature regime more usually associated with northern boreal conditions. This is borne out by records of the northern boreal/sub-arctic spiders *Hilaria frigida, Valckenairia clavicornis* and *Rhaebothorax morulus* taken from the pool systems on Knockfin (E Milner pers. comm.). In the Monadhliaths, ground with this climate has been found with snow patches as late as July on north-facing aspects (NCC unpublished). Although there is extensive peat, conditions for its formation must be severe, in view of the combination of frost action and powerful scouring by frequent rain.

Conclusion

Present climatic conditions may differ in some degree from those of the earlier periods which saw the origin and development of these peatlands. Nevertheless, the present vigour of the bog surface as peat-forming vegetation across so much of Caithness and Sutherland suggests that the present climate is probably as favourable for the growth of blanket bog as at any previous time in its history. Where bog surfaces have lost this vigour, the cause appears to be mainly human disturbance, or just possibly a natural senescence of bog growth, rather than any shift in climate.

Caithness and Sutherland east of the Moine Thrust satisfy the essential combination of conditions for ombrotrophic bog development – cool, humid climate, gentle topography and acidic substrates – more extensively than any other part of Britain or Ireland. The only other peatlands of comparable size likely to have existed in these islands during the Flandrian period were predominantly of rich fen type – the Fenland of East Anglia and the Bog of Allen in central Ireland, both of which have been largely drained out of existence. Other extensive and important areas of low-level blanket bog include Barvas Moor on Lewis, Rannoch Moor in Perth and Argyll and the Wigtownshire–south Ayrshire Flows; but they do not compare in size with the Caithness and Sutherland Flows.

5 Human impact

The peatlands of Caithness and Sutherland are one of the most extensive examples of a near-natural landscape still surviving in Britain, and one not far removed from the original primaeval scene before early man began to exert a significant influence on our environment. As a region, Caithness and Sutherland nevertheless have had a long history of human occupation, as evidenced by the Neolithic burial chambers of the Grey Cairns, at Camster, and the discovery that Caithness flagstones were exported to the continent at about the same time.

The intensity and effect of many land-uses in pre-Clearance times is difficult to judge, and the relationships between man-induced changes and natural processes as factors affecting bog systems are still the subject of considerable debate. Nonetheless it is possible to identify two major activities which have undoubtedly played a long-established and significant part in determining the current state of vegetation and surface patterns on the Caithness and Sutherland mires – crofting and sporting estate management. Forestry represents a far more recent, and dramatic, type of land-use change. Although some of its impacts are similar to those of more traditional land-uses, afforestation is considered mainly in the next chapter.

The effects of game management and crofting tenure overlap, but together they are responsible for four key modifiers of the mire system – drainage, peat-cutting, burning and grazing. The phenomenon of peat erosion is considered in relation to these activities, and the possible effect on the peatlands of atmospheric pollution generated in distant regions is also discussed.

Drainage

Drainage has been general practice on wet ground for centuries. This is partly to improve the quality of grazing and partly to remove the hazard to stock. More recently, however, intensive drainage has represented the first stage in preparing open ground for afforestation. Because sites already completely ploughed for forestry were not included in the sites selected for our survey, Figure 17 refers mainly to the form of hill-drainage known as "moor-gripping" (Stewart 1980), rather than to the more intensive type of drainage required for forestry. Until the early 1930s the method was laborious, involving hand-digging. The development of crawler tractors and the Cuthbertson plough meant that extensive areas could be "gripped" in a short time. Many crofting communities therefore pooled their resources to hire drainage contractors, with all parties benefiting from the availability of

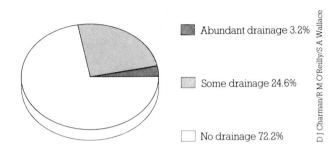

Abundant drainage 3.2%

Some drainage 24.6%

No drainage 72.2%

D J Charman/R M O'Reilly/S A Wallace

Figure 17 Proportion of sites in the NCC's Peatland Survey of Caithness and Sutherland affected by differing intensities of drainage.

government grant-aid designed to encourage land drainage for agriculture.

The extent to which this policy can be said to have been successful is vividly apparent on aerial photographs for many parts of Caithness and Sutherland – for example the area of Forsinard Flows north-west of Forsinard Station. Figure 17 shows that a quarter of the sites surveyed by the NCC had been drained to some degree, though few had suffered comprehensive drainage. The wide spacing of moor-grips means that such drainage is not generally recorded as "abundant". Consequently the 24.6% of sites with "some drainage" largely represent those which have been moor-gripped.

Recent advances in the understanding of peatland hydrology suggest that a thorough reappraisal of peat drainage is required, particularly in terms of its impacts on nature conservation value. The first indicators of change are often of no interest to (and are therefore not recorded by) developers, but these indicators may herald larger changes which then become of great significance to the developer.

Ivanov (1981), in providing the definitive modern work on peatland hydrology, emphasises the need to understand the impacts of Russia's long-established peat development programme on local and regional hydrologies and to consider the nature and implications of future schemes. He catalogues the effects of drainage thus: "Intensive drainage and lowering of the average water table . . . lead to the disintegration of mire systems through the desiccation of their peat . . . the main thickness of peat becomes extremely dehydrated, its temperature rises and biological processes leading to the decomposition of organic material are activated. Decomposition reinforced by the pressure of the peat's own weight (which, after the lowering of the water table, is no longer suspended in water) and by capillary tension, also resulting from lowering of the water table, leads to a shrinkage of the whole peat deposit, a gradual increase in its mineral content and the disappearance of its organic components."

Ingram (1982, 1983) and Ingram & Bragg (1984) combine much of their own original research with that described by Ivanov (1981) to suggest that recourse to normal soil hydrophysics is not appropriate when studying bog systems, because the hydrology of a bog is compartmentalised between the acrotelm and the catotelm (see Chapter 1). The fundamental role played by this "diplotelmic" (two-layered) structure in maintaining the stability of the entire bog unit is, they feel, widely overlooked by land managers, despite its extreme sensitivity to a wide variety of land-use practices.

The effects of peatland drainage fall into two broad categories. First, there is a change in profiles and gradients of the drained surface, sometimes extensive enough to affect the entire shape of the bog. This is the response most readily recognised by drainage engineers, although there are a number of features unique to peatland soils. Secondly, there is the much more subtle response of the living vegetation within the acrotelm. This latter response is often ignored completely, yet is probably the most important, and the unique, aspect of peatland drainage when the likely impact on the nature conservation importance of a site is being considered.

More so than with other soils, the effects of drainage on peatland are likely to be dramatic and irreversible only where the drainage system is regularly cleaned out, because the growing surface of *Sphagnum* moss will tend eventually to choke ditches which are not maintained and thereby to stabilise the hydrology of the area. However, there are circumstances where drainage has the effect of setting off a sequence of events which destabilise the hydrology. This can occur to such an extent that no further maintenance is required and the bog becomes self-draining.

The physical response to drainage

Hobbs (1986) details the various factors which an engineer will encounter when working with peat soils and demonstrates that, for many aspects of its behaviour, peat is similar to an unconsolidated clay. However, he identifies certain marked peculiarities, not least the high water content of peat bodies, but also, after drainage, the sequence of primary consolidation, followed by shrinkage, secondary compression and finally wastage or subsidence.

Primary consolidation is usually the major response of a soil to increased loading. As indicated by Ivanov's (1981) comments above, this increased loading can result purely from drainage. Wet, unhumified peat soils certainly exhibit a rapid initial response, with consolidation of 1.5 m in a peat depth of 10 m within 12 months if the water table is maintained at 1 m depth (Hobbs 1986). Primary

consolidation occurs because void space within the soil is reduced as the weight of the overburden (in this case the layer of drained peat) compresses the wet soil beneath, leading to expulsion of water from these diminishing pore spaces. Igarashi, Akazawa, Matsushita & Umeda (1984) point out that unhumified peats typically have large void spaces and therefore tend to undergo substantial primary consolidation. This large void ratio is in contrast to conditions in clayey soils, where primary consolidation is the only marked response to loading; the scale of response is thus much smaller in clay soils.

Shrinkage Where loading is caused by drainage, the layers thus removed from regular inundation experience physical shrinkage of structural parts. Hobbs (1986) recorded this shrinkage as typically 35-45%. Amorphous peat shrinks more than unhumified peat because its fibres are not aligned in any way. Unhumified peats, on the other hand, show marked lateral shrinkage but little vertical shrinkage because individual *Sphagnum* stems, which tend to remain upright in unhumified peats, have little capacity for vertical shrinkage. Shrinkage in such peats therefore tends to induce cracking rather than significant surface lowering. Only when the peat is significantly humified will both phenomena occur (see Figure 2 in Pyatt 1987). Hobbs (1986) illustrates the irreversible changes which occur to the peat colloids and structure once drying out has occurred by pointing to the usefulness of dried peat bales as stable, lightweight fill for use in conditions of permanent waterlogging. Despite constant inundation, which prevents oxidation and wastage (see below), the peat-fill can be relied on not to re-expand and thereby affect any graded contours.

Secondary compression begins once pore water pressure falls to zero above atmospheric pressure (Igarashi et al. 1984) and occurs as a "creep-like" process with gradual rearrangement of the peat fibres and steady loss of more tightly bound water from micropores (Hobbs 1986). The process occurs over a much longer period than primary consolidation and is linear with time on a log scale. Hobbs emphasises that this is the major response of peatland systems to loading (including drainage) but says that its effects are often omitted from engineering considerations in favour of the more dramatic and ubiquitous response (for most soils) of primary consolidation.

Wastage/subsidence Finally, and almost uniquely to peatland soils, there is the phenomenon of wastage. This is often difficult to separate from the effects of secondary compression and shrinkage, but arises when the organic components of peat oxidise to gaseous compounds and water, leaving only the tiny mineral component as a residue. Like secondary compression, this is a long-term process, one of the most vivid examples being the famous Holme Fen post in Cambridgeshire, where loss of peat has measurably lowered the ground level by almost 4 m since 1854 (Godwin 1978). The overall effect of subsidence is described by Prus-Chakinski (1962) and Eggelsmann (1975), who describe the general lowering of the mire surface on drained ground as a result of the various processes of shrinkage, subsidence and slumping.

Whilst these processes occur throughout an area of drainage, Pyatt (1987) notes that one of the most obvious effects is in the widening of original drain lines. An example of such a response can be seen in Figure 18, for a raised mire in Cumbria. The central drain was dug before 1939 and has been repeatedly cleaned out since. The width of the drain itself is only 0.5 m, but the effect on the mire surface gradient can be seen to extend to at least 100 m on either side.

Ingram's (1982) Ground Water Mound Model is based not on the average state of water balance, but on the very worst conditions of drought experienced by the mire. The long-term effects on surface gradients and stability of the entire system therefore depend on how the hydrology of the drained part of the mire behaves under such extreme conditions. Ivanov (1981) states that a mire surface which has its surface vegetation replaced by a non-peat-forming community and whose natural drainage remains (or is repeatedly) disrupted will experience gradual loss of peat until eventually all trace of an organic soil will be lost. In the case of forestry, the periods of site preparation at the first and second rotations will ensure complete disruption of the surface hydrology and encourage extensive wastage, whilst the phases of closed canopy will induce deep oxidation of the peat and extensive secondary compression as the weight of timber overburden increases. Whilst it is therefore possible to point to likely changes to the peat underlying forestry plantations, the implications for areas of open mire sharing the same hydrological unit as the plantation has been only partially answered.

The scale of consolidation and wastage around drain lines is often less in upland blanket bogs, which tend to be shallower and much more humified. They are presumably also less prone to surface drying, because the constant precipitation helps to keep the soil saturated for most of the time. The depth of drains and their configuration in an overall system are also important in affecting the rate of water removal and, hence, of lowering of the water table.

Ingram & Bragg (1984) point out that the acrotelm is so structured as to buffer the catotelm from all outside influences, so that the aerated layer never falls into the catotelm under natural conditions. In the event of drainage, only those areas which lose this thin surface layer will suffer the effects outlined above. Obviously, therefore, the important question is over what lateral distance will the acrotelm be disrupted?

The response of the acrotelm and surface vegetation to drainage

A recurring assertion through much of the literature on peat hydrology is that the effect of drainage is limited to a few metres either side of a drain and in general merely aids surface water run-off (Boelter 1972; Galvin 1976; Stewart 1980; Stewart & Lance 1983). Such apparently modest effects of drainage generally reflect situations where an acrotelm is no longer present at the peat surface, but the profound changes to both catotelm and acrotelm described here and above are most pronounced when a well-developed, *Sphagnum*-rich acrotelm is drained. Pyatt (1987) comments that "aeration of the fibrous layer improves as soon as the water table is

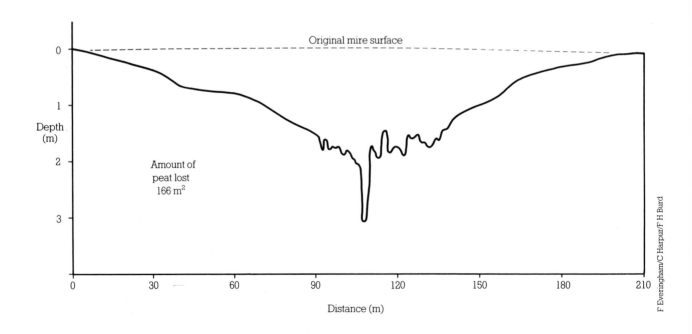

Figure 18 Cross-section of a drain cut into the peat of Wedholme Flow in Cumbria. The gradually sloping profiles on either side of the drain (which has been repeatedly cleaned out) indicate the extent of primary consolidation, secondary compression and wastage since the inter-war years. The horizontal scale has been compressed to display more clearly the extent of surface lowering.

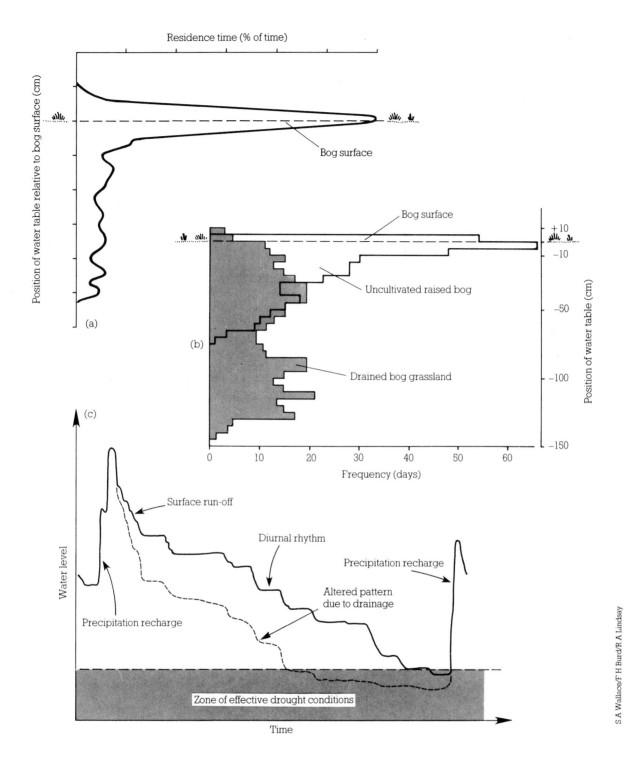

Figure 19 The effect of drainage on the water table in the acrotelm –
(a) Location of the water table in relation to the bog surface, expressed as proportion of time spent at particular depths ("residence time"). (Taken from Bragg 1982.)
(b) Pattern of residence times for bog water tables from a natural and an undrained bog in West Germany. (Taken from Ingram 1983.)
(c) Continuous recording of the water table, showing run-off and diurnal rhythm, from an undrained bog in Argyll (NCC unpublished data) and a generalised indication of the effect of increasing the surface run-off by, for example, drainage.

lowered". However, as Ingram & Bragg (1984) and Hobbs (1986) note, this fibrous surface layer is the acrotelm, and increased aeration (or reduced flooding) of this layer has profound ecological implications for the overall arrangement of species and surface patterns (microtopes) on a mire system, according to Ivanov (1981). He states (p. 199): "The maximum difference in mean long-term [water]

levels which does not lead to a change in the quantity or floristic composition of mire plant communities is very small. For several varieties of moss cover it is less than 4–5 cm."

The small scale of the niches taken up by bog plant communities has been discussed in Chapter 2, but Rydin & McDonald (1985) demonstrate that species typical of A1 hollows or T1 lawns, such as *Sphagnum tenellum*, are actually unable to grow at positions in the microtope just 10 cm above their normal niche. Clymo & Hayward (1982) also show that some of the more common bog *Sphagna* are extremely sensitive to desiccation. After 16 days of drought, plants of *S. papillosum* and *S. magellanicum* were found to be incapable of resuscitation, whilst *S. rubellum* showed some recovery response. Only *S. imbricatum* seemed entirely unaffected by the event. This accords with field observations of drained peatlands where scattered *S. imbricatum* hummocks may still be found although the majority of the *Sphagnum* cover has been lost. This species and *S. fuscum* nevertheless become more vulnerable to fire once the water table is lowered.

The proportion of time during which the water table stands at any given depth in the peat is known as the "residence time". In an undisturbed bog, the water table lies within a few centimetres of the ground surface for more than 90% of the time (see Figure 19a); the surface layers are thus said to have a high residence time. Drainage changes this pattern of residence times (see Figure 19b).

A typical sequence of water table movements producing a curve such as that shown in Figure 19a is displayed in Figure 19c. Also shown is the effect of increasing the rate of surface water removal – commonly asserted as the only effect of drainage. From Figure 19c it can be seen that drought events experienced by the *Sphagnum* carpet are determined by the rate at which water is lost from the surface layers between rain events. If the rate of loss is increased, by drainage for example, drought conditions between rain events will increase in frequency and become more prolonged. Such a change in acrotelm hydrology can be expected to have a significant effect on the surface vegetation, as predicted by Ivanov.

The outcome of such changes is not necessarily loss of *Sphagnum* in itself, and Ivanov explores alternative responses by mire systems to changed hydrological circumstances, particularly in terms of the relationship between hydrological stability and surface pattern ("arrangement of microtopes"). Ivanov demonstrates that the resilience of mire systems to hydrological change depends almost entirely on the presence of at least two distinct elements in the surface pattern, each having markedly differing hydraulic conductivities. Under conditions of increasing water content, the acrotelm requires a large proportion of the surface to possess a high rate of surface seepage, and therefore the aquatic element of hollows and pools, which have very high hydraulic conductivities, increases to form the dominant microtope across the mire. Where conditions become increasingly dry, the rate of surface seepage through the acrotelm must decrease, and so the mire surface becomes dominated by ridge and hummock communities, which have lower hydraulic conductivities.

This alternating pattern of "strip-ridge", as Ivanov terms it, forms an interconnected mosaic whereby the stability of each part of the pattern depends on the stability achieved by the sections of pattern further upslope (Scottish Wildlife Trust 1987). Equally, the rate of water percolation downslope is determined by the abundance of low-conductivity ridge structures. Such features become more abundant in the natural transition from flat mire expanse to the sloping mire margin, providing hydrological stability to the latter.

The effect of drainage anywhere within this system, therefore, is to impose a new set of gradients to which the acrotelm must adapt, if it can, though there is always the additional danger of catastrophic change such as the formation of erosion complexes within pool systems or the occurrence of bog-bursts in high-rainfall areas.

The first response to drainage involves the reduction, or even loss, of the wetter element within the mire surface pattern. However, although such flexibility can occur over areas which are dominated by hollows and shallow pools, the deeper A3/A4 "endotelmic lakes" consist of physical structures which cannot alter their surface area. Such areas of pattern therefore become unstable, leading to a lowering of the water level in the lake and an accompanying fall in the mean water table in surrounding parts of the microtope. The presence of peat 'cliffs' around larger *dubh lochain* in Caithness and Sutherland is common where part of the mire has suffered damage.

The general pattern of loss of hollows resulting from drainage is illustrated by Woike & Schmatzler (1980); see Figure 20. The possibility that partial drainage can alter the entire surface pattern is consistent with the changes observed by Chapman & Rose (1986) at Coom Rigg Moss (see Chapter 6). Tubridy (1984) also demonstrates a marked correlation between absence of pools and presence of peat-cuttings on Mongan Bog in County Offaly (see Figure 21). Only on the side of the bog furthest from extensive peat-cutting are bog pools common.

Such changes may also explain a number of cases where anomalous species distributions point to the original presence of pools or hollows on mires which no longer possess such features. Thus Cors Fochno, near Aberystwyth, was intensely drained on the west side in the early 1960s. It has since been found to support *Rhynchospora fusca* and the damselfly *Ceriagrion tenellum* only in flooded peat-cutting hollows, yet both are typical of bog pools and are reputed to have occurred originally on the mire expanse. The site shows no evidence of such pools today, having only shallow *Sphagnum* hollows (Dr A D Fox pers. comm.).

The sometimes dramatic effects of drainage within pool systems can be seen in a number of localities in Caithness and Sutherland. Single moor-grips or forest drains entering pools on the edge of a pool complex have caused them to deteriorate.

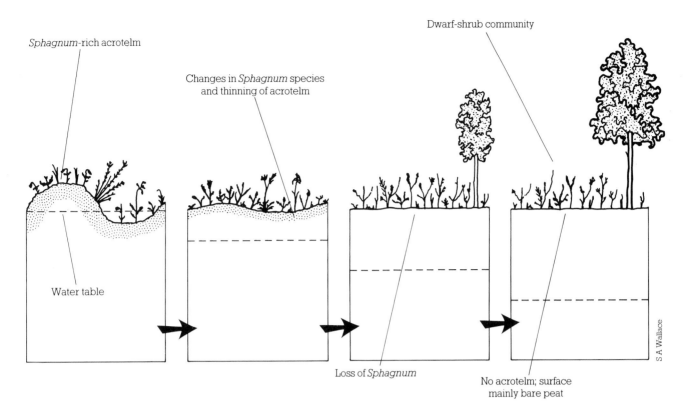

Figure 20 Changes in the surface and vegetation of an ombrotrophic bog with lowering of the water table (after Woike & Schmatzler 1980).

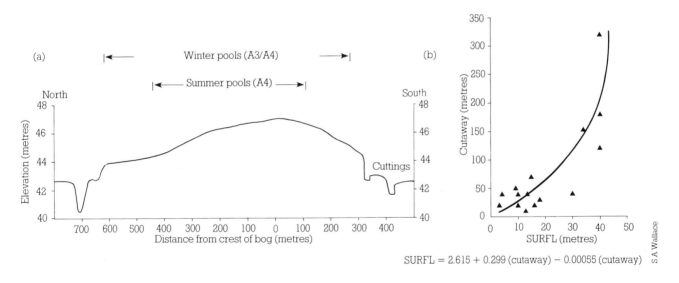

SURFL = 2.615 + 0.299 (cutaway) − 0.00055 (cutaway)

Figure 21 Relationship between the distribution of winter pools and the removal of peat by turf-cutting (for fuel) from the south side of Mongan Bog, County Offaly – (a) distribution of pools and location of cuttings; (b) regression analysis showing significant asymetry of pool distribution correlated with distance from peat-cuttings. (Taken from Tubridy 1984.)

Peat-cutting

Another of the more obvious impacts, which can show clearly for hundreds of years, is the widespread cutting of peat for fuel. Extensive peat banks are still worked by residents of Wick and Thurso along the Camster road, but a number of sites in both Caithness and coastal Sutherland attest to extensive past working. Rattar Moss beside the

Castle of Mey, for example, has clearly been completely cut over and subsequently abandoned, allowing an interesting, if modified, vegetation to regenerate. The same is true for such sites as Loch Hempriggs, south of Wick, and Moss of Greenland, east of Castletown.

In Shetland it is not unusual to find peat banks far removed from any likely habitation, past or present, with traditional 'peat-tracks' indicating the route taken by the peat-cutters and their peat-laden cattle or ponies. Little evidence was found from the central peatlands of Caithness and Sutherland to indicate that pre-Clearance peat-cutters had strayed far from the immediate vicinity of the straths. Figure 22 shows that only 5% of sites examined had distinct evidence of peat-cutting. Commercial extraction of peat is restricted to a single operation in Caithness, using the 'sausage peat' method, but an experimental peat-fuelled power station was operated for some years in the district during the 1950s, and there are suggestions that peat-fuelled power stations may be considered seriously in the future.

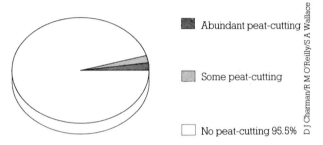

Figure 22 Proportion of sites in the NCC's Peatland Survey of Caithness and Sutherland affected by various intensities of peat-cutting.

Burning

Both of the traditional land-uses of the Flow Country are based on forms of grazing: crofting depends on sheep-grazing, and sporting estates on grazing by deer and grouse. In order to maintain or enhance the quality of this grazing, both employ fire as a management tool. This has undoubtedly been the oldest form of human impact on these mires, even to the extent that it has been suggested as the origin of their treeless character. Burning is also the most widespread of the land-use practices: Figure 23 reveals that only just over one third of sites examined had no obvious signs of recent burning. More than 10% were severely burnt, with peat showing a greasy bituminous layer as described by Conway & Millar (1960) for Burnt Hill in the northern Pennines.

The difficulty in assessing the true extent and impact of burning is that the ecosystem response to fire is still poorly understood. Although this is surprising in view of the large amount of work done in relation to grouse, deer and sheep management over the years, it is perhaps less so when the sources of variability in

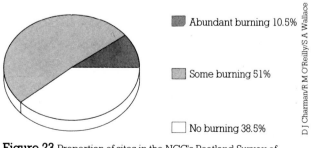

Figure 23 Proportion of sites in the NCC's Peatland Survey of Caithness and Sutherland affected by various intensities of burning.

'fire events' are considered, e.g. wind-speed, air temperature, ground temperature, degree of waterlogging, chemical composition of the vegetation, fire temperature, depth of burn, fire speed and nature of the peat surface (Eigner & Schmatzler 1980; MacLean, Woodley, Weber & Wein 1983; McVean & Lockie 1969).

Fire affects three major aspects of the peatland ecosystem –

- nutrient cycling;
- hydrology;
- vegetation pattern.

Nutrient cycling

There are two distinct phases in the response of nutrient cycling to fire. The first is concerned with redistribution of nutrients during the fire, and the second concerns the subsequent longer-term impact on the cycle (MacLean et al. 1983).

Changes during the fire

Loss of nutrients through volatilisation and smoke
This can include significant losses of carbon, nitrogen and sulphur, as well as cations such as potassium, magnesium and calcium. Phosphorus is not lost in great amounts, but losses increase in step with increasing fire temperature (Allen 1964). MacLean et al. (1983) consider that such volatilised materials are generally not returned to the site of the fire, but blown to other areas, as are significant quantities of mineral-rich fly-ash.

Accumulation of nutrient-rich ash on the peat surface
The ash content of many dwarf shrubs is high in phosphate and cations such as potassium and calcium. Where the bryophyte surface remains largely intact, the high cation exchange ability (CEA: see Chapter 1) of *Sphagnum* tends to bind the newly-deposited minerals and prevent large-scale losses. Where the peat surface has been significantly degraded, the post-fire sequence of events often results in a net loss of nutrients from the ecosystem.

Deposition of waxes/bitumens During the passage of the fire, a layer of bitumens derived from peat waxes (Clymo 1983) may condense on the peat surface. This forms a water-repellent film and effectively protects the lower layers from leaching (Chistjakov, Kuprijanov, Gorshkov & Artsybashev 1983). However, any ash layer is more likely to be lost in surface run-off because downward leaching into the peat profile is more difficult.

Post-fire changes

Nutrient leaching Where the organic surface mat has been destroyed, losses through leaching can be highly significant. Allen (1964) considers that regular losses from smoke and leaching together can result in a rate of depletion which would rapidly remove all available nitrogen from the system. A single fire can remove 45 kg/ha of nitrogen, leading Allen to suggest that nitrogen loss is the most serious consequence of burning.

However, being highly mobile, phosphorus is also susceptible to leaching (MacLean *et al.* 1983; Burke 1975). Most, but not all, of these losses can be made good from atmospheric input within a 10–12-year cycle of burning, and phosphorus and nitrogen are therefore liable to suffer gradual depletion under such a regime. This is a particular problem in oceanic areas such as Caithness and Sutherland because such regions have a relatively low input of particulate matter, generally rich in phosphorus and nitrogen, compared to more continental areas. Precipitation is instead rich in mineral salts derived from the sea (Groenendael *et al.* 1975; Bellamy & Bellamy 1966). Thus, whilst mineral salts are replaced rapidly, the two major nutrients limiting to plant growth, nitrogen and phosphorus, are liable to suffer serious depletion in western areas under all but the longest fire cycles.

Other nutrient effects The normal pattern of nutrient cycling is altered after fire by a number of factors relating to changes in decomposition rate. First, the nutrient release from ash deposits increases the pH of the surface layers, thereby improving conditions for bacterial rather than fungal decay (Fraser 1948). Through its lowered albedo (reflectance), a blackened peat surface tends to absorb heat more easily, thereby increasing the average temperature of the upper profile. This again tends to increase the rate of decomposition (MacLean *et al.* 1983; Hobbs 1986), whilst Komarek (1971) states that increased temperatures on blackened tundra soils stimulate the rate of nitrogen fixation.

Komarek (1971) also states that increased levels of calcium, phosphate and potassium in the ash deposit greatly stimulate the activity of nitrifying bacteria. Coulson & Butterfield (1978) have subsequently demonstrated that higher nitrogen concentrations lead to increased microbial activity, which in turn increases the nutrient flux. However, Hobbs & Gimingham (1987) point out that, although burning may produce a greater availability of plant nutrients, these are also more prone to losses through leaching on a surface where the moss layer has been lost.

Hydrological impacts

MacLean *et al.* (1983) state that the active surface layer becomes deeper after fire, whereas McVean & Lockie (1969) comment that the surface layer of oxygenated peat is destroyed or reduced by burning. Ingram & Bragg (1984) also describe the effect of burning on the diplotelmic mire, stating that many mires have been so severely burnt that the surface layer or acrotelm has been destroyed, creating what they term a single-layered (haplotelmic) mire. The difference between these

two views appears to centre on the definition of the "active layer" or acrotelm. MacLean *et al.* (1983) refer simply to the zone of water table lowering, irrespective of its structure. Ingram & Bragg (1984), on the other hand, are referring to the formal concept of an acrotelm, which comprises a highly-structured profile from the surface to the acrotelm base, overlying amorphous peat of the catotelm (see Chapter 1).

Severe burning undoubtedly destroys the genuine acrotelm and exposes varying depths of the catotelm to oxygen penetration. In cases where the catotelm peat was relatively unhumified before a fire, subsequent loss of the protective acrotelm can result in much deeper atmospheric penetration in the short term. However, the generally increased level of decomposition arising from this will eventually increase humification and reduce hydraulic conductivity of the catotelm peat to a point where the layer of oxygen penetration, as defined by MacLean *et al.* (1983), is reduced, though it is generally still deeper on average than that experienced within an undamaged acrotelm. The point should also be made that any oxygen penetration whatsoever into catotelm peat exposes it to the combined processes of wastage and erosion.

Brown (1983) emphasises the ease with which burning can induce severe gully erosion and thereby give rise to increased sediment loads in previously clear rivers or lakes.

Vegetation changes

The underlying assumptions behind the use of burning as a management tool on moorland systems are that it removes old, unpalatable vegetation and adds a certain amount of fertiliser to the ground in the form of ash, the two effects combining to stimulate fresh growth. Whilst fresh growth of grasses and sedges is undoubtedly stimulated by fire, the response of heather is more variable and the overall range of species produced does not always represent a steady improvement of grazing quality.

Pearsall (1950) and McVean & Lockie (1969) list the factors which affect the vegetation's response to burning on peat as –
* temperature and duration of the fire;
* type of ground (degree of drainage, slope, altitude);
* interval since the last fire.

A Guide to Good Muirburn Practice (DAFS 1977) recommends that burning be carefully controlled, with sufficient manpower, and that areas of deep peat, particularly those with patterns of pools and hollows, should not be burnt under any circumstances. McVean & Lockie (1969), however, point to the problems of implementing such recommendations: "Present day economics of grouse moor and hill-sheep farming management preclude the employment of the necessary staff to carry out moor burning in the way that past experience has shown it should be done." Even in Crampton's (1911) time the problem of uncontrolled burning in the Caithness peatlands was recognised: "The licence to burn is frequently abused, not only by burning at a time later than is allowed by law, to the danger of nesting birds, but also by burning too extensively and indiscriminately."

The problem is little better today. Unlike forestry, sporting interests receive no subsidies, and even agricultural support does not allocate resources to the manpower required for safe and efficient burning. Sporting, grazing and nature conservation would all benefit if the supervision of fires was better supported. Some estate keepers have expressed concern that the quality of the ground is steadily declining as a result of current burning practices, but, with the present staff reduced to a handful of estate workers, they also felt that this state of affairs was unavoidable if the deer were to be kept on the estate for the stalking season.

A well-managed fire will clip off the above-ground vegetation but leave the peat surface and below-ground parts untouched. Damage only occurs when the fire affects or enters the bryophyte-rich ground layer. When this happens, a whole range of effects comes into play. Pearsall (1950) states that burning tends to decrease the cover of *Sphagnum*, encourage the development of vascular plant tussock-formers such as *Eriophorum vaginatum* and induce an uneven surface, and that the increased nutrient flux encourages other bryophytes such as *Aulacomnium palustre*, *Polytrichum* spp., *Campylopus introflexus*, *Pohlia nutans* and *Ceratodon purpureus* to colonise the peat surface.

Evidence from Moor House, in the Pennines, indicates that, although *Eriophorum vaginatum* rises to dominance over a seven-year period after fire, it then declines in favour of *Calluna*. This then achieves maximum cover 11 to 17 years after the fire (Rawes & Hobbs 1979). In Sutherland and, to a lesser extent, in Caithness, the place of *Eriophorum vaginatum* is largely taken by *Trichophorum cespitosum*, whilst the dwarf shrub sward is a more open and mixed type than that typical of the Pennines. The fire succession is analogous in northern Scotland, in that *Trichophorum* tends to rise to dominance at the expense of dwarf shrubs. In the west, where *Molinia caerulea* is often the codominant with *Calluna* on shallow peats or peaty gleys, burning also promotes its ascendancy by altering the competitive balance with *Calluna*. Grazing, combined with fire, favours the monocotyledons at the expense of the dwarf shrubs.

Clymo & Duckett (1986) have established that *Sphagnum* regrowth can occur from stem fragments some 10-20 cm below the peat surface. If a fire were to burn into the *Sphagnum* carpet to below this depth, regeneration would be unlikely. The rate of regeneration on Glasson Moss NNR, Cumbria, which suffered a disastrous fire in 1976 (Lindsay 1977), indicates that eight years or so are required for significant numbers of new *Sphagnum* shoots to appear and only after 10 years are sensitive species such as *Sphagnum pulchrum* able to show significant signs of recovery (NCC unpublished data). It seems likely that a fire interval of at least 20 years would be required for the site even to hold its own as a *Sphagnum*-rich peatland, while recovery of the features typical of an intact mire surface would take much longer. A few hummocks of *S. imbricatum* were present on Glasson Moss in 1956 but now seem to have disappeared, and *S. fuscum* was much reduced in abundance in 1987.

The behaviour of fire within peat is reviewed by Wein (1983), who states that peat will ignite at a moisture content of 20-30% and temperature of 270-280°C. However, after five minutes' heating at 50-60°C, he found that lethal temperatures for most plant propagules were experienced up to 5 cm into the peat, whilst under drier conditions the peat ignited and lethal temperatures reached a depth of 12 cm. He points out that, after fire, the ground became drier because the fire-front had caused evaporation and irreversible drying-out of peat which had not ignited but experienced high temperatures. Lethal temperatures were thus more easily reached and penetrated further in the event of a second fire over the same area. Maltby (1980) describes the slow regeneration of vegetation on the North Yorkshire Moors, where severe fire in the 1976 drought killed large numbers of seeds within the peat by heating them above their lethal temperature.

Rowe (1983) considers the range of strategies adopted by different plants to fire and describes four basic types –

● resisters, such as *Eriophorum vaginatum*, which can actually tolerate and survive fire; there are few examples of this strategy in Britain;

● endurers, such as *Arctostaphylos uva-ursi* and *Empetrum nigrum*, which regenerate from below-ground organs;

● evaders, which are species able to set seed in the peat and germinate after fire;

● avoiders, such as *Hylocomium splendens*, which are species which cannot tolerate fire in any form and rely on long fire cycles to allow reinvasion and recovery from populations surviving elsewhere.

All but the first of these strategies fail, however, when fire gets into the peat. When this happens, the fire can burn for a few days to several months (even years in some documented cases from the U.S.S.R.: see MacLean *et al.* 1983, p. 84). The constantly humid climate of Caithness and Sutherland means that fires of such extreme duration are not likely, but even a fire of a day or so under the wrong conditions can reduce an extensive area of former grazing to a state of relative species-poverty and expose the unstable bare surface to the highly erosive action of heavy rainfall.

Where burning has been severe but the peat has not suffered a long, smouldering fire, the surface layers tend to be reduced to a state of almost complete humification, which is recognised by its gelatinous, rubbery texture (Hobbs 1986). McVean & Lockie (1969) point out the difficulty experienced by higher plants in becoming established in such a layer, where the water is either bound too tightly to the peat to be usable by the plants or forms a surface gel of such high water content that the roots suffer anaerobic waterlogging. The development of an algal skin on the peat surface also promotes surface water run-off.

In such circumstances, colonisation is generally by deeper-rooted species such as *Eriophorum angustifolium* or species which can grow on the waterlogged surface. In the west, the high mineral content of rainwater appears to encourage algae such as *Zygogonium* to colonise such areas before other species, thereby rendering further colonisation very difficult. A similar phenomenon is described by Boatman & Tomlinson (1973) for western bog pools, where algae out-compete aquatic *Sphagna*. However, where *Zygogonium* does not become the dominant immediately, the commonest species is *Sphagnum tenellum*, which appears to act as a form of 'scar-tissue' on such surfaces. It is common on wet, burnt surfaces from Dartmoor to Shetland, but it is found at its most abundant on heaths where wet bare peat is common or on areas of formerly dry bog where the water table is slowly returning to a position near the peat surface. Thus it has become extremely common on Roudsea Woods and Mosses NNR in Cumbria since a series of dams was installed across several old drainage ditches. In time, this *S. tenellum* sward will generally give way to a mixed carpet of *Sphagnum* species, as observed, for example, on Cors Fochno in Wales (Dr A D Fox pers. comm.).

In Caithness and Sutherland *Sphagnum tenellum* is most frequently found in the "microbroken" complex (see Chapter 10, Community 23), forming a mixed mat with *S. cuspidatum* over a wet, bare peat surface. This might in time be expected to reduce the rate of water flow through the erosion channels, thereby also reducing the risk of rain-scouring, and eventually to form the basis of a regeneration complex (see later section on erosion). Its ability to act as an agent of recovery after fire appears to be limited in eastern parts of the two districts, whereas in the west it regularly forms an association with *Campylopus atrovirens* and mat-like *Racomitrium lanuginosum* over wet bare peat. *Sphagnum compactum* often behaves similarly and is a characteristic species of the shallow peat of wet heaths in many areas.

Rowe (1983) points out that some of the severest fires recorded in the boreal forests had little effect because the ground was either wet or frozen, and Allen (1964) states that areas of *Sphagnum* are only exceptionally affected by fire because the genus is generally only dominant over areas which are permanently wet. In natural circumstances the fire

frequency for any particular area of peatland ecosystem in Nova Scotia and Maine is of the order of once in every 400 to 500 years, and the major initiator is lightning, usually between the months of May and September (Wein & MacLean 1983).

On the other hand, Wein (1983) states that the frequency of deep-burning fires increases when the ground is drained, and, as raised mires in the Solway region have dried out during recent decades, so they have become ever more prone to damaging fires. Although in a completely natural system the fire frequency may be extremely low, widespread use of moor-gripping and the repeated action of man-induced fires on the margins of peatland sites render many of the Caithness and Sutherland peatlands more prone to fire damage than in former times. This is reflected in the abundant evidence of recent burning found during our survey (see Figure 23).

Grazing and manuring

Blanket bogs are characterised by low primary (plant) production and the low nutritive quality of their vegetation (Heal and Smith 1978). While they thus have low carrying capacity for large herbivores, most British blanket bogs form part of the grazing range for sheep and/or red deer or are used as grouse moor. Burning regimes usually form part of the management for these animals. Grazing is mostly of a low intensity, except where blanket bogs are associated with substantial areas of high-quality grazing land, which may create a spill-over effect.

The impact of grazing *per se* on blanket bog vegetation is not well known. Its obvious effects, in combining with fire to favour the competitive balance of plants such as *Eriophorum, Trichophorum* and *Molinia* against dwarf shrubs, have been noted. Grazing must, though its extractive effect, help to maintain nutrient poverty and high acidity in the vegetation and the surface layer of peat. Except where animals may transfer nutrients from adjoining more fertile ground, the effect of dung and urine is probably one of localised enrichment which, over a long period of time, averages out as a pattern of recycling rather than addition. Several coprophilous mosses (e.g. *Splachnum* spp. and *Tetraplodon mnioides*) are characteristic of dung and other animal remains on blanket bog.

Conspicuous green flushes of vegetation often occur in pools and spongy hollows where sheep or deer have drowned and their decomposed remains have produced nutrient enrichment. Some blanket bogs which have had long-established and large colonies of breeding gulls have been subjected to substantial enrichment by calcium, nitrogen and phosphorus, but it is not known whether former gull colonies on some of the Caithness flows produced measurable effects of this kind. Individual tall bog hummocks are often used as favourite perches by peatland birds and defecation sites for foxes, and the associated nutrient enrichment may modify the hummock community (T3). White-fronted and greylag geese are selective grazers on *Rhynchospora alba* and *Eriophorum* spp., but their long-term effects on these species are unknown.

Conspicuous sheep and deer tracks across many bogs point to the influence of trampling when this is highly concentrated, and the possible effect of this factor in initiating peat erosion is noted below. Nevertheless, over most of a blanket bog surface trampling is usually light and unlikely to have marked effects.

Erosion

Peatland ecologists have long debated whether the phenomenon of blanket bog erosion, so widespread in the British and Irish uplands, is a natural condition or one initiated by human activity of some kind. The high-level plateaux are most affected by erosion, a general feature of high-level blanket bogs in Britain noted by Tansley (1939), Bower (1962), Tallis (1964b, 1981), McVean & Lockie (1969), Taylor (1983), Bowler & Bradshaw (1985) and many others. Peat erosion is extensive in Caithness and Sutherland, and Figure 24 shows that more than half the sites examined during the survey contained erosion and that of these just over a quarter were severely eroded. The phenomenon is widespread, but not evenly so.

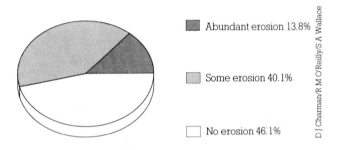

Abundant erosion 13.8%

Some erosion 40.1%

No erosion 46.1%

D J Charman/R M O'Reilly/S A Wallace

Figure 24 Proportion of sites in the NCC's Peatland Survey of Caithness and Sutherland affected by various intensities of erosion.

It is clear in some instances that adverse management can initiate peat erosion and that, once begun, such degradation may be beyond the control of land managers. One of the most dramatic effects of burning is its ability to reduce a formerly *Sphagnum*-rich mire to a maze of deep erosion gullies. Excessive drainage has also proved to be a major cause of erosion in parts of Sutherland. This does not necessarily mean that erosion is always man-induced; sometimes it may be a natural end consequence of bog development, but which influence is predominant in any one locality is often unclear.

There are much wider understanding and agreement on the subsequent agents of erosion than on the initiatory causal factors. The role of wind, desiccation, frost and rain have long been identified

as key elements in the erosion process (Geikie 1866; Moss 1913; Osvald 1949; Bower 1962).

Tallis (1981) records rates of erosion from the blanket peats of the Peak District of between 10 and 25 mm per year. Perhaps the most dramatic descriptive and pictorial evidence of the role played by heavy rain in the erosion sequence is the account given by Hulme & Blyth (1985) for an area of Shetland blanket bog. After a month of dry weather, they noted that erosion gullies had been baked into a 'mud-crack' pattern of polygonal flakes varying from 10-200 mm in diameter and 1-20 mm in thickness. At the onset of heavy rain the erosion channels rapidly filled with running water. The majority of the peat flakes were lifted from the peat surface by this water and washed away downslope through the erosion complex. Within one hour, most of such dislodged peat had entered main stream-courses. Hulme & Blyth (1985) recorded that up to 20 mm thickness of peat can be lost thus in a single storm. They also highlight the importance of this mud-crack and outwash process in exposing bare peat which is normally relatively protected from rain-scouring by algal mats.

Bower's (1962) classic account of peat erosion reviews a range of erosion types and suggests a series of possible causes, these being fire damage, climatic change, inherent hydrological instability and atmospheric pollution. Crampton (1911) favoured climatic change towards drier conditions as an explanation for many apparently moribund mire systems in Caithness, but there is no supporting meteorological evidence and Bowler & Bradshaw (1985) demonstrate that peat development in the Wicklow Mountains of Ireland is as vigorous as ever, even in areas of intense erosion. Taylor (1983) reviews a range of evidence gathered since Bower's original investigations and concludes that the process of headward erosion of watercourses is probably a major cause of erosion complexes, linked to the vulnerable topographic location of many blanket bog units. However, he considers that biotic factors such as burning, grazing and atmospheric pollution are probably important in initiating erosion in certain localities.

A probable example of burning-induced erosion can be seen near the western shore of Loch Rimsdale in central Sutherland. A well-patterned area of mire, rich in *Sphagnum* hollows and with no evidence of erosion, can be identified on the RAF's 1948 aerial photographs. The site was visited during 1980, after extensive spring fires, and the system was found to be completely surrounded by badly burnt peat, with the pools system itself almost totally destroyed. Most ridges had been broken down to little more than low hags, and the pools were reduced to an erosion network of gullies. Whilst no proof can be provided to show that burning caused this breakdown, it seems the most likely factor in view of the rapid change since 1948 and the abundant evidence of fire damage within and around the site.

Burning is also recognised as a major initiator of

erosion in the Peak District, where problems of peat erosion are extreme (Phillips 1981; Tallis 1981). Crampton (1911) and McVean & Lockie (1969) highlight the particular problems of fire in habitats and localities where growth is slow or the growing season short, such as the higher plateaux and wet blanket bog, the latter authors attributing much of the widespread blanket peat erosion on upland plateaux in Britain to this factor.

The increased level of erosion in the west (see Chapter 12) may also be related to the lack of atmospheric nitrogen- and phosphorus-rich particulate matter in such regions, as discussed in Chapter 1 (Groenendael *et al.* 1975). Repeated burning on an area may need to be on a much longer time-cycle in the west in order to allow a longer period of nitrogen and phosphorus accumulation. If insufficient time is given for this recovery between fires, the nutrient leaching possible in areas of such heavy rainfall and the consequently poor plant vigour and vegetation renewal may lead to breakdown and erosion in the event of another fire.

Yalden (1981) describes how preferential sheep-grazing at the edges of bare peat expanses can increase the area of the exposed peat and points out that the sharp hooves of a sheep exert twice the pressure of a human. In view of the results described by Slater & Agnew (1977) for the effect of trampling on *Sphagnum*, it appears that trampling pressure from grazing animals could on occasion be a contributory factor to erosion, by acting as the catalyst to its onset. Perhaps most sinificant is Dr M W Holdgate's (unpublished) observation that the only areas of significant peatland erosion that he noted in the islands of Tierra del Fuego were associated with the world's most southerly sheep farm.

During our survey, evidence was found in many areas or ground severely trampled by red deer. On the basis of observed damage resulting from the single passage of 20 or so deer across a previously surveyed area, it is clear that the regular passage of even small numbers across areas of patterned bog could induce breakdown of ridges and subsequent erosion. The extensive erosion encountered in the mires around Ben Armine may be partly due to the large numbers of deer which use this area, though the problem appears to be exacerbated by widespread burning. This effect of trampling is particularly important when the movements of animals are restricted. Mire systems which are adjacent to natural barriers such the steep eastern face of Ben Armine or artificial barriers such as forestry fences will inevitably be more prone to erosion by trampling than sites in a more open position.

Two forms of hydrological instability which explain some examples of erosion have been well documented. The first of these is the "bog-burst" and the second the features known as "sink-holes" or "swallow-holes". John Leland in his itinerary of about 1535-43 describes the great bog-burst of Chat Moss

in Lancashire (Smith 1910, pp. 42-43), when this large raised bog suddenly turned liquid and literally spilled out over the surrounding countryside, causing widespread damage and some deaths. Chunks of peat washed down the River Glazebrook were even reported to have reached the shores of Ireland. Since Leland's time a number of similar occurrences have been documented, and the evidence for such events can be seen today on aerial photographs. It seems almost certain, for example, from the jumbled nature of its surface patterns and the almost floating nature of the surface, that the small bog beside the road at the south-eastern tip of Loch Meadie, Altnaharra, has suffered a bog-burst.

In normal circumstances, the cation exchange ability of peat retains the bog in a coherent mass, despite the fact that the water content may exceed the liquid limit of the structure (see Chapter 1 and Hobbs 1986). In effect, the bog is a liquid mound held together by strong attractive forces in the peat. A bog-burst appears to occur when these forces are exceeded, as may occur with exceptionally heavy rainfall or if the integrity of the peat matrix is altered in some way (Hobbs 1986). Areas of quaking mire could be expected to be prone to the phenomenon if disturbed, yet the available evidence suggests that bog-bursts have always been rather unusual and chance events. The small example at Altnaharra is therefore particularly interesting.

On a small scale, as at Altnaharra, the process appears not to have induced more widespread damage and erosion, but, as Taylor (1983) points out, many mires are highly prone to such instability by their topographic position. Bog-bursts or peat slides from large upland plateaux could be expected to result in widespread erosion. In fact evidence of such erosion is hard to find, and it appears that the steady headward erosion of streams is the more usual cause of erosion in such locations. Landslips after heavy rain, where relatively steep slopes (often with soligenous mires or sometimes where drainage has broken the root mat) become over-charged with water and suddenly slump away, are much more common. They are usually quite small, but in 1983 such landslips cut back into the edge of the plateau blanket bog on Pennygant Hill, in the central Southern Uplands of Scotland, and resulted in substantial erosion of both mineral soil and peat over an area of several hectares.

A rather different type of erosion is described by Crampton (1911), whereby certain pools amongst the normal *dubh lochain* appeared to be linked to underground 'pipes' in the peat, often causing the affected pool and those in the immediate vicinity to drain away. This peat-piping and its associated sink-holes are currently the subject of investigation by the Institute of Hydrology and Dundee University. It is thought that two types of sink-hole exist, the first representing the last vestige of a watercourse which has been overwhelmed by peat growth and the second resulting from sub-surface erosion along natural lines of weakness at the peat base or within the peat, which then emerges as a sunken hole at the peat surface.

Evidence of the first type is possibly seen towards the northern part of Blar nam Faoileag, in Caithness, and at the foot of An Teallach in Wester Ross, where parts of the mineral terrain would clearly have supported a watercourse but the area is now swamped by peat. Along the line of the ancient watercourse a series of sink-holes can be seen which appear to have developed in harmony with the peat cover rather than as erosion features which have developed after peat formation.

However, evidence of the second type is far more abundant, particularly on high-level plateaux and intensely dissected sites. Here the hydrological stability of the pool system appears to be genuinely disrupted by sink-hole formation. Indeed it is possible to create a sink-hole. Dr D A Goode (pers. comm.) found that a pool on Knockfin Heights which had been sampled with a soil auger the previous day was completely empty 24 hours later, the water apparently having drained away down the auger hole. Such a phenomenon reveals just how sensitive parts of the system can be to either natural or artificial breaching of their hydrological integrity.

It thus seems that erosion may sometimes be a natural process, either representing the final stage in bog development or forming part of a long-term cycle of erosion and regeneration. Bowler & Bradshaw (1985) found evidence of rapid regeneration within peat erosion in the Wicklow Mountains, and there is considerable evidence on Moor House and elsewhere in the Pennines and in the Migneint in North Wales of regenerative phases in certain locations.

The fact that erosion appears to be a natural part of peatland development and hydrology, at least in some instances, requires that representative examples of the full range of erosion types should be conserved. They form an important part of studies on catchment hydrology, environmental monitoring and peatland ecosystem dynamics, and, in situations where peat erosion is man-induced, it is important to understand the details of the process for the possible insights that this may yield for improved moorland management practices.

Acid deposition

An important contributory factor to erosion identified in the Peak District and elsewhere in the Pennines is the impact of acid deposition on blanket bog vegetation, particularly *Sphagnum* species. Although bog systems are naturally acidic (Clymo 1983), this acidity is derived from organic rather than mineral acids. A substantial volume of evidence has now been published exploring the relationships between acid deposition, *Sphagnum* vigour and acidification of waters (e.g. Press & Lee 1982; Press, Ferguson & Lee 1983; Battarbee, Flower, Stevenson & Rippey 1985).

Early accounts of conditions on the Pennines at the turn of the century describe enormous quantities of soot falling on the vegetation from factory chimneys located down on the Lancashire Plain. Conway (1949) noted that the average figure in 1948 for Dore and Ewden, near Sheffield, was about 0.4 g per m^2 per month. However, such events were not restricted to the Pennines, and records exist of "black rain" falling in Scotland during 1862 and 1863. Brimblecombe, Davies & Tranter (1986) suggest that these deposits probably came from locations many hundreds of kilometres from the sites of deposition, and they point to more recent records of "black rain" in the Cairngorms area which also appear to be derived from distant sources.

Tallis (1964c) records the decline and extinction of some *Sphagnum* species in the Pennine blanket bogs since the description by Moss (1913), establishing, amongst other things, that the once-abundant *Sphagnum imbricatum* has completely vanished from the southern Pennines during the last 150 years. The most common species in the modern vegetation recorded by Tallis was *Sphagnum recurvum*, which is a species of high sulphate tolerance (Ferguson, Lee & Bell 1978; Smart 1983). Although Tallis recognises that climatic change may be the cause, he points to the correlation between the Industrial Revolution and the beginning of *Sphagnum* decline.

Ferguson *et al.* (1978) consider the loss of *Sphagnum* in such blanket bog areas to be the outstanding vegetation change in Britain attributable to atmospheric pollution. Work at Manchester University and Abisko Field Station in Sweden has concentrated on the physiological mechanisms behind such effects and has revealed that *Sphagnum* species are sensitive to increased levels of sulphate and bisulphite (Ferguson *et al.* 1978; Lee, Press, Woodin & Ferguson 1986). However, the most marked effects of acid deposition appear not to be related directly to the sulphur content and associated acidity, but instead to levels of deposited nitrate (Woodin 1986).

Woodin (1986) has established that, in unpolluted conditions, *Sphagnum fuscum* rapidly assimilates all nitrate deposited during precipitation. Ammonium is also readily assimilated, despite the fact that *Sphagnum* species possess only a single ammonium assimilation pathway (Meade 1984). Higher plants occasionally rely on other strategies for their scource of nitrogen (e.g. the insectivorous sundews *Drosera* spp.), but most depend on subsequent remineralisation of nitrogen within the peat. Thus the bulk of nitrate deposition, whether natural or as a pollutant, tends to have its primary effect on the *Sphagnum* layer rather than the higher plant cover (Woodin 1986).

Woodin has established that nitrate levels above the optimum cause an uncoupling of nitrate reductase activity, which leads to increased concentrations of nitrogen in the tissues, a reduced ability to immobilise the inorganic nitrogen supply and reduced growth, though without any outward sign of damage. She points out that the resulting increased availability of nitrogen in a system where normally only ammonium is in ready supply may have widespread effects on the higher plant cover.

Measures of acid deposition in northern Britain suggest that levels are low (Fry & Cooke 1984), but the peatlands of Caithness and Sutherland are considered by Woodin (pers. comm.) to be prime "acid deposition sensitive" ecosystems, because they have –

- a non-calcareous, highly resistant bedrock;
- acid soils with low buffering capacity;
- water bodies (dubh lochans) with low alkalinities;
- a short growing season;
- a solute supply of largely atmospheric origin;
- high altitude (in places);
- high precipitation, including considerable occult (mist and fog) deposition

(Tomlinson, Brouzes, McLean & Kadlecek 1980; Grant & Lewis 1982; Kling & Grant 1984; Gorham, Bayley & Schindler 1984).

The last factor, that of occult deposition, is particularly significant because it has been shown to expose vegetation to much higher concentrations of solutes than those measured in rainfall (Skeffington & Roberts 1985). Mrose (1966) states that coastal fog in Germany has a lower pH and solute concentrations six to ten times higher than those measured in rain. Moreover, Woodin (1986) has demonstrated that the physiological response of *Sphagnum* to simulated occult nitrate deposition is much greater than its response to similar amounts of nitrate in rain.

The implications for Caithness and Sutherland are clear. Whilst it is most unlikely that concentrations of pollutants ever reach lethal concentrations in the region, the increased cumulative stress imposed by even occasional acid rain events is likely to render the vegetation less resilient to burning and drainage. Recovery times are likely to be longer, and particularly so on the higher plateaux, where the cumulative effects of regular, if very low volume, occult deposition are liable to give rise to a particularly sensitive vegetation cover. Failure to recognise this sensitivity, coupled with too frequent and poorly controlled burning, may have combined with the slow regenerative powers of western and upland mires to produce the widespread erosion found today in the region.

Erosion is a widespread feature of western mires in Ireland, where acid deposition is low. Osvald (1949) describes many erosion features similar to those in north-west Scotland, and Bowler & Bradshaw (1985) explore the possibility that erosion in the Wicklow Mountains is a product of reduced peat growth or acid deposition. They establish that peat regrowth is currently as rapid as the fastest recorded rates for the Pennines over the last 5000 years and also that acid deposition products are at sufficiently low levels to make it unlikely that erosion is a product of atmospheric pollution. Bowler & Bradshaw's evidence from Ireland gives no information about the regularity of burning or intensity of sheep-grazing, and the authors offer no alternative cause for erosion to their original hypotheses of reduced peat growth and atmospheric pollution.

6   Forest history

The degree to which the area of the Caithness and Sutherland peatlands was once forest-covered and the reasons for its present treelessness have become matters of some interest. The evidence for Post-glacial (Flandrian) spread of forest across Britain has been documented by Godwin (1975), and various studies have gradually filled in the picture for Scotland. In many parts of the British uplands, there is direct visual evidence, from tree remains buried in the peat, that ground now occupied by treeless blanket bog was once covered by forest, at least in part. Ecologists have been concerned to understand how and when this transformation in vegetational character occurred.

The original extent of forest

Whilst the evidence from tree remains points to the former extensive occurrence of forest in northern Scotland, recent work suggests that this was by no means continuous, even within the altitudinal limits for tree growth (c. 300–400 m at present, but probably higher at the Climatic Optimum). The widespread occurrence of Scots pine *Pinus sylvestris* stumps in Sutherland blanket bogs suggest that pinewoods were once fairly extensive in this District (i.e. during the Boreal period and probably much later). Many of the remains indicate small-sized trees, suggesting that Scots pine was here approaching its natural climatic limit. The scarcity of even fragments of surviving pinewood amongst the very patchy present-day native woodlands of Caithness and Sutherland led McVean & Ratcliffe (1962) to suggest that, during the period of the last 2500 years, the predominant forest type of the region has been of birch *Betula pubescens*, with rowan *Sorbus aucuparia*, hazel *Corylus avellana*, willow *Salix* spp. and alder *Alnus glutinosa*. Durno (1958) reported pollen analyses from five peatland sites within central Sutherland and Caithness. The absence of data for absolute pollen frequency makes it impossible to gauge the extent of tree cover at any site, but the consistent average excess of birch pollen over pine pollen at each site suggests that birch has been the more important forest species throughout the region during the whole Flandrian period.

Moar (1969a, b) examined two sites in Orkney and one in the extreme north-west of Sutherland (Scourie) for evidence of past tree cover. In Scourie he found a high percentage of arboreal pollen consisting of birch as the forest dominant, together with pine and mixed oak forest, all of which showed a marked decline but not until the Sub-boreal. He concluded that the forest cover was extensive in west Sutherland until quite recent Post-glacial times.

On Orkney, by contrast, the pollen data suggest that tree cover was never extensive during Flandrian times and that birch and hazel scrub in sheltered spots was the main woodland type.

Peglar (1979) describes a pollen diagram taken from the Loch of Winless in central Caithness. She deduces from the results, which show very little arboreal pollen throughout the profile, that the area has a similar forest history to Orkney (Moar 1969) and Shetland (Johansen 1975; Birnie 1984), namely that there is no evidence of significant forest cover in the Flandrian. She concludes that the area, which currently borders one of the largest expanses of low-lying flow land in the Caithness-Sutherland Plain, was "probably the least forested area of mainland Britain throughout the Flandrian".

Peglar's findings are confirmed by the direct visual evidence from peat profiles exposed down to the underlying mineral soil along new forest roads cut in the flows of the Thurso River catchment: over long distances there are no traces of tree remains, indicating absence of Post-glacial forest cover. Occasional remains of pine and birch are to be found in more favourable situations close to streams, where there was probably more shelter and fertile soil. This contrasts with the situation, farther west, where pine and birch remains are often plentiful in newly exposed peat faces. The reasons for this earlier lack of woodland cover in central Caithness are not yet understood. The earlier scarcity of woodland cover in Orkney, Shetland and the Outer Hebrides has been assumed to result from climatic severity, including the wetness, high winds and lack of summer warmth associated with extreme oceanicity.

Forest decline and the development of blanket bog

As far back as the time of Leland in 1538–43 (e.g. Smith 1910, pp. 16–17), writers have commented on the presence of tree stumps within or beneath areas of deep peat. The massive 'bog oaks' which have been unearthed from drying peat in the Fenland and many other records of woody deposits at the base of raised bog profiles led Tansley (1939) to construct one of the classic sequences of raised mire development, involving the development of carr and oak woodland over terrestrialised basins and then subsequent swamping of this woodland by the rising water table and renewal of bog growth at the onset of the warm but wet Atlantic period (7500 BP).

Geikie (1866) and Lewis (1905, 1906, 1907) describe many examples of tree remains within Scottish peats, the former citing a number of cases where he considers buried tree-stumps to represent forest swamped by peat development. He suggests that this came about when Britain became separated from the continental land mass and thus lost its continental climate. Geikie noticed that in Scottish bogs there were often two distinct tree layers, one on the underlying mineral substratum and the other about half way up the peat profile, and he called these the Lower and Upper Forestian Layers. The clear implication was that, after a phase of active bog growth with no forest, conditions again favoured the spread of trees across the drying bog surface, but that a further increase in wetness then suppressed the forest in favour of bog. In Scandinavia, Blytt (1876) and Sernander (1908, 1910) later interpreted basal and upper tree layers in bogs as evidence of cyclical climatic change – dry Boreal, wet Atlantic, dry Sub-boreal, wet Sub-atlantic (see Godwin 1975). It was tempting to apply this intepretation to the British situation, but the ecological evidence has proved to be a good deal more complex.

Lewis (1910) describes extensive birch remains at the base of the peat in Caithness and Sutherland and, though stating that his "upper forest zone" with *Pinus sylvestris* is present in Caithness and Sutherland, gives no evidence for this. He remarks that some of the "upper forest zone" records for the area are represented by *Betula alba* L.(i.e. *B. pendula*) rather than *Pinus sylvestris* and that the zone is in fact absent except in the area towards Morven and Ben Alisky. Crampton (1911), in his account of the Post-glacial succession of Caithness (pp. 13–16), draws on Lewis's (1910) proposed sequence of events to describe a landscape at first covered by birch *taiga*, then its gradual paludification as the climate ameliorated. He proposes an interruption to this peat growth due to a period of drier climate, leading to the expansion of pine over many of the bogs. The subsequent loss of this woodland he takes to be the result of climatic change.

The occurrence of tree remains, mainly of Scots pine and birch, at the base of blanket bog peat is fairly general across Scotland. Their frequent association with charcoal remains has led some ecologists to speculate that the forest was not overwhelmed by the natural, climatically generated growth of bog, but that its disappearance was the result of human land-use, which paved the way for soil acidification and peat accumulation. Moreover, while many of the deeper blanket bogs began to form around the onset of the Atlantic period, there is a wide range of date of origin, spanning several thousand years, and this militates against the hypothesis of control by cycles of climatic wetness and dryness. Evidence has accumulated to suggest that initiation of blanket bog is a result of Neolithic, Mesolithic or Bronze Age forest clearance (Conway 1954; Simmons 1963; Tallis 1964a, 1975; Smith 1970; Birks 1970, 1972; Moore 1973a; Simmons & Cundill 1974; Moore & Wilmott 1979). Much of this evidence, however, concerns peats from England or Wales. Further north, in Orkney, Keatinge & Dickson (1979) attribute a decline in tree pollen around 5000 BP to increasing windspeeds and a deteriorating climate, although they consider that agriculture contributed in later stages to the decline of woodland cover.

Birks (1975) has studied the distribution and age of pine stumps in Scottish bogs and found that basal remains are of widely varying age (7400–2000 BP). There are also wide variations in the presence, abundance, vertical distribution and age of pine remains at levels above the basal peat. Birks identifies two distinct time patterns. Pine stumps in the north-west of Scotland all appear to date from 4500 BP to 4000 BP, whilst those from the south and east of Scotland show a much wider range of ages, from 7000 BP to 2000 BP. She speculates that the synchronism of the north-west pine stumps indicates climatic change, concurring with Pennington (1974) that such relatively sudden and comprehensive loss of tree cover is more likely to be a natural response to climate than due to man's influence, whilst loss of tree cover farther south and east in Scotland requires additional explanation.

Pears (1975), in attempting to establish the original tree-line for Boreal forests, gives a wide range of dates for supposedly concurrent Post-glacial events, but points out that local topography and slope geometry can play a major role in buffering individual areas from overall climatic trends for extended periods of time. On this basis, he finds his results in close agreement with those of Birks (1975). Onset of blanket bog formation can thus still be climatically determined, even when spread over thousands of years.

Paludification can be a continuing and observable process. George, Earl of Cromertie, (1711) is one of the earliest authors to record an apparent sequence similar to Tansley's (1939), but for blanket bog. He describes the overwhelming of a pinewood in the "Parish of Lochbrun" by a developing moss within the space of 15 years. The trees were old and dying when he first encountered them and, by the time of his second visit, had apparently been blown over by strong winds, to be absorbed into the growing moss, which itself subsequently proved to be a good source of peat fuel.

While it is far from clear that all blanket bog in Britain is a climatic phenomenon alone, even such workers as Dr P D Moore (1968, 1973a, 1984), who have studied blanket bog origins for many years, remain equivocal about man's role. There are undoubtedly remains of charcoal at the bottom of many blanket bog deposits (Tallis 1975), but it is not yet possible to distinguish fires started by Neolithic or Mesolithic man from those arising through natural catastrophes such as lightning fires (a major source of fire in northern boreal ecosystems: Wein & MacLean 1983). If it is proposed that the blanket bogs of Britain and Ireland are anthropogenic, rather than a product of the climate, it must also be explained how other areas of treeless blanket mire around the world have come about and why the origins of British-Irish blanket bog should be different.

Perhaps it is best to regard the process of bog initiation as resulting from both factors, climatic wetness and human impact, with the balance of their influence varying geographically and possibly also in time. What cannot be disputed is that the oceanic climate of Britain and Ireland has played a major role in generating a landscape type which is now regarded in other countries around the world as characteristic of cool, oceanic areas and for which Scotland and Ireland are generally considered to be the 'type' locations. Such a landscape is entirely restricted in other parts of the globe to regions which have the same climatic pattern, whether there is a history of human activity or not.

Present lack of forest cover as a natural condition

Regardless of whether human forest clearance sometimes preceded blanket bog initiation, it is inescapable that the subsequent scale of this bog development in Britain could only have occurred under a climate strongly favourable for ombrotrophic peat growth. In addition, trees cannot persist or establish themselves under the extreme conditions of waterlogging and *Sphagnum* dominance which have characterised so many of the main flow areas, often for thousands of years. Birks (1975) has reviewed the physiology of Scots pine and points out that it can be killed by a single wet season. She concludes that most British blanket bogs are unsuitable for pine establishment and growth without artificial ground treatment.

In the boreal forest zone of Scandinavia and Canada there is abundant evidence of the natural relationship between tree cover and ombrotrophic mire development. Depending on the steepness of the gradient from dry ground to soaking *Sphagnum* surface, there is a variable transitional zone of increasingly depauperate trees at the bog-edge, ending with tiny, stunted individuals in 'check' scattered sparsely over the bog centre. On some of the larger mires, even this checked growth is confined to a peripheral zone. Where bog development is so extensive as to restrict development of seed-bearing trees over large areas, the possibilities for even such abortive colonisation are much less.

Zoltai & Pollett (1983) comment that the tree cover within the Atlantic Oceanic wetland region of Canada, which is characterised by extensive blanket bog, is restricted to stream-courses or sheltered depressions. They illustrate the region (p. 262) with a photograph showing a completely treeless landscape, yet the human impact on the area in prehistoric and historic times has been slight. Botch & Masing (1983) describe the West Kamchatka Province as dominated by blanket bog and quite treeless, even though one of the major types is a relatively dry *Cladonia*-dominated mire. Pisano (1983) illustrates both the expanses of *Sphagnum magellanicum* bog and the cushion mires of Tierra del Fuego (pp. 314 and 319). In his caption to the

photograph of the *Sphagnum magellanicum* mires, he notes the *Nothofagus betuloides–N. pumilo* forest limited strictly to the line of the watercourse, whilst the high-level *Donatia* cushion mires are attended by a scrubby development of *Nothofagus* on rocky outcrops. Dr M W Holdgate (unpublished) states that the area is perhaps no more than 10% wooded. The Norwegian blanket mire plateaux are unwooded, as are those of Iceland and the Faeroes. There are, nevertheless, some areas of blanket bog in other countries which have sparse or stunted growth of trees (see Chapter 3).

On the extensive flows of east Sutherland and Caithness, the record in the peat itself demonstrates irrefutably that a treeless blanket bog landscape, barely distinguishable from that of today, has existed for at least the past 4000 years. Many pool systems have demonstrably occupied the same positions, relatively unchanged, for a large part of this time. The remaining question is about the former extent of tree cover on the shallower peat of the bog edges and the wet heaths of steeper ground and on the mineral soils of dry slopes and stream-sides. Most probably there was a patchy growth of woodland in these better-drained situations. Its extent would have increased westwards and towards the coasts and main straths, as the bog areas became increasingly dissected or replaced by ground of different character, more suited to tree growth. This patchwork of woodland is, however, likely to have been far more restricted than the area covered by woodland which existed before the bogs began to form. The patchwork has been largely cleared by man, probably beginning mainly around 2100–2600 BP (Birks in press), and has been prevented from re-establishing itself by continuous grazing and repeated fires.

The conclusion is, therefore, that in the absence of man some parts of the Caithness and Sutherland peatlands would today have had more woodland cover (mainly of a *taiga* birchwood kind) than at present, but that other quite large areas would have been almost as treeless as they are today. Whatever its origins, the flow landscape is undoubtedly an ancient one. There are few places in Britain now where it is possible to look across a landscape and share much the same view as Neolithic man. Up to 1979, this was still possible over much of Caithness and east Sutherland.

New afforestation

Afforested ground is quickly transformed from bog to forest. When the trees close to form thicket woodland at 10-15 years, the original vegetation is almost totally destroyed by the dense shade and litter fall. Observations on failed plantations of lodgepole pine killed by pine beauty moth infestation show that, after this short time under scrub, the peat has dried so much that the immediate changes are to a surface vegetation quite different from that of the original bog community. Vascular plants typical of drier ground become abundant (e.g. *Calluna, Trichophorum, Molinia, Eriophorum vaginatum*), evidently growing from buried seed, and often also the invasive rosebay willowherb *Chamaenerion angustifolium*. When the forests are cleared in the normal rotation, the best that can be hoped for is that a damp heath community of similar kind re-establishes itself, but this will only persist for a short while, since it is clearly intended to retain this land under forest indefinitely.

Whether a blanket bog community, with high *Sphagnum* cover, could ever regenerate is thus largely an academic question. The peat surface will continue to waste and contract downwards as described in Chapter 5. Cracking of the peat under the young trees is already widespread (Pyatt 1987), and such structural changes may become more marked with time. Possibly, if all the key points in the drainage system were blocked, water tables would begin to rise and conditions for recolonisation of *Sphagnum* might return, first in flooded drains. It could take a long time for an acrotelm to redevelop and active bog growth to be resumed more generally on a ploughed and deforested area, and, where patterned surfaces have been destroyed, some form of erosion would be more likely to result.

For all practical purposes, the planted ground ceases to be bog. It remains to consider the effects of afforestation on the ground not actually covered with trees – the enclaves of unplanted bog, the adjoining bogs outside the plantations, and the streams and lakes within the catchment containing forest. The linear systems of rides within the forest are far too narrow to represent the original peatland communities, for they inevitably dry out and become heavily modified, even though many of the original species may persist for a time (Ratcliffe 1986b).

Effects of forestry on the vegetation of adjacent mire systems

It is only relatively recently that large-scale afforestation has been able to invade areas of prime peatland and that cultivation techniques have become available to plough deep, wet peat right up to the edge of pool systems. There are, accordingly, no forests in Caithness and Sutherland old enough to enable any critical judgement to be made about their effects on adjoining peatlands. However, in Northumberland and Galloway large forestry plantations already exist in close proximity to areas that were in the past considered as good examples of peatland systems, although they are very different from the flows of Sutherland and Caithness. So far the only detailed attempts to assess changes after afforestation have been in the large plantation area in west Northumberland generally referred to as Kielder Forest. This is an area of about 50,000 ha, of which almost 40,000 ha is planted with conifers. A small proportion of the remaining area is remnant blanket bog, too wet to afforest during the planting period. The assessments of changes in Kielder are from two sources.

Chapman & Rose (1986) repeated a 1958 survey of Coom Rigg Moss (Chapman 1964) to assess vegetation changes on this site up to 1986. At the time of the 1958 survey, afforestation had occurred on only one side of the site. Subsequently this National Nature Reserve was to become almost completely surrounded by conifer plantations, with some planting actually on the hydrological unit of the mire itself.

The original survey used a grid to locate sample areas, random quadrats being taken within these areas. Fixed-point photography allowed some direct comparison of the overall appearance of particular areas, but the small number of original photographs did not permit extensive use of this method.

At a community level, Chapman & Rose (1986) found that what had originally been a wet peatland vegetation had become, over the intervening years, a mosaic of community types dominated by either *Calluna vulgaris, Deschampsia flexuosa* or *Eriophorum vaginatum. Calluna* showed little overall change in abundance but had increased in some areas while decreasing in others. *Deschampsia flexuosa* showed an overall increase, this being concentrated in several patches at the edge of the site. *Eriophorum vaginatum* showed an overall decrease, but, in the areas over which it is now a dominant, it has taken on a dense tussocky form of growth, very different from its appearance in the mid-1950s. Other individual species were found to have suffered dramatic changes in their pattern of distribution or abundance. Some of the more important species changes are discussed below.

Perhaps the most striking change recorded was the apparent extinction during the intervening period of *Sphagnum imbricatum* and *Drosera anglica* , both species generally regarded as indicators of high-quality undamaged mire. More than 75 individual hummocks of *S. imbricatum* were identified and mapped in 1958, whereas, despite a thorough search, no such hummocks were recorded in 1986.

Drosera anglica is a species typical of pool margins and low ridge (T1/A1 transition: Figure 8). Chapman (1964) recorded a series of shallow pools dominated by *Sphagnum cuspidatum* in central and northern parts of the site. Chapman & Rose comment that these *Sphagnum cuspidatum* hollows could not be found in 1986 and that *Sphagnum cuspidatum* had all but vanished. A photograph taken in 1958 shows an example of such a hollow in the foreground, amongst a vegetation type which is typical of soft, wet mire. Chapman & Rose (1986) found neither the structure nor the vegetation type.

Amongst the bog 'constants' that have declined, *Drosera rotundifolia* shows perhaps the most dramatic change, diminishing from 55% frequency at the sample points to 4% – a relative decrease in its abundance of 90%. *Sphagnum magellanicum, S. papillosum, S. capillifolium, Odontoschisma sphagni* and *Narthecium ossifragum* have all declined by at least 35% in the intervening 38 years,

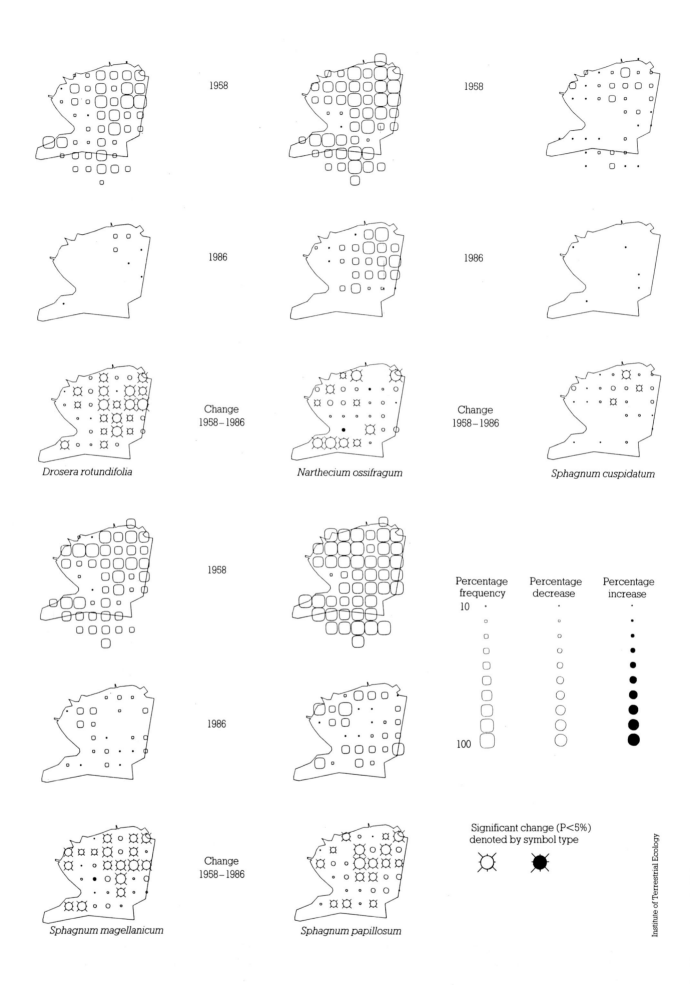

Figure 25 Changes in species abundance on Coom Rigg Moss recorded for the period 1958–1986. (Taken from Chapman & Rose 1986.)

Species	1958	1986	Relative change	Absolute change	Z	Number of significant squares
Drosera rotundifolia	54.85	3.71	−51.14	51.14	14.87	19
Sphagnum magellanicum	62.86	16.57	−46.29	49.14	12.51	17
Sphagnum papillosum	85.43	37.43	−48.00	48.57	13.05	16
Sphagnum capillifolium	62.23	22.00	−40.29	44.29	10.79	16
Odontoschisma sphagni	46.86	12.00	−34.86	40.00	10.12	16
Narthecium ossifragum	72.00	34.86	−37.14	40.00	9.85	11
Eriophorum vaginatum	82.86	47.43	−35.43	37.14	9.84	10
Calluna vulgaris	38.86	34.57	−4.29	36.86	1.18	12
Lepidozia setacea	49.71	20.00	−29.71	35.43	8.25	11
Eriophorum angustifolium	74.57	43.14	−31.43	33.71	8.45	8
Andromeda polifolia	49.71	22.00	−27.71	31.71	7.64	7
Erica tetralix	86.57	61.14	−25.43	31.14	7.66	9
Sphagnum tenellum	54.57	32.00	−22.57	29.43	6.03	4
Calypogeia trichomanes	35.14	8.86	−26.29	26.86	8.39	6
Trichophorum cespitosum	50.29	37.43	−12.86	26.00	3.43	2
Mylia anomala	34.00	43.43	9.43	25.43	2.56	5
Vaccinium oxycoccos	54.86	53.14	−1.71	22.29	0.46	2
Gymnocolea inflata	22.00	6.57	−15.43	20.00	5.83	3
Deschampsia flexuosa	2.00	17.43	15.43	18.29	6.89	7
Sphagnum cuspidatum	18.57	1.43	−17.14	17.14	7.56	3
Pleurozium schreberi	2.29	15.14	12.86	15.14	6.03	4
Cephalozia bicuspidata	14.29	7.71	−6.57	14.57	2.78	1
Empetrum nigrum	12.86	7.14	−5.71	12.00	2.52	3
Cephalozia connivens	7.71	4.28	−3.43	10.86	1.91	1
Polytrichum commune	6.29	12.00	5.71	9.71	2.62	0
Calypogeia fissa	5.14	4.29	−0.86	8.29	0.54	0
Aulacomnium palustre	7.43	5.14	−2.29	8.00	1.25	1
Sphagnum recurvum	6.29	4.29	−2.00	7.14	1.18	2
Molinia caerulea	2.00	4.00	2.00	5.43	1.55	1
Sphagnum subnitens	1.71	4.00	2.29	4.57	1.82	0
Polytrichum juniperinum	3.14	2.86	−0.29	4.29	0.22	0
Rhytidiadelphus squarrosus	0.57	3.71	3.14	3.71	2.87	1
Hypnum cupressiforme	0.86	2.86	1.43	3.14	1.52	0
Cladonia uncialis	3.14	0.00	−3.14	3.14	3.34	0
Cladonia impexa	2.29	1.14	−1.14	2.29	1.16	0
Vaccinium myrtillus	0.29	1.14	0.86	1.43	1.35	0
Galium saxatile	0.00	1.43	1.43	1.43	2.24	0
Pohlia nutans	0.29	0.86	0.57	1.14	1.00	0
Carex panicea	0.29	0.86	0.57	1.14	1.00	0
Sphagnum palustre	0.00	1.14	1.14	1.14	2.01	0
Carex echinata	1.14	0.00	−1.14	1.14	2.01	0
Plagiothecium undulatum	0.00	0.86	0.86	0.86	1.74	0
Juncus acutifolius	0.29	0.29	0.00	0.57	0.00	0
Campylopus flexuosus	0.29	0.29	0.00	0.57	0.00	0
Phragmites australis	0.57	1.14	0.57	0.57	0.82	0
Agrostis stolonifera	0.29	0.29	0.00	0.57	0.00	0
Zygonium ericetorum	0.29	0.00	−0.29	0.29	1.00	0
Riccardia pinguis	0.29	0.00	−0.29	0.29	1.00	0
Plagiothecium denticulatum	0.29	0.00	−0.29	0.29	1.00	0
Dactylorhiza maculata	0.00	0.29	0.29	0.29	1.00	0
Pinus sylvestris	0.00	0.29	0.29	0.29	1.00	0
Nardus stricta	0.00	0.29	0.29	0.29	1.00	0
Parmelia physodes	0.00	0.29	0.29	0.29	1.00	0
Carex rostrata	0.29	0.57	0.29	0.29	0.59	0
Deschampsia cespitosa	0.29	0.29	0.00	0.00	0.00	0

Table 2

Percentage frequencies of species present at Coom Rigg Moss National Nature Reserve in 1958 and 1986, together with percentage changes over this period and the significance and extent of these changes. (Taken from Chapman & Rose 1986.)

some by more than 50%. The original and present distributions of some of these species can be seen in Figure 25, with a quantative measure of change. Table 2 lists all the species recorded, their relative change and the statistical significance of that change.

A different approach to the problem was adopted by Charman (1986), who sampled 15 mire sites within the plantation area, all of which were completely surrounded by forest. Significant correlations existed between the numbers of ombrogenous mire species and the sizes of the mires. There were also indications that fewer species occurred on sites that had been surrounded by trees for longer periods of time. R Smith & D J Charman obtained 510 samples from 34 sites. These so far unpublished data confirm the earlier work, finding correlations between area, age of plantation and shape of site, on the one hand, and occurrences of ombrogenous mire species at a cover of greater than or equal to 5%, on the other. Large round or square sites surrounded by young plantations hold more mire species than small irregularly-shaped sites surrounded by mature plantations. A similar but converse relationship was found for species mainly of dry moorland communities.

It seems clear that the vegetation on mires which become surrounded by plantations can change over a relatively short period of time. What are not yet clear are the mechanisms by which these changes occur. In the case of the Kielder sites, there has been a change in management associated with the forestry operations. Prior to extensive plantings the moorland was grazed at low stocking rates and would have been lightly burnt occasionally, even on the wet areas (Chapman & Rose 1986). This would have reduced dominance of any species, such as *Calluna vulgaris*, which might otherwise smother more sensitive mire species.

Chapman & Rose found that the various existing vegetation types at Coom Rigg were correlated with peat depth and slope, whereas the vegetation types in 1958 showed no such correlation. They suggest that cessation of grazing and burning may have allowed these hidden influences in the vegetation pattern to be expressed. However, this does not explain the loss of pools from the site or of 'typical' mire species from the deepest areas of peat. Another possibility is that the water supply to the mire is reduced or its retention impaired. Forestry operations involve ploughing and the cutting of deep drains, not always restricted to the area eventually planted. Drains adjacent to mire systems may cause sufficient water table drawdown to affect particular species or types of surface pattern (see Chapter 5). On some of the Kielder sites there are also drains which cut across the mire surface. The effects of drainage have been considered in detail in Chapter 5. It may also be possible that the increased evapo-transpiration due to the surrounding conifers reduces any surface seepage to the mire. This may be particularly so where plantations are upslope of mires. Seedling invasion of the drier parts may become a problem, as at Belleray Flow in Kielder

Forest, further reducing water supply by evapo-transpiration and interception by the canopy.

Most coniferous plantations are refertilised during each rotation, usually by air. This inevitably involves some drift onto adjacent areas, particularly if they are pockets of open land in the forest. Williams, Davis, Marrs & Osborn (1987), for example, record drift of up to 1000 m from herbicide sprayed from helicopters. Enrichment ensuing from fertiliser drift, combined with possible increased aeration from water table drawdown, would tend to result in increased oxidation and breakdown of surface peat and the decline of some *Sphagnum* species. It may also mean that nutrient conditions are no longer optimal for other peatland plants.

Microclimatic change has also been suggested as a possible causative factor. Afforestation reduces windspeed and may 'trap' moisture before it reaches the mire, particularly if it is in the form of mist or fog. Snow-lie is also reported to last much longer in isolated pockets within forests, and drifting along the edges of forests can result in the same effect, particularly along north-facing plantation edges (R Soutar pers. comm.). Bragg (1982) has demonstrated that, when there is snow cover, the water table generally falls; free water does not readily become available again until snow-melt.

There is no proof that any of the above factors are the cause of the vegetational changes in Kielder Forest. It is, however, extremely unlikely that such changes would have been so rapid without afforestation. The nearest comparable site outside the forest is Butterburn Flow, and no such changes were recorded there. Future work is planned to elucidate the mechanism by which these effects occur, to include grazing and burning trials as well as investigations into hydrology, climate and peat chemistry.

Impact on the mire margin

A major effect of forest drainage is the destruction of the mire margin complex, typically consisting of water-tracks (endotelmic seepages) and surface seepage, which together form the transition either to mineral ground or the next mire macrotope. These are naturally the main areas of water run-off from the mire edge and generally lead fairly rapidly to main watercourses. As a result, these are also the areas typically used in forest drainage schemes as the location for collector and feeder drains, catching the water as it flows from the main areas of ploughing and taking it to the major watercourses. In an ecosystem complex as limited in variety as blanket bog, the loss of this significant source of relative diversity, particularly in the invertebrate fauna, represents a serious reduction in the importance of the mire as a whole. Too often the margins are assumed to be expendable, yet, as discussed in Chapter 2, the mire expanse–mire margin gradient is one of the key features integral to a mire unit (Sjörs 1948; Malmer 1985).

New plantations thus appear to have considerable potential for affecting adjoining unplanted peatlands, especially where there is physical continuity of the peat body and catchment. There may, however, be beneficial effects, especially on bogs in different catchments, from the cessation of moor-burning which is usually required. The Silver Flowe in Galloway has benefited from a reduction in both fire and grazing since the adjoining but mostly separate catchment was afforested, and its vegetation is now in excellent condition. Much more work on the effects of afforestation on adjacent, unplanted ground is needed before general conclusions can be drawn.

While non-patterned flow at low altitudes is evidently the favoured ground for new planting, the leaving of numerous unplanted islands containing pool and hummock systems cannot be assumed to secure these as naturally-developing enclosures for the future. Any similarity to open peatlands within the boreal forests of Fennoscandia is superficial and misleading (see Stroud *et al.* 1987, Figure 6.1). Some of these unplanted pool systems are already tapped

by drains, and the previous section has indicated the strong possibilities of adverse change.

Above all, there is no case, in ecological or any other terms, for arguing that afforestation is here restoring a more natural condition or putting back what was once present. The establishment of a cover of exotic trees, made possible only by treatments which radically alter the physical habitat and kill the existing natural and semi-natural vegetation, comes close to environmental engineering. The contrast between the resulting product and the real, natural boreal forest of Fennoscandia or Canada – or even the Highlands – has been described and illustrated recently (Nature Conservancy Council 1986, pp. 53–54). Indeed, the two have little in common, apart from the presence of trees.

Present distribution of new forest

The total area of Caithness and Sutherland peatland either planted or approved for planting is believed to be 67,000 ha, representing 17% of the total peatland area (Stroud *et al.* 1987). Not surprisingly, in view of factors such as altitudinal limits and suitability

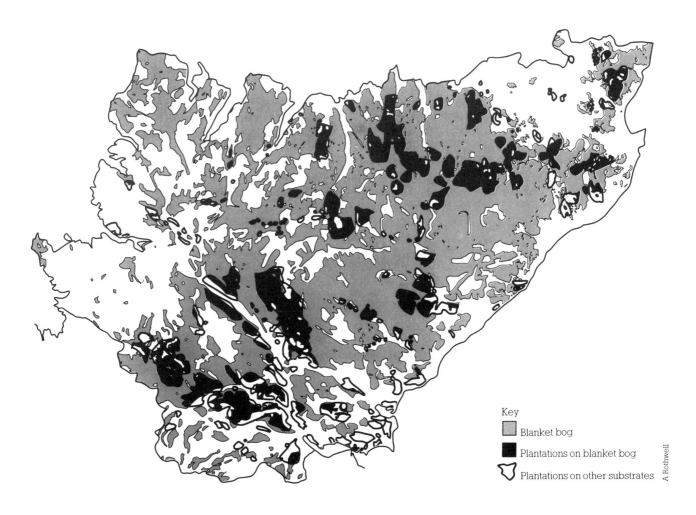

Key
■ Blanket bog
■ Plantations on blanket bog
▽ Plantations on other substrates

A Rothwell

Figure 26 Extent of blanket bog in Caithness and Sutherland, with areas of forestry (including land in Forestry Commission ownership or with Forest Grant Scheme approval) established on peatland and elsewhere.

of soil types, the distribution of forestry in the region so far is not uniform, although it is widely scattered, thereby spreading its effects over a large number of catchments. However, Figure 26 reveals that almost the entire pressure from recent forestry in the two districts has fallen on ground which is in the heart of the Caithness and Sutherland peatland complex.

Bioclimatic zones such as O2.H1/A3 are devoid of forestry because of altitudinal limitations, as are zones associated with the Moine Thrust, whilst the majority of the hyperoceanic O1 zone is also unafforested, almost certainly because most of it is in small units of ownership which preclude large-scale economies of planting. In the west much of the area is presumably too steep and rocky. Exposure to westerly gales may also be a limiting factor, but new planting round Loch Urigill, Ledmore, suggests that this is not a major consideration.

Clearly there are limitations other than land-class type which determine the nature of land acquired and planted, but it is obvious that the wetter types of land are more likely to be considered for sale to forestry interests than others.

7   Peatland distribution and area

Basis for reassessment

Some statistics on the approximate extent and distribution of the peatland resource in the region, based on the soil maps produced for the Soil Survey of Scotland, have been presented by Angus (1986). The figures of peatland loss to forestry presented by Angus particularly emphasised the vulnerability of low-lying blanket bog in the Flow Country because he was able to show that the major pressure from forestry was clearly directed towards land below the 250 m contour. To develop this exercise further, the NCC required a more accurate assessment of the extent of peatland soils in the Flow Country, because evidence gathered during the course of its Peatland Survey of Caithness and Sutherland indicated that high-quality pockets existed that failed to meet the required size criterion for "exploitability", which was the primary purpose of the Soil Survey for Scotland assessment (see Chapter 8).

Angus's report used the soil units of the Macaulay Institute for Soil Research (MISR) – now the Macaulay Land Use Research Institute – to map a range of peatland categories. In mapping "peat" Angus used the MISR map units 3 (basin and valley peat), 4 (undifferentiated peat), 4d (deep peat > 100 cm) and 4e (eroded peat). There is no problem in using these categories to identify peatland for our purposes. Difficulties arise, however, with the next category, of "peaty soils", which includes a number of MISR map units, all of which have some peat but where either it does not constitute full cover or it is less than 50 cm deep.

For example, a large part of the region, particularly in Sutherland, is covered by MISR soil unit 23 (Bibby, Douglas, Thomasson & Robertson 1982). This is excluded from Angus's definition of "peat" but it is described by Bibby *et al.* (1982) as –

Type 1: "deep peat broken up by areas of peaty gleys, peaty podsols and shallow peat";

Type 2: "smooth slopes with shallow peat and peaty gleys . . . codominant and closely associated", with deep peat less common.

Type 1 is more common in Sutherland and Caithness. From such a description alone it is clear that a good proportion of this soil unit may have sufficient peat cover to form areas of significant peatland interest. This is also true of most of the other "peaty soil" categories. Units 26 and 29, which form the majority of the rest of the "peaty soils" in east Sutherland and Caithness, also have appreciable shallow and occasional deep peat elements. Unit 395, which covers most of the Lewisian Gneiss in

west Sutherland, is mainly rocky, undulating ground with many small pockets of peat. The NCC's extensive Peatland Survey has shown that certain areas of MISR "peaty soils" are of importance for nature conservation and in this sense are little different from the deeper peats.

The MISR 1:250,000 map and Angus's report both use a scale which is only capable of detecting soil units occupying areas greater than 100 ha. This scale of mapping is often not appropriate for identification of more restricted peat deposits, which again may be of high conservation interest. This, incidentally, is probably one of the reasons for the low representation by MISR of basin and valley peats, which tend to occur as small units. For example, a valuable site at Loch Laxford does not register on the MISR map because of its relatively small size.

The peatland distribution described below represents an attempt to allow for all the above factors and to map peatland extent for conservation purposes. The categories defined by the MISR are designed particularly for the mapping of exploitable peat resources.

Methods

The method followed was to examine the MISR soil units mapped at 1:50,000 scale and then to look more closely on 1:25,000 Ordnance Survey maps at those areas where "peaty soils" occur. The large scale of the later MISR series of maps means that many of the smaller areas of deep peat excluded from the 1:250,000 map available to Angus(1986) are now shown. From the descriptions given in Futty & Towers (1982), gradient was considered to be the most important determinant of peatland occurrence within "peaty" soil units. Knowledge of wide areas, gained during the peatland field survey and through examination of air photographs, was also used in interpreting the MISR soil units. In this way the marginal and mixed soil categories were divided into peat and non-peat units. The MISR peat distribution for the north-eastern section of Caithness, corresponding with O.S. sheet 12 (1:50,000 scale), was accepted as the best estimate of peatland in conservation terms.

The 1:50,000 maps produced in this way were then photo-reduced to produce a version at 1:250,000 still maintaining the detail of the larger-scale maps. Figures for the actual areas of peat and of peat/ forestry overlap could then be calculated by using a planimeter on the 1:250,000 map with a forestry overlay at the same scale. These figures were checked by means of the Arc/Info computing system.

Results

The results are shown in Figure 27. The total extent of peatland is calculated as 401,375 ha. The total percentage peatland cover of the region is approximately 52.5%. From the map it is clear that the total area of peatland is much larger than the region identified by the RSPB as its "study area" (Royal Society for the Protection of Birds 1985; Bainbridge, Minns, Housden & Lance 1987).

Key

■ Blanket bog

D J Charman/F Everingham/R M O'Reilly

Figure 27 Peatland distribution in Caithness and Sutherland, based on the soil maps of the Macaulay Land Use Research Institute. All of soil categories 3, 4, 4d and 4e are included, together with parts of other categories which represent a mosaic of thin and deep peat. Deep peat within these 'mosaic' soil categories was identified on the basis of the NCC's Peatland Survey combined with an assessment of the topography displayed on 1:25,000 maps.

8 The Nature Conservancy Council's Peatland Survey of Caithness and Sutherland

The account by Crampton (1911) of the Caithness "moorlands" contained the first ecological description of the blanket bogs of this region, though it was generalised. Surprisingly, when Tansley (1939) compiled his *magnum opus, The British Islands and their Vegetation*, he made scant reference to the immense peatlands of Caithness and Sutherland and dealt with western Ireland as the classic area in his treatment of low-level blanket bog. Pearsall (1956) published a detailed description of two small areas of patterned blanket bog in Sutherland, but his account gives no impression of the abundance and diversity of blanket bog within this District. For many years after interest in peatland ecology developed in Britain, the importance of this far northern part of Scotland seemed to escape notice. Surveys by the Scottish Peat Committee (Department of Agriculture and Fisheries for Scotland 1965, 1968) to estimate workable peat resources were made in the 1950s, but then this concern died away. Ratcliffe (1964) gave another generalised description of these blanket bogs, drawing attention to their immense area (the largest in Britain) and the frequent occurrence of patterned pool-hummock surfaces.

During the last few years, the international importance of Britain's blanket mire habitat has become increasingly evident, with the result that it has become the focus of much greater attention than previously, emerging from relative obscurity (see Chapter 3 and Moore 1984) to be recognised as one of Britain's most important terrestrial habitats (NCC 1986).

Previous peatland surveys by the original Nature Conservancy and subsequently the NCC have been limited to the identification of exemplary sites within the range of variation shown by the peatlands of Caithness and Sutherland. Goode & Ratcliffe (1977) give an indication of the peatland types to be found in the region, but their account is limited to seven outstanding sites chosen on the basis of knowledge then available.

Extensive habitat survey had not been part of the research policy of the former Nature Conservancy, but, when the Nature Conservancy Council was set up anew in 1973, it accepted the need for systematic survey of semi-natural habitats as the necessary basis for a comprehensive conservation programme. A small peatlands survey team of two people was accordingly set up in 1977, with the remit to cover the whole of Britain. The advance of moorland reclamation and afforestation made it seem inevitable that the hitherto intractable flows of Caithness and Sutherland must eventually come under pressure for development. Recognising the supreme importance of the blanket bogs of this region, the NCC initiated a pilot study of the Caithness peatlands in 1978, to develop an appropriate methodology.

Problems over access limited the first two years' work to isolated areas of peatland within the Caithness agricultural plain. In 1980, however, a major programme of peatland survey for Caithness and Sutherland was launched and continued over the seven field seasons up to 1986. The original team has expanded to number six as the maximum at any one time – some of the authors of the present report and John Riggall, Fiona Burd, Sarah Garnett, Bob Missin, Sara Oldfield, John Ratcliffe, Jane Smart and Sylvia White. An additional survey team was organised by the Scottish Field Survey Unit and led by Liz Charter. This study has been supplemented by detailed botanical surveys of peatland sites conducted for the North-West Scotland Region of the NCC by Dr R E C Ferreira.

Methods

The approach adopted for the NCC's Peatland Survey of Caithness and Sutherland is similar to that used for the NCC's Welsh Wetland Survey (Ratcliffe & Hattey 1982), where a programme of stratified survey and sampling was employed. This procedure involves, first, the delimitation of the complete resource for possible survey. The mapping of the peat deposits of Caithness and Sutherland is described in Chapter 7. The next stage consists of assessment to discard unsuitable areas. The entire region of Caithness and Sutherland was therefore examined by using the post-war air photographs housed at the Scottish Development Department. Sites were deleted from the survey programme only where –

● some other land-use had completely destroyed the peatland interest;

● they showed erosion in such an advanced state that extensive bedrock or sheets of bare peat were exposed, leaving little peat vegetation; thus sites with slight or moderate erosion were surveyed;

● the slope evident from stereo-photographs indicated that the peat was likely to be extremely thin, but, even then, only if it showed no signs of extensive flushing or any type of surface patterning;

- information obtained from local sources indicated that the area contained no peatland interest.

Finally, in the field, sites were stratified according to the level of peatland information they revealed. If, on initial survey, mire systems held very little interest, owing perhaps to recent damage, or were extremely uniform, the range of information gathered was limited and the time spent on such a site was much less than on one with good representation or a wide range of morphological, surface pattern or vegetation features.

Aims

The survey aimed to identify and visit all peatland areas of significant interest to nature conservation within Caithness and Sutherland, to produce descriptions and evaluations of each area (identifying prime peatland areas) and to draw up a detailed classification of the blanket bog and vegetation types present. This was intended to provide the basis for a comprhensive conservation programme, having regard to both national and international requirements and including the peatland "key sites" already listed in *A Nature Conservation Review* (Goode & Ratcliffe 1977).

Selection of sites for survey

By using a combination of existing knowledge, 1:25,000 maps, LANDSAT satellite imagery and air photos, 399 sites (mesotopes) were identified for survey. A further 84 areas were dismissed at an early stage because of signs of damage obvious on air photo images (see Figure 28).

At each site several features were noted, in order to allow comparison between sites and an assessment of the relative value of each site.

1 Mire unit morphology (mesotope)

This was characterised according to hydromorphology and geomorphological location (see Chapter 2), to give a number of broad categories –

- watershed
- saddle
- valleyside
- low watershed/valleyside
- spur
- ladder fen
- minerotrophic fens

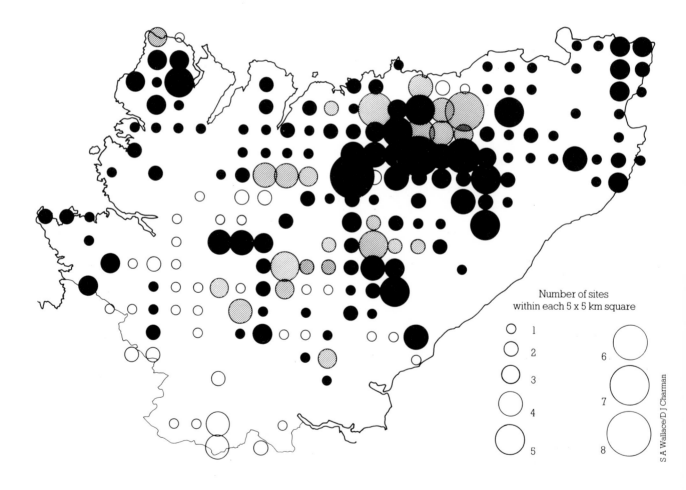

Figure 28 Distribution of sites examined on aerial photographs, displayed by 5 km squares. Open circles indicate sites examined but not selected for field survey, hatched circles indicate a combination of surveyed and unsurveyed sites within the 5 km square, and filled circles represent 5 km squares where all sites examined were surveyed in the field.

68

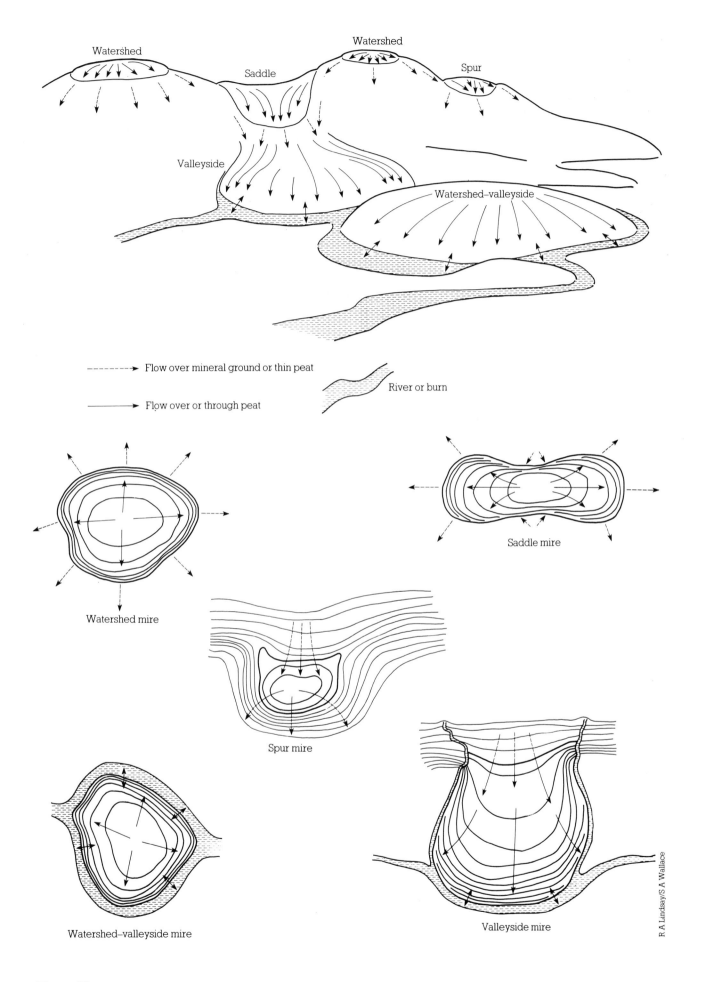

Watershed

Watershed

Saddle

Spur

Valleyside

Watershed–valleyside

- - - - - - → Flow over mineral ground or thin peat

──────→ Flow over or through peat

River or burn

Watershed mire

Saddle mire

Spur mire

Watershed–valleyside mire

Valleyside mire

R A Lindsay/S A Wallace

Figure 29 Hydromorphological bog types (mesotopes) – generalised location within the landform, with an indication of surface water flow patterns, and generalised pattern (as seen from above) of surface water "flow-nets" (Ivanov 1981).

The general morphology and pattern of flow-nets for each of these is illustrated in Figure 29.

2 Surface pattern (microtope)

Ten discrete zones were identified for sites which possessed surface patterning, according to previously published accounts (see Chapter 2). Zones recorded were –

- T5 peat mounds
- T4 erosion hags
- T3 hummocks
- T2 high ridge
- T1 low ridge
- A1 *Sphagnum* hollows
- A2 mud-bottom hollows
- TA2 erosion channels
- A3 drought-sensitive pools
- A4 permanent pools

The relative abundance of each zone was recorded on the DAFOR scale (Dominant, Abundant, Frequent, Occasional, Rare).

3 Vegetation

The vegetation within the mire expanse and the mire margin was sampled by using 1 m^2 quadrats adjusted in shape to record visually homogeneous vegetation within each (separate) zone. These data were analysed by TWINSPAN (Hill 1979) followed by recombination of the "end groups" to produce noda which could usefully be identified in the field. The resultant groups were compared with existing classification systems including the National Vegetation Classification communities (Proctor & Rodwell 1986).

4 Damage

All damage to the bog surface and surrounding ground was recorded, with notes on the degree of damage, ranging from absent through to severe, in the following categories –

- burning
- erosion
- drainage

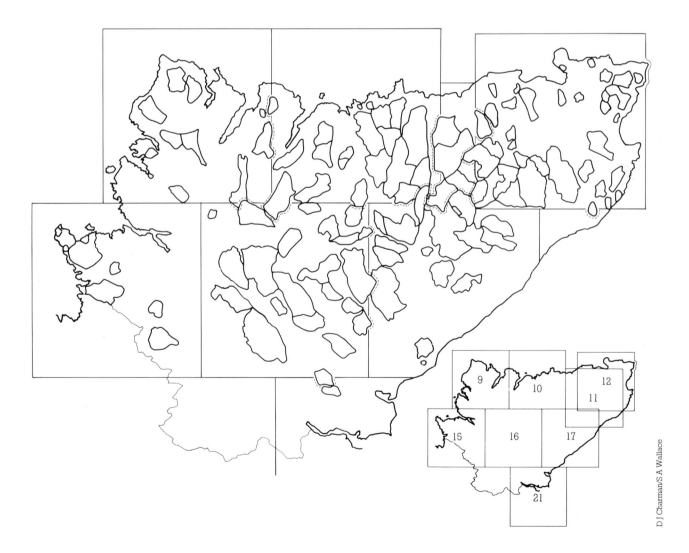

Figure 30 Distribution of mire complexes (macrotopes) identified for detailed quadrat analysis during the NCC's Peatland Survey. Inset key shows 1:500,000 Ordnance Survey map coverage and map numbers.

- grazing/trampling
- afforestation
- peat-cutting

5 *Sphagnum cover*

An assessment of the total *Sphagnum* within the
T (terrestrial) zones was made in the field –

0 – no significant *Sphagnum* cover;
1 – *Sphagnum* present;
2 – significant cover (patchy in extent);
3 – extensive to continuous cover over large areas of
the site.

6 Quaking ground

This consists of *Sphagnum*-rich surfaces which show
almost no sign of disturbance and which have such a
high water content and low level of humification that
the mire surface quakes when being traversed. It
indicates a high degree of naturalness. Three
categories were identified –

1 – present in small areas;
2 – common, scattered throughout site; higher ridges
not quaking when walked over;
3 – extensive areas of quaking ground, making
walking through the site very difficult; most of the
ridges quaking, even the higher areas.

7 Notable plant species

Certain species are regarded as important owing to
their localisation or as indicators of naturalness/lack
of damage to the bog surface. Others indicate
certain conditions (e.g. flushing or oceanicity) and
some show bias in geographical distribution
(sometimes linked to oceanicity).

The preliminary work attempted to identify as many
as possible of what appeared to be significant mire
units (mesotopes), for subsequent field study. These
mire units were grouped into the seven topographic–
water flow categories of Section 1 above. Within
each mire unit, the detailed surface pattern
(microtopes), vegetation and other key features
were analysed according to the standard lists in
Sections 2 to 7. Mire complexes (macrotopes) were
then defined on the basis of hydrological boundaries
(e.g. rivers or lake margins), where possible, but
based on other limits where ecological
discontinuities (such as pronounced changes in
slope and vegetation or occurrence of rock
outcrops) appeared on air photographs, peat/soil
maps or 1:25,000 Ordnance Survey maps (Figure 30).
This is the method adopted by Moen (1985) in
Norway. Each mire complex contained at least one
deep peat area, and some contained many such
systems forming extensive mire complexes. While
former mire units which are now largely afforested
have been omitted, many of those included for
survey contain some forest.

The process of classification was then based, as in
Norway and Canada, on the variation between
individual mire units (mesotopes) according to the
differences displayed by their detailed surface
structures (microtopes). The mire complexes,
(macrotopes) were subsequently classified on the
basis of the combination of differing mesotope and
microtope features.

9 Mire features of note in Caithness and Sutherland

One of the striking features about the peatlands of Caithness and Sutherland is the contrast between the apparent uniformity of the terrain when seen from a distance, particularly from a car or train window, and the bewildering maze of patterns, pool types and other surface features which it is possible to encounter when walking across such terrain. Even then, it is quite possible to walk within a few metres of a huge, complex pool system and not realise this, because the low-lying nature of such patterns, the very flat nature of most bog expanses and the consequent lack of high vantage points make it almost impossible to obtain an extensive view of the bog surface and its patterns from ground level. It is ironic that a habitat which is characterised by wide vistas and unobstructed views should itself be so difficult to see. Despite these problems, or perhaps because of them, two particular structural features which have so far received little attention in the published literature, and therefore deserve special mention, were identified during the course of the survey.

Ladder fens

The limited view of the overall arrangement of surface features on a bog can make it particularly difficult during field survey to obtain an accurate idea of the pattern type. It does not require a great deal of extra height to overcome this problem – 20–30 m above the central part of the bog often suffices – but there are many practical difficulties in obtaining reasonably standardised views from the relatively low altitudes required to resolve the smaller elements of surface pattern. Without doubt the most effective means of recording this type of information is through the use of aerial photographs, but the most standardised, clearest and most comprehensive cover is that of the Ordnance Survey, which, unfortunately, is taken from too high an altitude for complete resolution of all important features. A more useful scale was adopted for the complete aerial photo-coverage of Britain carried out immediately post-war by the Royal Air Force, but the quality of image is sometimes poor.

Nevertheless, it was during the course of routine searches through the RAF photo-coverage that a particular arrangement of mire patterns was encountered in Sutherland which did not fit easily into any type previously described in the literature for Britain. The aerial photographs showed a system in which the ridges and pools were quite markedly straight and parallel, as opposed to showing the more typically arcuate trend of ombrotrophic linear patterning. In addition the areas always appeared to lie within a slight zone of seepage (see example in Figure 7).

In Caithness and Sutherland, the peatlands are predominantly of the blanket bog mesotope, but typically aggregated into large and often complex macrotopes. In places there are numerous small areas of soligenous and valley mire, adjoining or mixed with the blanket bogs. During the vegetation survey in the field following the initial selection of sites from aerial photographs, a number of patterned surfaces were encountered which did not fall easily within the class of ombrotrophic mire, as they were dominated by *Molinia caerulea*, *Carex rostrata* and occasionally *Carex lasiocarpa*. The vegetation was typical of the soligenous areas which characterise the mire margins of ombrotrophic bogs, but the structure of the patterns was much more formal than that generally found in soligenous conditions. It was instead the strip-ridge pattern characteristic of ombrotrophic mires, with long, narrow ridges lying at right angles to the obvious direction of water seepage. Water clearly passed down through the system from one pool to the next, but the lack of a central watercourse meant that such movement must be either through or over the ridges.

Re-examination of the aerial photographs for these sites confirmed that the areas of unusual, parallel patterning noted during the initial aerial photographic search and these strongly patterned *Molinia–Carex* mires were in fact the same.

The similarity of these patterns and general hydromorphology to the *aapa* mires of Fennoscandia is quite striking. However, the overall vegetation and scale of patterning are somewhat different.

Stratigraphic work, by one of the present writers (D J Charman), to determine the origin and developmental history of these systems has only just begun, but examination of several such sites during the course of the Caithness and Sutherland survey has already revealed what may be different stages in the development of a ladder fen.

Ladder fen development

The range of soligenous sites examined which show various stages of linear ridge formation suggests that ladder fens may originate from single-channelled poor fens which lie between two lenses of peat or a lens of peat and an outcrop of mineral ground. As the peat builds up beneath the area of poor fen and the gradient thus becomes shallower, the watercourse becomes increasingly meandering, not unlike a mature lowland river. Eventually the peat builds up to a point where the gradient is sufficiently low, and the rate of water flow thus sufficiently reduced, to allow the peat ridges caused by the wide meanders to grow right across the watercourse. Thereafter,

Simple soligenous flush on mineral soil

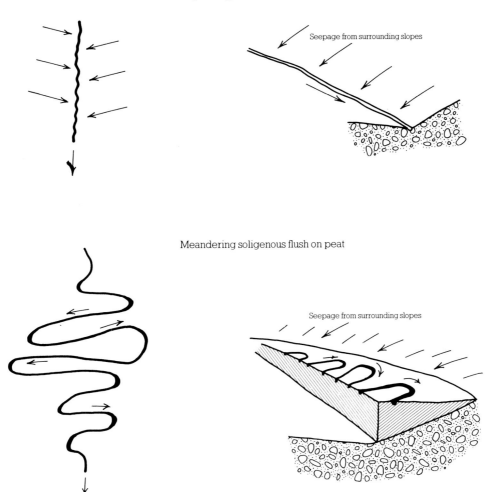

Seepage from surrounding slopes

Meandering soligenous flush on peat

Seepage from surrounding slopes

Ladder fen on deep peat

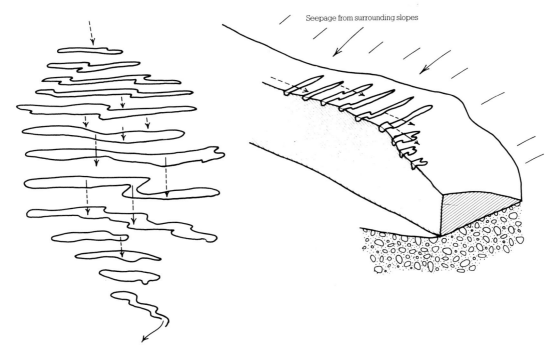

Seepage from surrounding slopes

R A Lindsay/S A Wallace

Figure 31 Suggested sequence of ladder fen development (see text)

water movement is by seepage over and through the ridges (see Figure 31).

However, this type of site is so little studied, and the observations above are so tentative, that an authoritative picture of the developmental history of ladder fens must await the detailed results of work at Southampton University.

In September 1986 the International Mire Conservation Group visited two ladder fens during the course of their Second Field Symposium. The Group considered that, though the type has affinities with the *aapa* mires of Fennoscandia and the ribbed fens of central Canada, it is more closely related to the oceanic ladder fens of eastern Canada (Dr Stephen Zoltai pers. comm.), whilst being a distinct type in its own right. IMCG members called for the few examples identified to be given the highest conservation status.

Caithness peat-mounds

Although the majority of structural features are so low-lying that they do not stand out from the overall expanse of the bog surface, one type of structure has given rise to occasional comment in the literature precisely because it is so strikingly obvious even from a considerable distance. It is probable that these structures have not attracted more attention before now because they are so easily mistaken for small outcrops of *Calluna*-covered mineral ground.

Goode & Lindsay (1979) describe the structure and vegetation of so-called peat-mounds from Lewis in the Outer Hebrides. Similar features have been recorded from Shetland (Spence 1974; Goode & Field 1973), but none of these accounts provides a satisfactory explanation for the origins of such structures. Zoltai & Pollett (1983) describe "peat-mounds", as opposed to *palsa* mires, from the Canadian Mid-Arctic Wetland Region, but these are, like them, associated with a permanent ice-core. Ruuhijärvi (1960, 1983) describes structures from Finnish northern boreal mires which are essentially large *Sphagnum fuscum* hummocks but which are distinct from *palsa* mires in lacking an ice core. Dierssen (1982) relates these to Icelandic *thufa* described by Schunke (1977) and gives an

illustration of a Norwegian example (Dierssen 1982, Plate 80). Whilst these are clearly much smaller features than Scottish peat-mounds, which may rise to two or three metres, the physiognomic similarity between *palsa* mires (which attain the same or a higher order of height), peat-mounds and *thufa* is as yet unexplored.

The most detailed account to date of Scottish peat-mounds is provided by Robinson (1987), who describes the stratigraphy of three mounds in eastern Caithness. The peat mound "field" near Keiss, Caithness, does not support a clearly defined area of *dubh lochain* as might be expected on such a gently-contoured plateau. Instead, it has relatively deep peat which is covered by a homogeneous blanket bog vegetation type dominated by *Eriophorum vaginatum*, dwarf shrubs and a limited range of *Sphagna*. The mounds are scattered across this otherwise smooth plateau and are made striking by the luxuriance of their dwarf shrub vegetation, beneath which are generally hypnoid mosses rather than *Sphagna*.

Robinson (1987) explores a number of possible mechanisms for their development, but suggests that they may be a result of localised ponding, climatic change and fire. From his discovery that some of the mounds have a tightly matted layer of *Eriophorum* and *Sphagnum* towards the base of the structures, he proposes that certain areas of the bog surface were able to remain waterlogged even after a climatic shift around 5000 BP which led drier conditions to prevail. These localised areas of waterlogging were, he suggests, able to promote more rapid peat growth and therefore rose above the surrounding bog surface. Robinson considers that burning would then have accentuated this process, resulting in development of the high mounds which can be seen today.

The area around Keiss is the best example of a peat-mound "field" in mainland Britain. Such "fields" are also found in Shetland (Spence 1974; Goode & Field 1978; NCC unpublished), Orkney (NCC unpublished) and Lewis (Goode & Lindsay 1979; NCC unpublished), but the mounds at Keiss are unusual in being located within a matrix of remarkably vigorous blanket bog vegetation.

10   Analysis of vegetation communities

Although the survey was essentially concerned with ombrotrophic vegetation, a number of fen systems were sampled in the course of the work. In addition, the transitional types, such as ladder fens, were recorded in some detail. Thus a certain proportion of the overall data-set describes minerotrophic vegetation.

This report does not discuss the minerotrophic vegetation in any detail, because a more comprehensive review of Scottish fens is required before their status can be assessed. The provisional communities are presented here in tabular form for completeness, but, other than ladder fens, will not be further commented on.

The vegetation analysis derived a total of 33 ombrotrophic vegetation types, with two more for ladder fens, which together can be grouped into 13 broad categories. These can be grouped into five structural types, reflecting the small-scale structures of the mire surface discussed in Chapters 1 and 2.

Tables 3a and 3b are synoptic tables showing the communities identified from the analysis, based on the quadrat data for plant species collected during the survey. The communities are described according to species constancy rather than abundance as is usual in such phytosociological tables.

The five structural types are –

- thin peat communities;
- peat-mounds/high hummocks;
- *Sphagnum*-rich hummocks and ridges;
- runnels and damaged mire;
- hollows and pools.

Each vegetation type is compared below to plant communities described by Dierssen (1982) and by Proctor & Rodwell (1986).

1 Thin peat communities

Where mineral ground protrudes through areas of deeper peat, a number of characteristic communities can be found, including the rare *Arctous alpinus–Calluna vulgaris* dry heath. However, where ground is essentially still wet and forms an integral component of the blanket mire hydrological unit, a wet heath community characterised by *Juncus squarrosus* is common.

Vegetation group 1 – thin peat

Community 1 – *Juncus squarrosus* community

Ericetum tetralicis (see Dierssen 1982); M15/15d – *Sphagnum compactum* wet heath, *Juncus squarrosus–Dicranum scoparium* sub-community (Proctor & Rodwell 1986)

This community becomes more common towards the west of the Flow Country, where even slopes receive sufficient rainfall and run-off to form wet heath over thin peat. The community is also characteristic of peat-cuttings where the subsoil has almost been exposed, leaving just a thin peat covering. In time, under such conditions, the wet heath component could be expected to succumb to *Sphagnum* colonisation and redevelopment of peat.

Juncus squarrosus is a major component, but not entirely constant, and the community is sometimes found as a low, thinly scattered *Calluna* sward beneath which is a bryophyte carpet of *Plagiothecium undulatum*, *Pleurozium schreberi*, *Rhytidiadelphus squarrosus* and feeble growths of *Sphagnum cuspidatum*. *Carex nigra* is also found in such conditions, this last and the previous species pointing to the essentially flushed nature of the community.

2 Peat-mounds/high hummocks

This structural type merges with the previous one because the communities which characterise peat-mound summits are similar to some of those found on moist, bryophyte-rich hill slopes. On mire systems proper, the communities are restricted to the very highest levels of the microtopography or appear where the mire has suffered extensive lowering of the water table.

The other major category within this broad type is the highest of the bryophyte hummocks, namely the *Racomitrium lanuginosum* hummock. On undamaged mire it forms the highest element unless peat-mounds are present, whilst on damaged sites it is characteristic of dried-out hummocks or the summits of erosion hags.

Vegetation group 2 – Bryophyte-rich slopes and peat-mounds

Community 2 – *Empetrum nigrum–Hylocomium splendens–Sphagnum rubellum*

M19c – *Calluna vulgaris–Eriophorum vaginatum* blanket mire, *Vaccinium vitis-idaea–Hylocomium splendens* sub-community (Proctor & Rodwell 1986).

This community is typical of both peat-mound summits and bryophyte-rich hill slopes. From a

Structural type	1	2					3						
Vegetation group number	1	2		3			4				5		
Surface pattern zone		T5		T4/T3/T1			T3/T2				T2/T1		
Community number	1	2	3	4	5	6	7	8	9	10	11	12	13
Species name													
Juncus squarrosus	IV												
Carex nigra	III												
Luzula spp.	I												
Juncus effusus	I												
Polytrichum juniperinum	I												
Sphagnum recurvum	I												
Hylocomium splendens		III											
Rhytidiadelphus squarrosus	I	II											
Rhytidiadelphus loreus		IV	I										
Pleurozium schreberi	II	V	IV				III						
Hypnum cupressiforme		IV	III						II	I			
Empetrum nigrum		IV	IV	I									
Hypogymnia physodes		II	I						I				
Rubus chamaemorus			II										
Calluna vulgaris	III	V	V	IV	V	V	V	V	V	V	IV	IV	IV
Erica cinerea	I			I	II								
Cladonia arbuscula		II	II	II	I								
Cladonia impexa	II	IV	IV	III	V	V	V	III	IV	V	I	III	IV
Racomitrium lanuginosum	II		I	V	V	IV	IV		II	II	I		
Trichophorum cespitosum	I	II	I	III	IV	IV	IV	III	IV	IV	III	III	V
Potentilla erecta					IV	III					II		
Molinia caerulea					V	III	III				IV	I	
Lycopodium selago				II		II							
Sphagnum fuscum			I				V						
Pedicularis sylvatica					II								
Mylia taylorii									I				
Sphagnum imbricatum								V	II				
Cladonia uncialis	I		I	III	II	IV			II	III	II	I	IV
Mylia anomala			I					II	II				
Eriophorum vaginatum		IV	IV	II			IV	IV	IV	II	II	III	II
Sphagnum rubellum	I	IV	III				III	V	V	IV	IV	IV	II
Sphagnum papillosum			I				IV	II	III	II	V	IV	
Narthecium ossifragum	I		II		II	V	IV	IV	IV	IV	IV	IV	IV
Erica tetralix		IV	III	III	III	IV	V	IV	V	IV	IV	IV	IV
Drosera rotundifolia	II	II	III	I	V	V	V	IV	II	III	IV		
Sphagnum tenellum		II	II			I	III	II	IV	III	II	II	II
Odontoschisma sphagni			I						IV	II			
Pleurozia purpurea	I					III	III		I	II	I	I	
Myrica gale			I			I				I	II	II	III
Arctostaphylos uva-ursi													
Polygala serpyllifolia											I		
Sphagnum magellanicum	I								I				
Betula nana			I										
Eriophorum angustifolium	III	IV	IV	III	II	IV	IV	IV	V	V	III	IV	IV
Sphagnum subnitens			I					II	II			I	
Aulacomnium palustre		IV	I										
Bare peat	III		I	III		III	III			II		II	V
Campylopus atrovirens													
Cerex panicea					I								II
Sphagnum compactum													IV
Lepidozia setacea									III				
Schoenus nigricans													
Carex pauciflora											I		
Drosera anglica			I			I		II	II	II	I	III	III
Sphagnum pulchrum													
Sphagnum cuspidatum	III						I		I				
Rhynchospora alba													
Carex limosa													
Eleocharis multicaulis													
Drosera intermedia	I												
Rhynchospora fusca													
Sphagnum auriculatum													
Menyanthes trifoliata									I				
Utricularia vulgaris													

Table 3a

Synoptic table showing the structural types, vegetation groups, surface pattern zones associated with them, and plant communities in which the listed species occur. The Roman numerals indicate the level of percentage constancy displayed by species in each community: V – 100-81%; IV – 80-61%; III – 60-41%; II – 40-21%; I – 20-1%.

							4			5									
6					7		8			9					10			11	12
T1					T1		T1/TA2			A1					A2			A2/A3	A4
14	15	16	17	18	19	20	21	22	23	24	25	26	27	28	29	30	31	32	33
IV	IV	IV	IV				III	II											
		II																	
	IV		III				I												
			II				II												
	III	III	II		II		IV	V	V										
II			III		II	V	III					II					II		
	II						I												
I																			
III	V	II	III			V	I			III			IV						
III	IV	IV	III	IV	IV	V	III	V					V	III		II			
III	IV	II	III	III		V	II	III					IV						
	IV	IV	IV			V													
V	IV		II	IV		IV	I		V										
	II																		
				III			I											I	
	II	III					II												
	V																		
IV	IV	IV	II	III									V						
		III																	
III	IV	V	V	IV		V	IV	IV		III	II	V	V	V		V	II	III	
III																			
					V	IV	III		IV					V		IV			
					IV		I												
							II												
					II		I												
						V													
			IV																
	III		V				II				II	V						I	
	II		V	IV			II	II	V	V	V	V	V	IV	III	IV	III	V	
			II	IV										IV		IV	IV	II	
										II					V		III		
							I									III			
			IV							II				II		II		IV	
	II		IV				III			III		III		V	II			II	V
																		I	

Community number	1	2	3	4	5	6	7	8	9	10	11	12	13	14	15
Species name															
Carex rostrata	III	III			II	IV	II	IV	IV	V	V		IV	V	
Potamogeton polygonifolius		II	V	IV		II	IV	II	V	V			II		II
Menyanthes trifoliata	IV	II		III		II		V	III	V	V	V			
Equisetum fluviatile			II			II			III	III	III	V	III	V	
Ranunculus flammula		II		III		II		V	II	IV		II	V	V	
Potentilla palustris				II				IV	V	V	V	V	III	V	
Carex limosa		III	III			II	V		IV	IV	V				
Carex panicea			III	IV	II	II	II			V					
Eriophorum angustifolium	III	V	II	IV	III	III		II							
Erica tetralix	V	III	III	II	IV										
Sphagnum recurvum			II		III	IV				II		V			
Carex lasiocarpa	II	V	II			II	III								
Carex demissa			II	V	V			II						III	
Scorpidium scorpioides				II	V				III	IV			III		
Sphagnum auriculatum	II		V	II		II				III					
Narthecium ossifragum	V		V		V	II									
Pedicularis sylvatica	II			II				IV						IV	
Pinguicula vulgaris	II		II		II	II									
Sphagnum papillosum	V		V			IV					III				
Potentilla erecta	II		II		II	III									
Myrica gale	III	V	IV			IV									
Trichophorum cespitosum	III	II	III		II										
Molinia caerulea	V	IV			IV			II							
Myosotis scorpioides								II			II	V		V	
Calluna vulgaris	IV	II			II	II									
Drepanocladus revolvens				II	III			II	II						
Drosera anglica		III	V		V	V									
Caltha palustris													II	II	V
Polygala serpyllifolia	II		II			II									
Juncus bulbosus		II			II			II							
Carex nigra			II					II	II						
Eleocharis multicaulis			V			III	II								
Drosera rotundifolia	III		II			III									
Sphagnum cuspidatum			III			IV									
Drosera intermedia		II		II											
Calliergon giganteum										II		II			
Hydrocotyle vulgaris										II			IV		
Empetrum nigrum			II			II									
Juncus articulatus				II					II						
Carex curta			II									V			
Chamaenerion angustifolium										III			II		
Eriophorum vaginatum				III			II								
Campylium stellatum					II					III					
Juncus kochii										II			III		
Mnium hornum										II				V	
Utricularia vulgaris			II			II									
Juncus acutiflorus												II		V	
Carex echinata			II			III									
Cardamine pratensis												II		V	
Galium palustre													III		
Succisa pratensis				II											
Sphagnum rubellum	III														
Polytrichum commune			II												
Racomitrium lanuginosum			II												
Filipendula ulmaria														V	
Odontoschisma sphagni				II											
Eleocharis quinqueflora					III										
Mnium punctatum														IV	
Salix spp.										III					
Bare peat	II														
Schoenus nigricans					III										
Sphagnum contortum				III											
Utricularia spp.											II				
Calliergon cordifolium														V	
Equisetum palustre				II											
Sphagnum subnitens						II									
Philonotis fontana														III	
Bryum pallens										II					

Table 3b

Synoptic table showing the provisional fen plant communities identified from analysis of the survey data, including two for ladder fens, in which the listed species occur. The Roman numerals indicate the level of percentage constancy displayed by species in each community: V – 100-81%; IV – 80-61%; III – 60-41%; II – 40-21%; I – 20-1%.

distance the community is characterised by its dwarf shrub sward, which may appear *Calluna*-dominated. However, on closer inspection *Empetrum nigrum* will generally be found as a codominant. Beneath this dwarf shrub layer, the dense bryophyte carpet is characterised by *Hylocomium splendens*, *Pleurozium schreberi*, *Hypnum cupressiforme*, *Sphagnum rubellum*, *Rhytidiadelphus loreus* and sometimes *Dicranum scoparium*.

A particular variant of this community occurs around the margins of some larger *dubh lochain* in Caithness. Where waterfowl, particularly Greenland white-fronted geese *Anser albifrons flavirostris* or teal *Anas crecca*, roost on the pools or breed on the margins, a bryophyte-rich halo forms a striking feature around the pool margin. The halo is dominated by *Aulacomnium palustre* but with many of the characteristic species of this community. A similar feature has been noted in Shetland, around pools used extensively by great skuas *Stercorarius skua*.

Community 3 – *Empetrum*–hypnoid mosses

This is a community more restricted to hill slopes, generally those which have been more regularly burnt, as indicated by the absence of *Hylocomium splendens*. *Rhytidiadelphus squarrosus* replaces *R. loreus*, and both *Hypnum cupressiforme* and *Sphagnum rubellum* are somewhat reduced. This is the only community in which cloudberry *Rubus chamaemorus* is recorded, although it is common on the high peat plateaux of the Highlands. The community represents, along with Community 2, the typical peat-dominated vegetation of relatively undamaged catchment slopes.

Vegetation group 3 – *Racomitrium* hummocks/hags

Community 4 – *Racomitrium lanuginosum–Cladonia*

Erico-Sphagnetum magellanici, subass. *Cladonia uncialis, Racomitrium lanuginosum* phase; M17b – *Scirpus cespitosus–Eriophorum vaginatum* blanket mire, *Cladonia* subass.

This is typical of the highest erosion hags throughout the two Districts, with a mat of *Racomitrium* capped by a sward of *Cladonia* species, although the absence of *Molinia caerulea* tends to mean that the type is commoner in the east. Bare peat is a common component of the surface.

Community 5 – *Racomitrium–Molinia* hummocks and hags

Pleurozio-Ericetum tetralicis, subass. *Racomitrium lanuginosum*; M15c – *Scirpus cespitosus–Erica tetralix*, subass. *Cladonia*

Racomitrium hummocks are more common in the western part of Caithness and in Sutherland because they occur on both natural and damaged mires, whereas in most of Caithness they are almost exclusively restricted to eroding mires (see Chapter 10). The *Racomitrium–Molinia* community is therefore also common in the west, but is largely absent from Caithness. It occurs as vigorous hummocks capped by oceanic indicators such as *Potentilla erecta* and *Pedicularis sylvatica*, together with *Molinia caerulea*, or as the summits of heavily eroded hags, where *M. caerulea* and *P. erecta* are joined by *Erica cinerea*.

Community 6 – *Racomitrium–Pleurozia purpurea*

Pleurozio-Ericetum tetralicis, fac. *Molinia*; M17a – *Scirpus cespitosus–Erica tetralix* blanket mire, subass. *Drosera rotundifolia–Sphagnum*

In central and western parts of the region, *Racomitrium* does not only occur as a hummock-former; it also grows as a loose mat on low ridges, where it characteristically mixes with *Pleurozia purpurea, Trichophorum cespitosum, Narthecium ossifragum* and *Molinia caerulea*. The type is similar in appearance to other undamaged low ridge communities and should not be confused with the mats of *Racomitrium* which dominate the surface of certain badly damaged sites. The associated species of these latter sites indicate clearly that they belong to Community 4 or 5.

3 *Sphagnum*-rich hummocks and ridges

The majority of communities within this category are characteristic of undamaged mires. The term "hummocks and ridges" is taken to mean all those parts of the mire surface which lie above the water table, other than erosion hags and peat-mounds. The structural type can be subdivided into five main vegetation types based largely on the dominant species of *Sphagnum*. Each of these can then be divided on the basis of characteristic species complements, to give a total of 14 community types, making this the richest of the major structural divisions. Such variety is not surprising in view of the fact that the bulk of niche partition for the blanket mire vegetation must occur within this structural span.

Vegetation group 4 – *Sphagnum* hummocks

Community 7 – *Sphagnum fuscum* hummocks

Erico-Sphagnetum magellanici, subass. typical, phase *Sphagnum fuscum*; M18b – *Erica tetralix–Sphagnum papillosum*, subcomm. *Empetrum nigrum–Cladonia*

Although *Sphagnum fuscum* is very local on a national scale, it occurs relatively frequently throughout the Flow Country. It is more commonly found in the west and is thus often associated with *Molinia caerulea*. *Eriophorum vaginatum* is a common associate in Caithness, and *Drosera rotundifolia* is a constant associate throughout the range. Some hummocks are low-growing or have lower slopes which extend across wet (T1) low ridge, allowing species such as *Pleurozia purpurea* and *Sphagnum tenellum* to form communities.

Community 8 – *Sphagnum imbricatum* hummocks

Erico-Sphagnetum magellanici, subass. typical, phase *Sphagnum imbricatum*; M17a – *Scirpus cespitosus–Eriophorum vaginatum* blanket mire, subcomm. *Drosera rotundifolia–Sphagnum*

This community is more central and eastern in its distribution, as reflected by the absence of *Molinia caerulea* and *Racomitrium lanuginosum* as associates. It is almost always accompanied by a greater or lesser proportion of *Sphagnum rubellum* and *Drosera rotundifolia* and is often capped by an open sward of *Cladonia impexa*. *Eriophorum vaginatum* is also a common feature of these hummocks.

Community 9 – *Sphagnum rubellum–Odontoschisma sphagni*

Erico-Sphagnetum magellanici; M17a – *Scirpus cespitosus–Eriophorum vaginatum* blanket mire, subcomm. *Drosera rotundifolia–Sphagnum*

Representing one of the typical communities found in the Flow Country, this occurs as a mixed mosaic of *Sphagna* beneath a dwarf shrub sward. There are no clear *Sphagnum* hummocks, but instead a generally high ridge formation of a somewhat dry nature, as indicated by the presence of *Hypnum cupressiforme* within the mixed *Sphagnum* carpet. In the survey this category is commonly used for the T2 high ridge level wherever more striking features are absent.

Community 10 – Mixed *Sphagna*

Erico-Sphagnetum magellanici; M17a – *Scirpus cespitosus–Eriophorum vaginatum* blanket mire, subcomm. *Drosera rotundifolia–Sphagnum*

This community represents high *Sphagnum rubellum* hummocks. Other *Sphagnum* species are generally represented only by scattered *S. tenellum*. *Cladonia* species are common, particularly *C. impexa*, whereas *Eriophorum vaginatum* is surprisingly sparse.

Vegetation group 5 – *Sphagnum*-rich high/low ridge

Community 11 – *Sphagnum papillosum–Molinia* ridge

Erico-Sphagnetum magellanici, subass. *Cladonia*, var. *Molinia*; M17a – *Scirpus cespitosus–Eriophorum vaginatum* blanket mire, subcomm. *Drosera rotundifolia–Sphagnum*

Typical of central and western parts, this represents the characteristic *Sphagnum papillosum* ridge over much of western Scotland. The mixture of *Potentilla erecta, Molinia caerulea* and *Myrica gale* emphasises the oceanic nature of the community.

Community 12 – *Sphagnum–Eriophorum vaginatum* ridge

Pleurozio-Ericetum tetralicis; M18a – *Erica tetralix–Sphagnum papillosum* mire, subcomm. *Sphagnum magellanicum–Andromeda polifolia*

This is the eastern and southern equivalent of the previous community, largely lacking the oceanic indicators but with significantly increased *Eriophorum vaginatum*. The type is common throughout Caithness, but it is also found on many mires across southern Scotland and northern England.

Community 13 – *Sphagnum compactum* ridge

Ericetum tetralicis; M16 – *Erica tetralix–Sphagnum compactum* wet heath

This occurs where *Sphagnum*-rich mire has been affected by burning and the majority of *Sphagnum* species have been lost. The link between this type and true wet heath/valley mire is indicated by the relative abundance of *Myrica gale*, which appears to be encouraged by mineralisation of the peat after burning.

Vegetation group 6 – *Sphagnum magellanicum* low ridge

Community 14 – *Sphagnum magellanicum–S. subnitens*

Erico-Sphagnetum magellanici; *Erica tetralix–Sphagnum papillosum* mire, subcomm. *Sphagnum magellanicum–Andromeda polifolia*

This occurs as two variants, the first of which is found in valley mires and seepage lines, where *Sphagnum magellanicum* and *S. subnitens* form a mosaic of oligotrophic hummocks within a more minerotrophic community. *Sphagnum tenellum* is a minor component of this type but is almost always present. The second variant is found on ombrotrophic mires, more usually in the west than in the east, and tends to occur as small stretches of ridge which support a mosaic of *Sphagnum subnitens, S. magellanicum* and *S. tenellum*, always within a few centimetres of the water table. It is thus characteristic of low-relief mire patterns.

Community 15 – *Sphagnum magellanicum–S. rubellum* ridge

Erico-Sphagnetum magellanici; M18a – *Erica tetralix–Sphagnum papillosum* mire, subcomm. *Sphagnum magellanicum–Andromeda polifolia*

Although closely allied to the second variant of the preceding community, this community is represented by a marked association between *Sphagnum magellanicum*, *S. rubellum* and *Cladonia impexa*. This is the typical community for *S. magellanicum* when it is free of extreme oceanic influences.

Community 16 – *Sphagnum–Arctostaphylos–Betula nana* dwarf shrub mire

Narthecio-Sphagnetum papillosi, phase *Arctostaphylos uva-ursi*; M19c(i) – *Calluna vulgaris–Eriophorum vaginatum* blanket mire, subcomm. *Vaccinium vitis-idaea*, var. *Betula nana*

Of all the communities recorded in the region, this is perhaps the most characteristic. Although the dwarf shrubs *Betula nana* and *Arctostaphylos uva-ursi* are found in other habitats in Britain, their occurrence together on a *Sphagnum*-rich mire system is almost unique to the region. The *Sphagnum* carpet is generally *S. papillosum*, though *S. magellanicum* is a common but scattered component.

Community 17 – *Sphagnum papillosum–Carex pauciflora*

Erico-Sphagnetum magellanici, subass. *Cladonia uncialis*, var. *Molinia*

In places where limited erosion has left the higher ridge areas with only restricted *Sphagnum* cover, being now dominated by Community 4 or 5, but the A2/A3 pools retain some water, this community may be found. It is most common in central parts and is not recorded from eastern Caithness. A vigorous growth of *Sphagnum papillosum* over areas of wet, bare peat at the T1/A2 margin is often accompanied by a short sward of *Carex pauciflora*. The type appears to be quite consistent and is accompanied by *Molinia*, emphasising its somewhat western trend.

Community 18 – *Rhynchospora alba–Sphagnum* low ridge

Sphagno tenelli-Rhynchosporetum albae, subass. *Sphagnum tenellum*; M18a – *Erica tetralix–Sphagnum papillosum* mire, subcomm. *Sphagnum magellanicum–Andromeda polifolia*

In the west of Sutherland and extending into the terrain associated with the Moine Thrust, conditions clearly become markedly oceanic. This community is typical of mires in these western parts, with an abundance of *Rhynchospora alba* and *Pleurozia purpurea* and a marked absence of dwarf shrubs.

Vegetation group 7 – Hyperoceanic mire vegetation

Community 19 – *Campylopus atrovirens* low ridge

Pleurozio-Ericetum tetralicis, fac. *Molinia*, var.

typical; M17 – *Scirpus cespitosus–Eriophorum vaginatum* blanket mire

This community is more typical of the hyperoceanic Hebrides. Goode & Ratcliffe (1977), Goode & Lindsay (1979) and Lindsay *et al.* (1983) describe it from Lewis and Mull, where it forms a characteristic component of the low-relief microtopography. It is recorded from a small number of sites in Caithness and Sutherland, but its distribution appears to be enhanced by severe burning.

Community 20 – *Schoenus–Molinia* mire

Pleurozio-Ericetum tetralicis, subass. typical, var. typical; *Schoenus nigricans–Narthecium ossifragum* mire

The distribution of *Schoenus nigricans* is discussed in the next chapter. The ombrotrophic community which it characterises was only recorded from a single site in the extreme north-west, by Loch Laxford. On this site, it takes up a position within the T1 zone, which is in contrast to its habit on Islay, where it occurs in both the T1 zone and as high as T2 tussocks.

4 Runnels and damaged mire

Vegetation group 8 – Runnels and damaged mire

Community 21 – *Carex panicea* damaged mire

Scapanio gracilis-Narthecietum ossifragi; M15 – *Scirpus cespitosus–Erica tetralix* wet heath

Throughout the majority of the Flow Country, *Carex panicea* is an indicator of damage when it occurs on unflushed peats. The range of vegetation types from which *C. panicea* mire is derived is diverse, but by the time *C. panicea* has become a significant component, very few other species remain. Bare peat is a common component, becoming increasingly so with the severity of damage sustained.

Community 22 – *Narthecium* runnel or overflow

Narthecio-Sphagnetum papillosi; M21a/M15b/M3

This represents a feature commented on by both Goode (1970) and Goode & Lindsay (1979) in areas of patterning in western regions, termed "overflows" or "runnels". The vegetation of these features, which are formed when water flows over a ridge to a pool further downslope, is characteristically *Sphagnum*-poor. The growth form of *Trichophorum cespitosum* under such conditions is not the tussock form, but instead it occurs as stands of individual stems grouped in an open sward. The most striking aspect of such features is the dominance of *Narthecium ossifragum*.

Community 23 – Microbroken mire

Sphagno tenelli-Rhynchosporetum albae, subass. typical

Where areas of patterning have been damaged but are not yet broken down into deep gullying, the anastomosing network of shallow channels between raised, dry erosion 'islands' has a tendency to collect and hold shallow areas of water. This network is generally colonised by an intimate mixture of *Sphagnum cuspidatum* and *S. tenellum*, sometimes with an open sward of *Trichophorum cespitosum*. The type is easily recognised from its morphology and species composition and is common throughout the two Districts.

5 Hollows and pools

The range of physical structure provided by pool formation gives a significantly larger range of niches for vegetation types to occupy than mire systems further south in Britain. Even so, the range of vegetation types derived from the analysis for the aquatic element of the microtopography is relatively limited. In the east, *Sphagnum cuspidatum* is almost exclusively the constant, whereas towards the west, where nutrient conditions become less extreme, a wider range of vegetation types is found.

Vegetation group 9 – *Sphagnum cuspidatum* carpets (A1)

This type represents the bright green-yellow swards which cover shallow treacherous depressions in the mire surface. The type also occurs as dense mats around the margins of deeper open-water pools, but in both cases the A1 'carpet' is distinguished from a looser, floating matrix of *Sphagnum* because the individual plants in a carpet are permanently bound in place. It is unusual to see surface water within an A1 carpet, but the structure is clearly an aquatic element in the microtopography.

Community 24 – *S. cuspidatum–Eleocharis multicaulis*

Eleocharitetum multicaulis, subass. *Sphagnum auriculatum*; M2 – *Sphagnum cuspidatum/recurvum* bog pool community

A type common in Caithness but also found abundantly in the Halladale catchment, its appearance is very similar to *Scheuchzeria–Sphagnum balticum* carpets in Fennoscandia. It is a very simple community, with few other species recorded. The type is not common in the rest of Britain, mainly, as far as can be determined, because eastern mires which would be expected to favour it have been extensively drained.

Community 25 – Pure *S. cuspidatum* carpets

Eriophorum angustifolium community, subcomm. *Sphagnum cuspidatum*; M2 – *Sphagnum cuspidatum/recurvum* bog pool community

This is a type characteristic of Caithness rather than Sutherland. It occurs as A1 hollows with a pure *S. cuspidatum* carpet extending throughout all or most of the hollow. It closely resembles carpets of *Sphagnum balticum*, a species which adopts the same habit in central and northern Europe. These pure *Sphagnum* carpets are typical of bog hollows further south in Britain and are recorded as far south as Esgyrn Bottom in Pembrokeshire and East Dart Head on Dartmoor.

Community 26 – Typical *Sphagnum cuspidatum* carpets

Eriophorum angustifolium community, subcomm. *Sphagnum cuspidatum*; M2 – *Sphagnum cuspidatum/recurvum* bog pool community

Found from east to west coasts, the community is recognised by its mosaic of *Menyanthes trifoliata, Drosera anglica, Eriophorum angustifolium* and occasional *Narthecium ossifragum* within the *S. cuspidatum* carpet.

Community 27 – *Sphagnum pulchrum* carpets

Erico-Sphagnetum magellanici, subass. *Sphagnum pulchrum*; M18 – *Erica tetralix–Sphagnum papillosum* blanket mire

Few mire species are entirely restricted to the transition zone between the terrestrial and aquatic phases within the microtopography. *Rhynchospora alba* and *Drosera anglica* are perhaps the commonest examples, but, of the *Sphagna*, only *Sphagnum pulchrum* is actually restricted to this zone within mire patterns. The distribution of this species is discussed in the next chapter, but its characteristic vegetation assemblage in Caithness and Sutherland is not markedly different from that in its other British stations (Ratcliffe & Walker 1958; Goode & Ratcliffe 1977).

Community 28 – *Sphagnum cuspidatum–Carex limosa*

Caricetum limosae, subass. *Sphagnum cuspidatum*; M2 – *Sphagnum cuspidatum/recurvum* bog pool community

Carex limosa occurs only rarely on the mire expanse in Caithness, and it is therefore excluded from a major part of the A1 hollow distribution. However, in central and western parts of the Sutherland plain this variant is found on some mires. The type is not found south of the Highland Boundary Fault, apart from an isolated outpost on the Silver Flowe in Dumfries and Galloway.

Vegetation group 10 – Mud-bottom hollow (A2) communities

This type covers a number of communities

characteristic of what is generally an oceanic feature in Britain. Of the three identified, only two are widespread in Caithness and Sutherland.

Community 29 – *Eleocharis multicaulis* mud-bottom hollows

Eleocharitetum multicaulis, subass. *Sphagnum auriculatum*; M1 – *Sphagnum auriculatum* bog pool community

The relatively firm substrate of the mud-bottom hollow provides a rooting medium for *Eleocharis multicaulis*, which then characteristically grows in a loose matrix of *Sphagnum cuspidatum* and *S. auriculatum*. The type is recorded from the central part of the region and is generally limited in Britain to a line north of the Great Glen.

Community 30 – *Rhynchospora alba* mud-bottom hollows

Sphagno tenelli-Rhynchosporetum albae, subass. *Sphagnum auriculatum*, var. *Rhynchospora alba*; M1 – *Sphagnum auriculatum* bog pools

Restricted to the far west, this nodum is the aquatic extension of the *Rhynchospora alba–Sphagnum* low ridge (Community 18) discussed above. It requires a firm mud-bottom to the hollow. Farther south in Britain its presence on mire expanses extends as far south as Wales, where shallow A2 hollows have extensive mats of *R. alba*, but it has not been recorded from the patterned mires of Dartmoor by the NCC's Peatland Survey (unpublished).

Community 31 – *Rhynchospora fusca* hollows

Sphagno tenelli–Rhynchosporetum albae, subass. *Sphagnum auriculatum*, fac. *Rhynchospora fusca*; M1 – *Sphagnum auriculatum* bog pools

Like *Schoenus nigricans* (see Community 20), the only location for this type in Caithness and Sutherland is in the extreme north-west near Loch Laxford. Here it forms both *R. alba–R. fusca* mixed swards and single-species stands within the mud-bottom (A2) hollows, in a manner characteristic of other British examples of this type within mire patterns (e.g. Lindsay *et al.* 1983).

Vegetation group 11 – *Sphagnum auriculatum* (A3) bog pools

These are distinguished from the next type by their tendency, during periods of extreme drought, to lose their free water and dry out. Under normal weather conditions, this community floats freely within an expanse of open water.

Community 32 – *Sphagnum auriculatum* bog pools

Eriophorum angustifolium community, subcomm. *Sphagnum auriculatum*; M1 – *Sphagnum auriculatum* bog pools

Where free water is present almost permanently and a loose matrix of aquatic *Sphagna* represents the major biomass of vegetation in the pool, *Sphagnum auriculatum* becomes a constant alongside *S. cuspidatum*. It varies from a sparse scattering of individuals within dominant *S. cuspidatum* mats in the east to pools entirely dominated by a loose matrix of *S. auriculatum* in the west. The companion species are *Menyanthes trifoliata* and *Eriophorum angustifolium*, but in the west *Utricularia vulgaris* agg. may be found in some pools. The type is found mainly within the blanket mire patterns of western Scotland; towards the drier south and east the dominant community type is the *Sphagnum cuspidatum* (A1) hollow (Vegetation type 9).

Vegetation group 12 – Deep pool (A4) vegetation

Community 33 – Deep pools

Permanently water-filled, many of these pools have no vegetation at all, apart from an algal community attached to the pool sides. The characteristic vegetation, where there is any, is *Menyanthes trifoliata*, which sometimes supports a column of *Sphagnum cuspidatum*, the whole mass floating loose in otherwise empty pools up to 4 m deep.

6 Flushes and ladder fens

Vegetation group 13 – *Molinia–Myrica* flushes and ladder fens

Ladder fens tend to occur on the margins of mire expanses (see Figure 7) and are usually dominated by what appears, at first sight, to be much the same vegetation as on many other parts of the mire margin, particularly the soakaways. The most charactersitic species of the ladder fen community is therefore *Molinia caerulea*. This fact alone is not sufficient to distinguish ladder fens from other mire margin communities. It is therefore necessary to take particular note of the microtopography.

Community 34 – *Molinia–Myrica* ridges

Although at first sight this community is typical of a *Molinia*-rich bog ridge, closer inspection reveals a number of distinctive features. The *Sphagnum* cover is markedly discontinuous, forming low hummocks, and the bare peat surface between is stained a dark, ochreous colour, which also stains the individual plants of *Sphagnum* in the hummocks. *Polygala serpyllifolia* and *Pedicularis sylvatica* are often present, and occasional plants of *Carex rostrata* or even *C. lasiocarpa* can be found growing through the ridges. In Scandinavia, *Trichophorum cespitosum* and *Trientalis europaeus* would be present in such a community (Professor H Sjörs pers. comm.).

Community 35 – *Carex rostrata–C. lasiocarpa* mud-bottom hollows

The linear hollows (solid mud-bottom "flarks") are often ochre-stained and generally support scattered *Carex rostrata*. The community may also have *Carex limosa* in the poorer variants or *Carex lasiocarpa* in richer examples. In Sweden these fen hollows, or "flarks", would also contain *Carex livida, Carex chordorhiza, Scheuchzeria palustris, Utricularia intermedia* and *Juncus stygius* (Professor H Sjörs pers. comm.).

11 Distribution of notable plant species

Information on the localities of particular species was collated by using the Revelation data-base, which contained species records obtained from the various sources described in Chapter 8. Several species were not recorded comprehensively during the survey, and the data-base can give only the most general indication of their distribution. For the species discussed, however, the data are reasonably comprehensive for the peatland sites surveyed. These species are chosen for individual consideration for several reasons –

Range

● Variation across the two Districts, indicating the variability and completeness of this peatland system

● Their relationships and importance to distribution in the rest of the UK and Europe

Rarity

● Regional, national and international status

● Some of the species are under-recorded for some of the more remote parts of the region. These data show the region to be more important for some species than would have been predicted from existing published information, e.g. Perring & Walters (1976) and Perry (1975).

Indicator value

● Some species appear to be restricted by certain environmental factors, e.g. altitude and hydrology.

When one is considering the distribution patterns of these species, it is important to take into account the uneven distribution of survey sites and peatland systems (see Figure 28). The maps in Figures 32–49 show only whether or not a species is recorded from each 1 km square. All records are from peatland sites, but some species occur in other habitats and so have a wider overall distribution.

Comments on British distributions are based on Perring & Walters (1976) and those on northern European distributions mainly on Fitter (1978).

Arctostaphylos uva-ursi

Regional (see Figure 32)

Mainly a central and eastern species on survey sites but with a more western total distribution (Perring & Walters 1976). The more westerly records are mostly not from mire sites, but from drier morainic

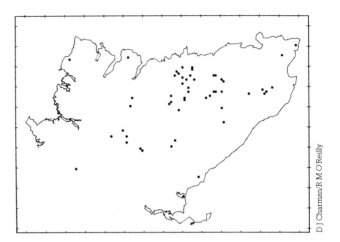

Figure 32 *Arctostaphylos uva-ursi*

ground, coastal and upland heaths, and other mineral soils and rocks, which are its more usual habitat in Britain. On mire sites it is almost entirely restricted to T2 high ridges and T3 hummocks.

National

Locally abundant in the Highlands, but now rare in the Southern Uplands, Cheviots, Pennines and Lake District (Perring & Walters 1976). Godwin (1975) notes that the majority of fossil records from Britain are from beyond its present southernmost limit and describes it as a species which was formerly widespread during the late Weichselian but whose range has since become restricted to northern and montane regions. Conolly & Dahl (1970) show that its present distribution in Ireland and northern Scotland corresponds to the 24°C maximum summer temperature isotherm.

Europe

Mainly in northern Europe and Iceland. Commonest on dry or very dry sites and typical of gravel ridges within pine–lichen forest.

Betula nana

Regional (see Figure 33)

Restricted to central parts of the region, with 45 records from survey sites. Found on high ridges and hummocks, often with *Arctostaphylos uva-ursi* or *Sphagnum fuscum*. The species is not common in Caithness, with only two records for the District.

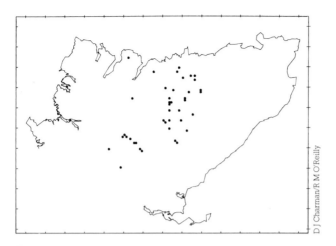

Figure 33 *Betula nana*

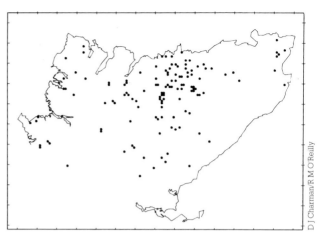

Figure 34 *Myrica gale*

National

Very local in the Highlands, with two isolated outposts in Northumberland and Durham, and recently (post-1930) only found in 46 10 km squares in Britain (Perring & Walters 1976). The survey reveals that 16 10 km squares have this species on peatland sites in the region. The survey record from A'Mhoine is the most northerly for Britain.

Europe

This is a circumpolar plant (if related taxa are included) associated with arctic-alpine mires and heaths. It extends as far north as 76° in Spitzbergen (Godwin 1975), and Conolly & Dahl (1970) suggest that its present distribution is limited by the 22°C maximum summer temperature isotherm. Drury (1956) and Cowardin *et al.* (1979) give examples of *Betula nana* bog from the Yukon delta, but it is absent from the blanket bog regions of Canada.

Myrica gale

Regional (see Figure 34)

The species has a widespread distibution on peatlands but occurs with greater constancy in central and western areas. Eastern locations tend to be on sites with some enrichment from water movement. It is one of the characteristic species of ladder fens.

National

Generally common in the north and west of Scotland, Lakeland, north-west Wales and western Ireland, but scattered and rather local through much of eastern Scotland and Ireland and the rest of England and Wales (Perring & Walters 1976). The northern extremity of its range is reached in the region, apart from two locations in Orkney.

Europe

Myrica gale has a distinctly oceanic to sub-oceanic distribution in Europe, Matthews (1937, 1955) describing it as "Oceanic Northern". Its occurrence throughout Caithness and Sutherland serves to emphasise the oceanicity of the entire region.

Vaccinium oxycoccos/Vaccinium microcarpum

These two species are difficult to distinguish in the field, so our peatland records have been amalgamated for the map.

Regional (see Figure 35)

Present only in eastern Sutherland and Caithness and with only 16 separate locations noted. *Vaccinium microcarpum* and *V. oxycoccos* are each recorded for only a single 10 km square in the region by Perring & Walters (1976). Although the nature of the sites varies somewhat, presence seems to be linked to wet, *Sphagnum*-rich margins around deep watershed pools with no lowering of the water table.

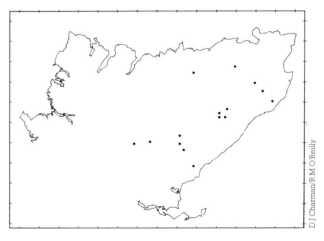

Figure 35 *Vaccinium oxycoccos/microcarpum*

National

Both species are here at the extreme northern limits of their distribution. *Vaccinium microcarpum* is present in only 19 10 km squares, mainly in Grampian Region. This species tends to occur further north than *V. oxycoccos* (Clapham, Tutin & Warburg 1962), which has its centre of distribution in northern England and southern Scotland.

Europe

V. oxycoccos is found in all of Fennoscandia, except the mountains, and further south and east in Europe, while *V. microcarpum* is found chiefly in central and northern Fennoscandia. Northern Scotland is an oceanic outpost of this distribution.

Drosera anglica

Regional (see Figure 36)

This is an example of a species which is ubiquitous in peatlands across the region, occurring in almost every 10 km square (Perring & Walters 1976). It occurs at or around the water table in the microtopography and also within flushes.

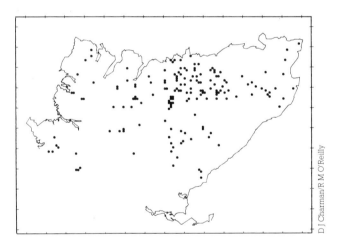

Figure 36 *Drosera anglica*

National

Widespread and common only in peatland areas of the north and west Highlands and western Ireland, and very local elsewhere. It is more continuously distributed within Caithness and Sutherland than anywhere else (Perring & Walters 1976). Its European distribution is mainly in northern and western parts.

Drosera intermedia

Regional (see Figure 37)

This is a notable component of wet, bare peat hollows in the west. It does not occur in Caithness

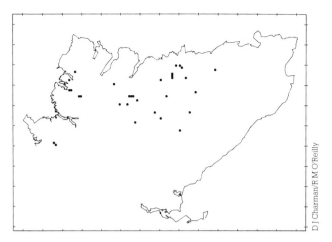

Figure 37 *Drosera intermedia*

except on the wet, bare peat of flush margins. There are a number of records for central Sutherland, but at least some of these may be in error, possibly mistaken for vegetative *Drosera anglica* or *D. x obovata*.

National

Generally a western but very local species, both in mainland Britain and in Ireland, but locally abundant in southern and eastern areas in its characteristic habitat, wet lowland heath (Clapham *et al.* 1962; Perring & Walters 1976). At its northerly limit in the British Isles in Sutherland.

Europe

In Europe it spreads no farther north than central Fennoscandia, except for two records east of the White Sea.

Rhynchospora alba

Regional (see Figure 38)

Scattered records were obtained from all but the far east of Caithness, but it occurs as a more constant component of western peatlands, generally on a low ridge with *Sphagnum papillosum* or in hollows just below the water table. It is, for example, abundant at Laxford Bridge.

National

Of similar distribution to *Drosera intermedia*, generally western in Britain and Ireland. It is frequent in some southern wet heathland locations, such as Thursley Bog on the Surrey Greensand and the New Forest valley mires. Sutherland is the northern limit of its British distribution, apart from an isolated record for Shetland.

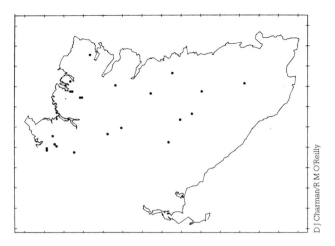

D J Charman/R M O'Reilly

Figure 38 *Rhynchospora alba*

World

It is found in most of Europe except northern Fennoscandia, north and east Russia and most of the Mediterranean. It does not occur in the Arctic. It also grows in Japan and in both Pacific and eastern North America, with a few scattered localities elsewhere.

Rhynchospora fusca

Regional

Recorded from only two locations, both close to Laxford Bridge. It grows in the aquatic zones, generally lower than *R. alba*, at A2.

National

A rare species, having its main populations on the south coast of England in Dorset and Hampshire and in western Ireland. It occurs at one or two locations near the west coasts of Scotland and Wales, but the Laxford records are not given by Perring & Walters (1976). The record for Cors Fochno in Dyfed is a recent rediscovery (Fox 1984) after its apparent disappearance from the site during the middle of this century. Interestingly, it has been found in an area of flooded peat-cuttings which mirror the conditions of mud-bottom hollows. A similar phenomenon is found at Thursley in Surrey, where *R. fusca* occupies flooded tank tracks left by post-war military manoeuvres.

World

Dierssen (1982) records the species from Ireland and Norway. Tubridy (1984) describes its occurrence in mud-bottom hollows on Mongan Bog, in County Offaly. It grows mainly in western Europe, where its northern, eastern and southern limits extend beyond those of *R. alba*. It is present in North America, but absent from the Pacific area.

Eleocharis multicaulis

Regional (see Figure 39)

Found in hollows and pools (A1–A3), with either *Sphagnum cuspidatum* or *S. auriculatum* or alone in the deeper water, this species is scattered across the two Districts.

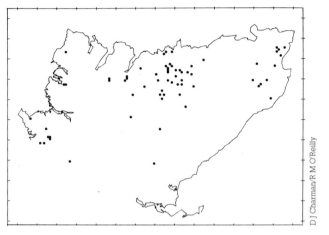

D J Charman/R M O'Reilly

Figure 39 *Eleocharis multicaulis*

National

It is another species fairly widespread in the far west of Britain and Ireland, but very local elsewhere and mainly on lowland bogs and wet acidic heaths, which provide important outposts in the New Forest, Surrey and East Anglia. It is not rare, but its distribution across Sutherland and Caithness reflects the oceanic conditions of the whole region.

World

Godwin (1975) describes the species as European–Atlantic. It extends above 60°N only on the Faeroes and in westernmost Norway (Professor H Sjörs pers. comm.).

Carex limosa

Regional (see Figure 40)

This species is present across both Districts but is more constant and abundant in the west, particularly in A2 mud-bottom hollows. In addition to such ombrotrophic conditions, it is also characteristic of flushed areas, especially sloping and ladder fens. Present in 34 10 km squares, though only 10 post-1930 records are shown by Perring & Walters (1976).

National

Mostly in northern and western Scotland and western Ireland, but scattered through northern

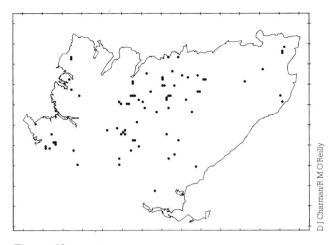

Figure 40 *Carex limosa*

England and Wales. However, the bulk of these records are for minerotrophic mires. The species does not occur in bog pools south of the Silver Flowe in Galloway and is almost completely restricted to the extreme west coast for its distribution within this microtope. Only in Caithness and Sutherland does it extend eastwards in blanket bogs.

World

Carex limosa is found in western mire systems in Ireland and in Norway (Moen 1985), but on the continent it is not at all an oceanic species, being recorded for instance in A1 and A2 hollows on Estonian mires (Masing 1984). Matthews (1955) classifies it as "Continental Northern" and provides a map (p. 139) showing its southern limit in Europe. Its world distribution is widely circumboreal.

Carex pauciflora

Regional (see Figure 41)

Present throughout the region but perhaps having a centrally based distribution, *Carex pauciflora* grows on low ridges, often with abundant *Sphagna*, typically in a *Sphagnum papillosum* T1 lawn.

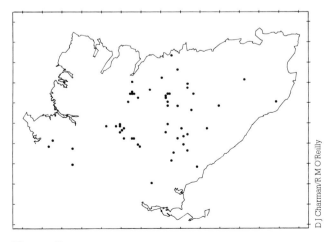

Figure 41 *Carex pauciflora*

National

Widespread and often common in ombrotrophic mires through much of the Highlands, but very local in south-west Scotland and northern England. Not recorded further north than Sutherland.

World

Sjörs (1983) describes *Carex pauciflora* as "doubtfully minerotrophic" and states that it occurs in most oligotrophic sloping and mountain mires in Sweden, whilst Botch & Masing (1983) recognise it as a species largely restricted to oligotrophic moss communities. The world distribution is similar to that of *Rhynchospora alba*, though it is probably less favoured by an oceanic climate.

Molinia caerulea

Regional (see Figure 42)

Present in almost every 10 km square in the region (Perring & Walters 1976), its occurrence on ombrotrophic peatlands is more westerly. Throughout the region, but increasingly towards the

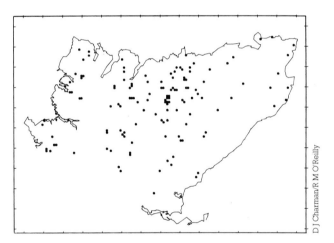

Figure 42 *Molinia caerulea*

west, this species is found most abundantly alongside burns and seepages, where it is encouraged to develop monotypic stands by the increased oxygenation of the peat (see Chapter 1). For the same reason, it is typical of the mire margin on many sites. On the mire expanse, however, it is quite markedly restricted to sites west of the Halladale, and it is not a common component of ombrotrophic expanses until west of the Naver. Its presence can be encouraged on a site by burning, and, like *Racomitrium lanuginosum*, its distribution has been artificially enhanced by man's activities in the area.

National

It is difficult to draw any useful conclusions from the map of Perring & Walters (1976), because the species records undoubtedly come from a wide range of sites other than ombrotrophic bog, but, from evidence gathered during the course of the NCC's SSSI Guidelines field survey throughout Britain (NCC unpublished), the mass occurrence of *Molinia caerulea* on ombrotrophic mire systems is a distinctly western phenomenon. Areas characterised thus are Dartmoor, west Wales, Cumbria, Dumfries and Galloway, the Inner and Outer Hebrides, and the extreme west coast of Scotland. Much the same is true of Ireland. *Molinia* on mire expanses tends to be rather sparse in growth, and the dense, tussocky habit develops where flushing with mineral-rich water occurs, especially when loaded with sediment.

World

Molinia caerulea is almost entirely restricted to Europe, where it is a widespread species.

Sparganium angustifolium

Regional (see Figure 43)

A species of deep, open water pools (A3–A4), it is generally uncommon over much of the region, and the records from the survey are western.

National

A western plant, especially abundant in the Western Isles, but local elsewhere.

World

Again this species shows the affinities of this region with more northern regions, as its centre of distribution is in Norway and Sweden, becoming rarer to the south, though recorded as far south as Spain.

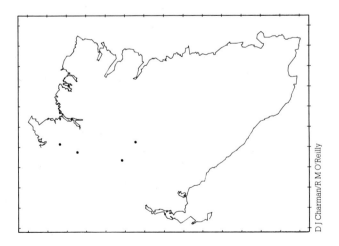

Figure 43 *Sparganium angustifolium*

Carex dioica

This sedge is common in richer minerotrophic mire and flush habitats throughout Scotland, but it has a quite distinct niche in the mires of Sutherland, Caithness and Wester Ross. Although it is not normally found on the mire expanse, it is often found on the T1/T2 ridges of base-rich ladder fens in these Districts. It is a species of Europe and western Siberia.

Carex lasiocarpa

C. lasiocarpa is typical of the mud-bottom hollows ("flarks") in slightly enriched ladder fens, though it grows through the ridges too. It is recorded from the mesotrophic fens of Caithness, where the shelly boulder clay tends to encourage rather more mineral-rich mire systems. Its occurrence within the central and western parts of the region is linked quite strongly with ladder fen systems, but it is also found in more typical seepages where there is a little base-enrichment.

Erica cinerea (see Figure 44)

Although very much a hyperoceanic species, *Erica cinerea* adopts a niche in Scotland which ensures that its roots are not subject to anaerobic waterlogging. Thus it smothers the thin peat cover of rock outcrops with vigorous growth in the far west.

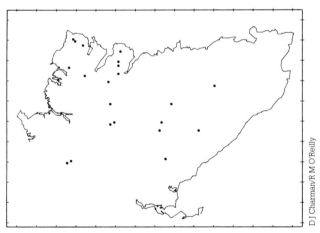

Figure 44 *Erica cinerea*

On mires, it only occurs on tall erosion hags or the cut edges of old peat banks (thus adopting the same niche as that taken by *Vaccinium myrtillus* in north-west England). Osvald (1949) shows it adopting much the same behaviour on eroding hummocks in the Lough Boleynagee area of Ireland. Although generally western, it occurs a considerable distance eastwards where the niche is available. Its European distribution is almost entirely restricted to the Atlantic seaboard, and there are records from Madeira and a single locality in north Africa. It is extinct in West Germany.

Rubus chamaemorus

This species is typical of Pennine and upland blanket bog (Eddy, Welch & Rawes 1969) and is also recorded extensively within Caithness and Sutherland by Perring & Walters (1976). Its presence on blanket bog, however, is restricted to more montane situations on the higher hills of Sutherland and the Morven range in Caithness, where it is often abundant, as well as in higher-level *Calluna* heath on shady slopes. It is sparse in *Calluna–Eriophorum vaginatum* blanket bog on the Knockfin Heights. During the survey it was recorded within the region only from the steep east-facing slopes of Ben Armine, in an association of *Sphagnum rubellum, Vaccinium myrtillus, Calluna* and *Listera cordata*.

Listera cordata

This is an often overlooked species on mires which, if the records for Caithness and Sutherland are any indication, occurs within T2/T3 *Sphagnum*-rich swards where the dwarf shrub layer is tall but open. Its occurrence on the Dubh Lochs of Shielton in Caithness is associated with this niche.

Schoenus nigricans

Sparling (1962, 1967a, 1967b, 1968) and Boatman (1960) examine the widespread occurrence of this species on western Irish blanket bog in some detail, pointing out that it can occur on ombrotrophic peats with a pH as low as 3.7. Lindsay *et al.* (1983) give a British location for *Schoenus nigricans* on blanket bog, in Islay, but further investigation of the site has revealed that there is a certain amount of flushing from nearby slopes. Sparling (1968) states that the records for Ireland are on "unflushed or slightly flushed blanket bogs". The latter accord with the conditions on Islay.

A single record for the species on ombrotrophic peats has also been found for mainland Britain, at Laxford Bridge in Sutherland. The site is a raised mire unit formed at the head of Loch Laxford, and the extensively patterned surface supports *Schoenus* tussocks at the T1 level. As on Islay, there is a suggestion of water flow through the pools in this part of the site, but the patterns are still quite typically ombrotrophic and the area concerned is clearly part of the ombrotrophic dome. *Schoenus nigricans* is a widespread species in Britain, especially in western Scotland, but most of its habitats are somewhat nutrient-rich and it is most abundant in base-rich habitats.

Pleurozia purpurea (see Figure 45)

A large number of survey sites in Caithness and Sutherland possess this species, and it appears to be almost uniformly distributed. From field observations it is perhaps more constant and more abundant in Sutherland and the west generally. It is common

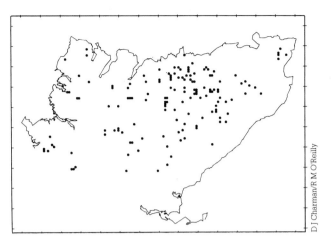

Figure 45 *Pleurozia purpurea*

throughout western Scotland and western Ireland but is totally absent from England and Wales. It has a highly disjunct world distribution in cool, humid regions, being found elsewhere in Europe in Ireland, Norway and the Faeroes, and also in Alaska, Pacific British Columbia, the Himalayas and the West Indies (Ratcliffe 1969).

Sphagna

One of the most important aspects of the peatland area is the abundance and variety of *Sphagnum* species present. Nowhere else in the British Isles is there such a large and continuous expanse of terrain dominated by this genus. Three species in particular are discussed here.

Sphagnum imbricatum and S. fuscum

Regional (see Figures 46 and 47) **and national**

Both these species are prominent hummock-formers (T3), and survey records show that they are most constant in central and eastern Sutherland and throughout Caithness, having a similar distribution.

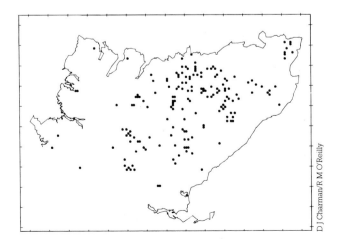

Figure 46 *Sphagnum imbricatum*

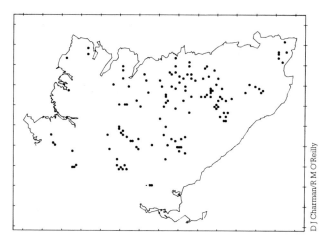

Figure 47 *Sphagnum fuscum*

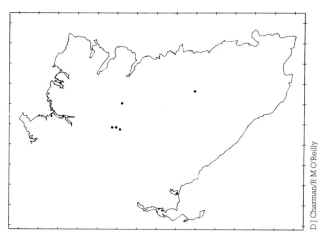

Figure 48 *Sphagnum pulchrum*

Both are noted as northern–continental species by Birks (1973) and Goode & Ratcliffe (1977). *S. fuscum* occurs at a generally higher level of hummock and over a wider range of altitude (0–1050 m) than *S. imbricatum* (mostly below 460 m). It is widespread in montane blanket bog in the Highlands. Caithness and Sutherland hold a high percentage of the British distribution of these two species. *S. imbricatum* is of particular interest, as it occurs widely and abundantly as a major component of south Pennine peat, although present-day vegetation is of a very different nature, lacking *Sphagnum* altogether (Tallis 1964c). The possible causes for this and the implications for Caithness and Sutherland are discussed in Chapter 5.

World

S. fuscum has a mainly circumpolar–boreal world distribution and is extremely frequent in Fennoscandia, whilst *S. imbricatum* is sub-oceanic and has a disjunct world distribution(Smith 1978). Flatberg (1984) has recently shown that the bog-dominant both in America and in western Europe is subsp. *austinii*. This deep brown subspecies is a hummock-former not only in Scotland but also in coastal British Columbia and adjacent Alaska.

Sphagnum pulchrum (see Figure 48)

This is a rare *Sphagnum* species, occurring only locally on the Solway mosses and in a few locations in north-western England and Wales, mostly on raised mires, and in valley mires in Dorset. Perry (1965) shows a single location further north than Wigtownshire, at Claish Moss, but our survey has discovered six locations, all in Sutherland. Most notably it is the dominant *Sphagnum* species around the low summit of Cnoc an Alaskie, where it grows in its typical position around the water table, at the T1/A1 transition. It grows in the altitude range of 120-300 m in Sutherland, mostly at the higher end of this range. This fits well with the range given by Perry (1965) of 8-300 m.

Sphagnum strictum

This most oceanic of the British *Sphagna* occurs widely in Sutherland, but mainly around the edges of the blanket bogs and on shallower peat or peaty gleys amongst steeper ground or moraines. It is typically found in wet heath communities with *Trichophorum, Molinia, Erica tetralix* and *Calluna* or in soligenous mires with *Molinia* and *Myrica*. The species is amphi-Atlantic and only slightly sub-oceanic in Europe. In Scandinavia it is probably most frequent in the uplands (approx. 200–700 m), where it is clearly minerotrophic, though mostly weakly so, and usually grows as a fringe at or slightly above the water's edge in "flarks" or pools.

Racomitrium lanuginosum (see Figure 49)

Large hummocks of this species are found throughout the mires of the two Districts, but in Caithness, except in high-level mires such as Knockfin Heights, it is generally associated with damaged, eroding sites. Towards the west it occurs more frequently on undamaged sites, even being found as part of the bryophyte layer within the T1 zone, but continuous cover on hummocks and ridges

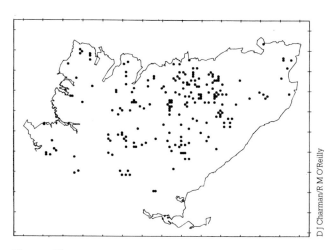

Figure 49 *Racomitrium lanuginosum*

tends to be an indicator of damage. Moore (1977) demonstrates that the large hummocks of *Racomitrium* on Claish Moss in Argyll have a very long history and are therefore likely to be entirely natural. Hummocks of *Racomitrium* are common in Ireland (Osvald 1949), but they are partly replaced on some raised mires by hummocks of *Leucobryum glaucum*, as at Mongan Bog in County Offaly (Tubridy 1984) and on blanket bogs in Connemara (Groenendael *et al.* 1975). This is an almost cosmopolitan moss, but it occurs as a community dominant mainly in highly oceanic areas.

Campylopus atrovirens

This common species of wet acidic rocks and mineral flushes in western Britain is also a widespread peatland species. It sometimes occurs on deep peat, but its more typical habitat is on disturbed, sometimes eroded, bog and on the shallower peats of wet heaths with *Trichophorum* and *Calluna*. It is an Atlantic species in Europe as a whole, though occurring as far east as the Black Sea.

Dicranum bergeri

This is a rare moss in Britain, regarded as an indicator of undamaged raised mires and a few low-level blanket bogs, where it forms conspicuous carpets or crowns low hummocks in association with *Sphagnum*. It was recorded from the Moss of Killimster, but during the present survey was found only at the Dubh Lochs of Shielton. It has a northern European distribution.

12 Analysis of site types

As a final stage in the analysis of peatland features, to provide a further basis for nature conservation evaluation, the variation between mire systems throughout the two Districts was examined on the basis of two major attributes. These were the vegetation groups derived from the earlier vegetation analysis and the information relating to microtopography obtained from survey. In the field, the surface structure is often the more striking and readily identifiable attribute because the vegetation almost invariably occurs as a complex mosaic within the structural patterns (see Chapters 1 and 2). By combining these, the overall character of the mire unit can be revealed, as illustrated by Lindsay *et al.* (1983) and Lindsay *et al.* (1985).

We assigned vegetation types derived from the floristic descriptions to individual sites. On the basis of information recorded on the original field sheet, these vegetation types were then allocated to particular zones within the microtopography. After

vegetation types had been allocated to each site, the information was transferred from the Revelation data-base into TWINSPAN, where each site was treated as a single sample, with attributes of vegetation type rather than species. The resulting data matrix thus consisted of 399 such samples, each with a record of one or more vegetation types. This second-order analysis of TWINSPAN output is a technique successfully employed by Ratcliffe & Hattey (1982) in the analysis of lowland wetland communities in Wales. The approach allows the broad spectrum of vegetation to be classified from all samples irrespective of sites and then the sites from which samples were taken to be classified in turn on the basis of the combination of vegetation classes each site contains.

The TWINSPAN analysis, at the first level of division, isolated eroding mire from *Sphagnum*-rich types. The distribution of these two major types (see Figure 50) reveals both the extensive occurrence of

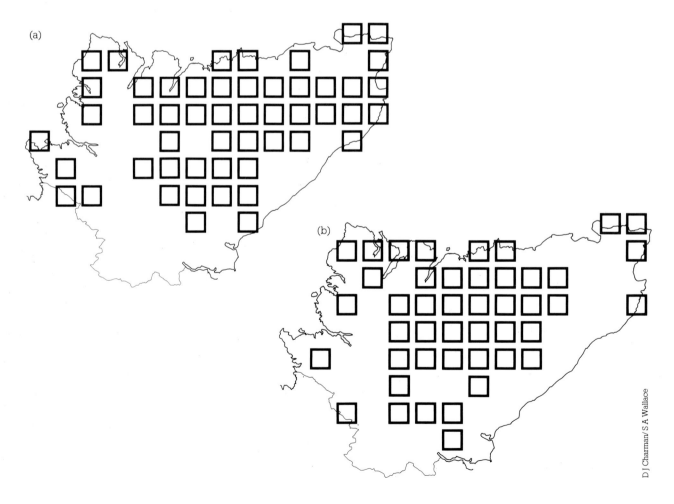

Figure 50 Distribution of sites (on the basis of 5 km squares) within the first major division of TWINSPAN for the analysis of site types from the NCC's Peatland Survey data. The two categories broadly represent – (a) *Sphagnum*-rich sites; (b) sites with some erosion or damage.

Comm. no.	Microtope and community type		Type 1	Type 2	Type 3	Type 4	Type 5	Type 6	Type 7	Type 8	Type 9	Type 10	Type 11	Type 12	Type 13	Type 14	Type 15
	Peat mounds	(T5)		I	I	I	I	I	I	I		I				IV	I*
	Erosion haggs	(T4)		V	IV	V	II	V	V	V	V	II	III		V*	IV	V*
	Hummocks	(T3)	IV	V	V*	V*	V	V*	V*	V*	IV*	V*	V*	III*	V*	V*	IV*
	High ridge	(T2)	V*	V	V*	V*	V	V*	V*	V*	IV*	V	V	V*	IV	V*	V*
	Low ridge	(T1)	I	IV	V	V	IV	V	V	V	V	IV	III	III	III	III	IV
	Sphagnum hollow	(A1)	V*	V*	V	V	IV*	V	V*	V	III	II*	V*	III	V*	V	IV
	Mud-bottom hollow	(A2)		IV*	IV*					V*	V*	IV	V*		V*	IV	IV*
	Erosion channel	(TA2)		III	III	III	III	IV	III	V*	V*	V*	III		III	II	II
	Drought-sensitive pools	(A3)		III	III	III	III	IV			V*	V*	III		III	IV	II
	Permanent pools	(A4)		II	I	I	I	II	III	V	V*	V*	II	III	III	II	I
1	Juncus squarrosus thin peat							II			I				II	I	I
2	Empetrum–Hylocomium splendens mounds/hummocks							II		II	III	I			III		I
3	Empetrum–hypnoid moss slopes and hummocks				I					II		I					I
4	Racomitrium–Cladonia hummocks and hags		I		II	II	II	II	III	II	III	II		III	III	III	III
5	Racomitrium–Molinia hummocks and hags			III	IV	II	II		III	IV	III	I		III	II	II	II
6	Racomitrium–Pleurozia wet low ridge				I		I	I	II		II	I	III	I	I	I	I
7	Sphagnum fuscum hummocks						II	II					III	III			
8	Sphagnum imbricatum hummocks		II	III	IV	IV	III	III	III	IV	III	IV	IV	III	III	II	III
9	Sphagnum rubellum–Odontoschisma dry ridges					II			II								
10	Mixed Sphagna (S. rubellum hummocks)			III	III	III	IV	III	III	III	III	III	III	III	III	I	II
11	Sphagnum papillosum–Molinia ridge			I		I		I	I	I	I	I	III	I	I	I	I
12	Sphagnum–Eriophorum vaginatum ridge			III	II			II	II	II	II	II	IV	II	II		
13	Sphagnum compactum ridge		III		I							I	V		I		
14	Sphagnum magellanicum–S. subnitens		III	II	IV	III	IV	III	IV	I	I	II	III	II	II	III	II
15	Sphagnum magellanicum–S. rubellum ridge				I	II	IV	III			I				I	I	
16	Sphagnum–Arctostaphylos–Betula nana mire				III			III									II
17	Sphagnum papillosum–Carex pauciflora			II	III	II	IV	I	IV	III	II	IV	V		I	I	II
18	Rhynchospora alba–Sphagnum low ridge			II	III			I				I					
19	Campylopus atrovirens low ridge		III	II	II												II
20	Schoenus–Molinia mire		I														
21	Carex panicea damaged mire		I					II				I				III	II
22	Narthecium ossifragum "tunnel"							I				I		V			III
23	Microbroken mire						III	III	III	III	III	II		III		III	III
24	Sphagnum cuspidatum–Eleocharis multicaulis					II	III	III	IV			IV	II			II	I
25	Pure Sphagnum cuspidatum carpets			I	I	IV	IV	II		I	II	I	II	III	II	I	I
26	Typical Sphagnum cuspidatum carpets			II			I	I		IV							I
27	Sphagnum pulchrum carpets				IV	II	III	I	II	I	I	I					
28	Sphagnum cuspidatum–Carex limosa		I	I	III	I	I	I					I			I	
29	Eleocharis multicaulis mud-bottom hollows			I	III				II	I			I			I	
30	Rhynchospora alba mud-bottom hollows		I					I	III		I				I		
31	Rhynchospora fusca mud-bottom hollows			II	II	II	II	IV	IV			III	III			II	II
32	Sphagnum auriculatum bog pools			II	III	II	I	IV	III	IV	III	IV	III		III	I	II
33	Deep pools		IV	III	IV					I	II						
34	Molinia–Myrica ridges (ladder fen)		IV	II	III	II			IV	IV	V						
35	Carex rostrata–C. lasiocarpa (ladder fen "flarks")		V	III	II				III	IV	V						

Table 4

Synoptic table showing the levels of constancy with which the microforms and communities occur in the site types identified in the Caithness and Sutherland blanket bogs. The Roman numerals indicate the level of percentage constancy displayed by microforms and communities in each site type: V – 100-81%; IV – 80-61%; III – 60-41%; II – 40-21%; I – 20-1%. Asterisks indicate microforms which are particularly abundant within a site type. Numerals relating to communities which characterise a site type are highlighted.

actively-growing mire over a wide area of the region and also the concentration of erosion in central and western mires, leaving the low-lying flows of Caithness relatively free from its effects.

In all, 15 site types were identified. These can be seen in Table 4, where the results are expressed in synoptic form because of size constraints, but the raw data are readily available on request. The majority of site records in the Revelation data-base were then assigned one of these site type codes, the exceptions being the true fen sites (as discussed previously: see Chapter 10), which are mainly found within the region of shelly boulder clay in the agricultural lowlands of Caithness.

Site types of Caithness and Sutherland

There follows an account of each site type.

Site type 1: Ladder fens (see Figure 51)

General appearance

These sites always lie on gently-sloping ground and are often characterised at the upslope limit of the site by a marked zone of upwelling or constricted flushing. The expanse of ladder fen forms a smooth floor to what is usually a gently-sloping and wide zone of water collection and seepage, but, unlike the more normal valley mire, is quite distinct in having no central watercourse. Instead the pools of open water lie at right angles to the direction of seepage. The site type is often best distinguished from a distance by the relative prevalence of taller species such as *Molinia caerulea, Carex lasiocarpa* or *Carex rostrata*.

Surface microtopes

The pattern is distinctly low-relief, with few T3 hummocks. The bulk of the ridges are a mixture of high and low ridge (T2/T1), but the nature of the surface is much more humified and solid than typical T1 ridge. A1 hollows are generally completely absent, and the aquatic phase is dominated by A2 mud-bottom hollows or "flarks". The ridges and flarks between them form narrow sinuous lines across the direction of seepage, but their overall trend is straight, rather than the typically arcuate pattern found on ombrotrophic surfaces.

Vegetation

The great majority of examples encountered can be classed under a limited range of vegetation types which are characterised by the abundance of *Molinia* and of the presence of *Carex lasiocarpa* or *Carex rostrata* within a background mosaic of

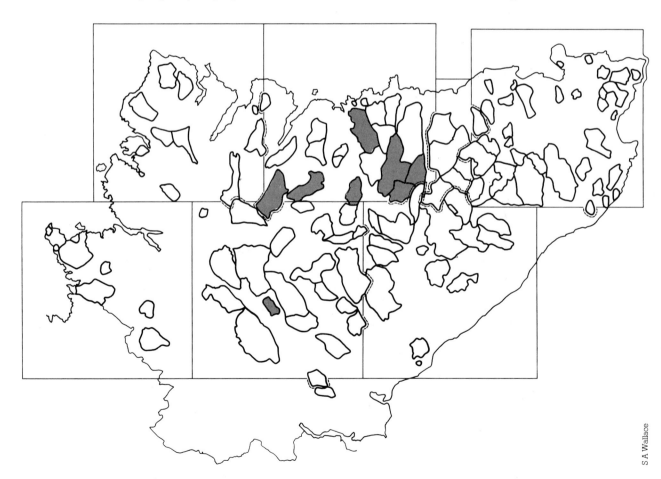

S A Wallace

Figure 51 Distribution of Site type 1 – Ladder fens. All macrotopes with a record for the type are tinted.

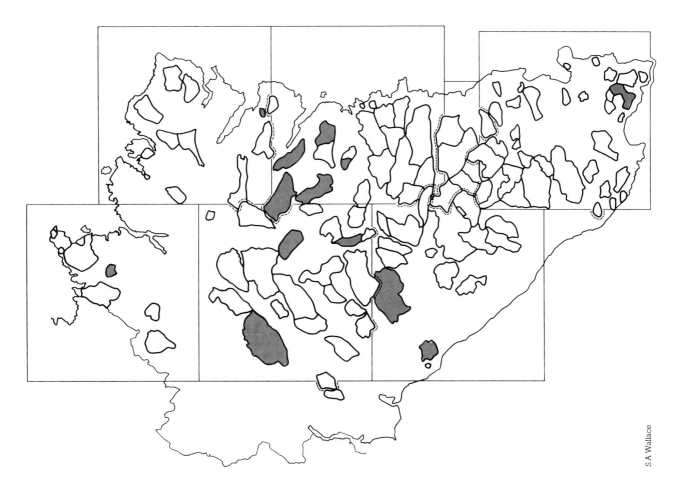

S A Wallace

Figure 52 Distribution of Site type 2 – Flushed bog and valley mire transition. All macrotopes with a record for the type are tinted.

Sphagnum papillosum, Erica tetralix, Potentilla erecta and *Narthecium ossifragum. Calluna*-dominated *S. imbricatum* hummocks (rather than the *S. fuscum* typical of such places elsewhere round the globe) occur as isolated mounds, as do occasional *S. rubellum* and *Racomitrium* hummocks.

Distribution

So far restricted to the bioclimatic zones O2.H1/B2 and H2/B2, records for this type indicate a distinctly central distribution, the centre of this distribution also falling within one of the most active areas of afforestation.

Site type 2: Flushed bog and valley mire transition (see Figure 52)

General appearance

This type spans the transition between ombrotrophic mire, valley mire and true ladder fen and as such has a somewhat variable appearance. It is mostly found as an anastomosing pattern of ridges and channels within a basin topography (which may lie on a saddle or spur), but it can, particularly when occupying a saddle, possess deep A3/A4 pools. Within a valley mire, on the other hand, it is recognised by the mosaic of hummocks and

channels lying between the zone influenced by the central water-track and the outer zone of ombrotrophic vegetation. A particular feature of this type in ombrotrophic conditions is the common occurrence of quaking mire.

Surface microtopes

These depend on the particular character adopted by the type, but within valley mires the major features consist of T2 mounds (as opposed to hummocks) and A2 channels, within which individual T3 hummocks and areas of T1 low ridge are common. In the case of more ombrotrophic saddle/spur mires, the relief may be somewhat less uneven, with wide areas of T2 ridge giving way to T1 around the margins of deep A3/A4 pools.

Vegetation

The characteristic vegetation type is *Sphagnum magellanicum* with *S. subnitens*, the latter forming T2/T3 hummocks, whilst the former dominates the lower T1 zone. Ombrotrophic examples of this mixture, usually more dominated by *S. magellanicum*, represent one of the few types where *Vaccinium oxycoccos/microcarpum* may be found in the two Districts. *S. imbricatum* and *Racomitrium* communities, particularly associated with *Molinia*, are common on ombrotrophic examples, but less so in valley mire conditions (though possible occurrence of the so-called "lax" *S. imbricatum* var. *affine*, often mistaken for *S. papillosum*, might repay further investigation). In valley mires the frequent presence of *Carex limosa* and *C. lasiocarpa* communities within the *Sphagnum*-dominated mounds, which are often predominantly of *S. subnitens* in such cases, provides a link with ladder fen communities. However, the arrangement of surface patterns differs fundamentally between the two types. In addition, the A2 channels are typically richer in species than in ladder fens, with occasional records of *Utricularia vulgaris*, *Eleocharis multicaulis* or *Rhynchospora alba* communities.

Distribution

The general trend is somewhat more western than for true ladder fens, though a record from the hills outside Brora indicates that this is not exclusively so. A single record from north-eastern Caithness represents the mixed valley mire complex of the Lochs of Auchengill, which shows a transition to ombrotrophic mire outwards from the central water-track.

Site type 3: Low-relief 'western' blanket bog
(see Figure 53)

General appearance

Of the two types characteristic of quaking mire, this is the commoner type. It is dominated by the middle range of microtopography, though occasional large *Sphagnum* or *Racomitrium* hummocks dot the mire expanse. Free water is generally limited to mud-bottom hollows, but deeper pools are often found where the gradient is gentlest. The ground is marked by a general feeling of softness, and *Sphagnum*, rather than free water, dominates the surface, though bare peat is also a common component at the T1/A1 transition.

Surface microtopes

Over the majority of the surface, T1 low ridge and richly-vegetated A1/A2 hollows form an intimate mosaic. Only where the gradient is gentlest and A3 pools form is there any clear orientation to the pattern. Areas of T2 ridge are abundant, but are unusually soft. T3 hummocks are the only feature to break an otherwise smooth appearance.

Vegetation

Dominated by a *Racomitrium–Molinia–Pleurozia purpurea* community, the ridges are markedly 'western' in their vegetation. The typical

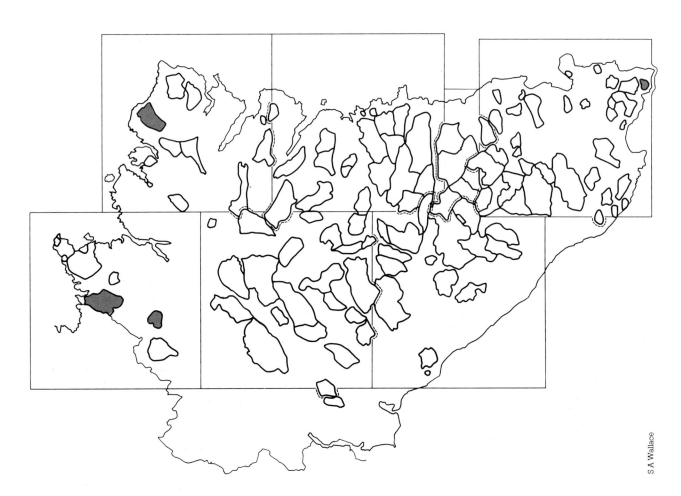

S A Wallace

Figure 53 Distribution of Site type 3 – Low-relief 'western' blanket bog. All macrotopes with a record for the type are tinted.

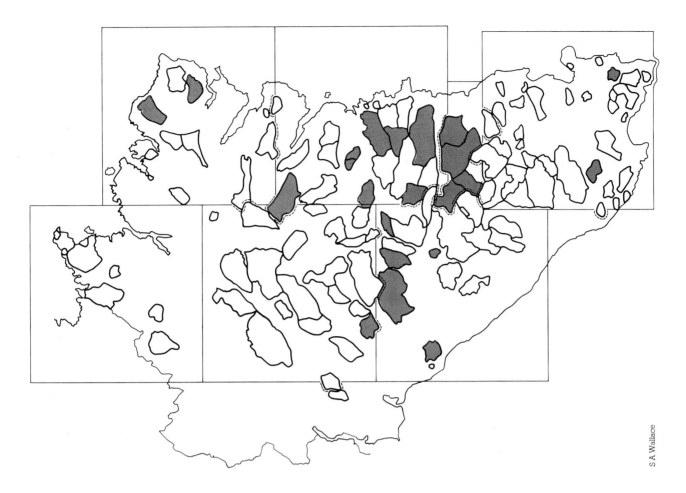

Figure 54 Distribution of Site type 4 – Low-relief northern boreal blanket bog. All macrotopes with a record for the type are tinted.

S A Wallace

Rhynchospora alba–Drosera intermedia mud-bottom hollows of western areas are also restricted to this type, and *Campylopus atrovirens* carpets, often associated with a mixed *Sphagnum* sward which includes *S. tenellum*, are characteristic. This is a type very similar to that described for parts of Coladoir Bog on Mull (Lindsay *et al.* 1983) and in mires on the Outer Hebrides (Goode & Lindsay 1979; Hulme 1985).

Distribution

Entirely restricted to the west coast, this type characterises the Sutherland peatlands west of the Moine Thrust. It is a type which could have been expected much more widely through central Sutherland if that geological boundary were not there.

Site type 4: Low-relief northern boreal blanket bog (see Figure 54)

General appearance

Found typically on spurs or saddles, this type appears initially similar to low-relief 'western' bog, but on closer inspection it is generally found to have a more 'corrugated' appearance than the western type. This appearance is derived from the more

clearly defined orientation of the surface microtopography. It also has more obvious *Sphagnum* and dwarf shrub layers than the western type. It frequently contains extremely soft quaking mire.

Surface microtopes

The dominant elements are T2 and T1 ridge, with A1 hollows. These combine to form a surface topography which is not as smooth as the more western type, being distinctly raised into a series of corrugations which generally reach T2 level. Higher T3 hummocks are scattered through this, and in places the corrugations give way to pools of A2 or A3 free water.

Vegetation

Far more strikingly dominated by *Sphagnum* than the western type, the general communities comprise various dwarf shrub–*Sphagnum* communities, including frequent *S. imbricatum* types. The characteristic vegetation, however, is *Sphagnum–Betula nana–Arctostaphylos uva-ursi*, which is common on both T1 and T2 ridges growing through the soft *Sphagnum* sward. This and the abundance of *S. papillosum* make it unique to Caithness and Sutherland as a blanket bog community. Also within the vegetation mosaic is the typical *S. cuspidatum* hollow community, with *Drosera anglica*, *Eriophorum angustifolium* and *Menyanthes trifoliata*.

Distribution

Largely shared out between the H2/B2 of both hyperoceanic and euoceanic zones, with an extensive area also within zone O2.H1/B2, this type is predominantly central, though with both western and eastern outliers.

Site type 5: *Eriophorum vaginatum* 'eastern' blanket bog (see Figure 55)

General appearance

One of the most characteristic site types of the two Districts, this is commonly found on watersheds and valleyside flows where the ground is dominated by high ridges and mud-bottom hollows or deeper pools. The usual surface is more firm than that described for the previous two types, being more akin to the solid ridges of a ladder fen. The extent of free water is an obvious feature, usually forming linear rather than rounded pools. The vegetation has a somewhat irregular appearance, owing to the presence of *Eriophorum vaginatum* tussocks mixed with dwarf shrubs at the higher levels of the microtopography.

Surface microtopes

Forming wide bands between A2/A3 pools, the typical surface is dominated by T2 high ridge. T3 hummocks are common as isolated features, and very occasional areas of erosion hags can be found, usually towards the margin of sites (e.g. Pearsall 1956). Although the majority of free water is in shallow A2/A3 hollows, more typical A3 pools are also found where the gradient is gentlest.

Vegetation

The most significant community recorded for this site type is the *Sphagnum pulchrum* complex, which mainly occurs towards the south-western limit of this site type. In more ordinary conditions the type is characterised by a *Sphagnum* mosaic within which *Eriophorum vaginatum* and *Odontoschisma sphagni* are common components together with frequent *S. imbricatum* and *S. rubellum* T3 hummocks. Aquatic phases are normally dominated by typical *Sphagnum* hollows, 'pure' A1 *Sphagnum cuspidatum* hollows or *S. auriculatum–S. cuspidatum–Menyanthes* pools.

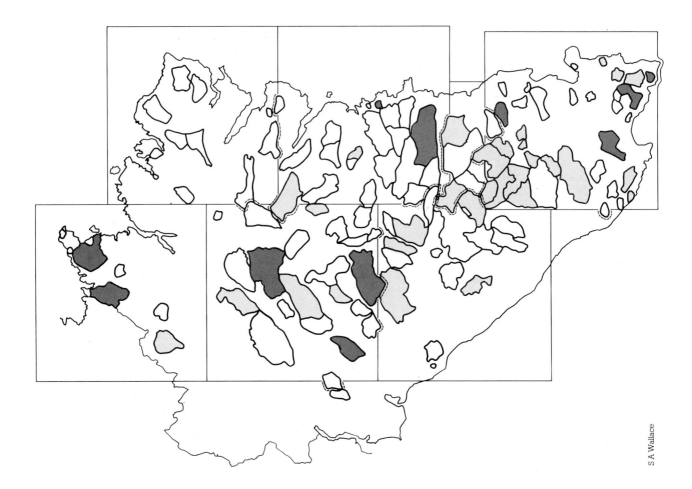

Figure 55 Distribution of Site type 5 – *Eriophorum vaginatum* 'eastern' blanket bog. The dark tint represents the macrotope which contains the largest example of the type within each bioclimatic zone. The light tint represents other macrotopes with records for the type.

100

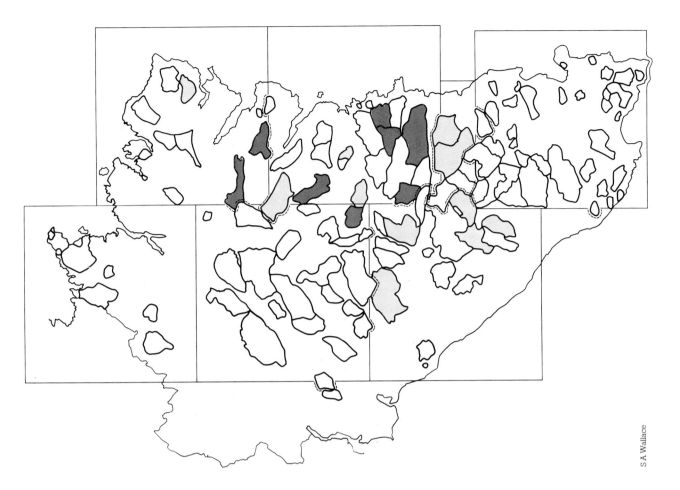

Figure 56 Distribution of Site type 6 – *Molinia–Sphagnum–Menyanthes* blanket bog. The dark tint represents the macrotope which contains the largest example of the type within each bioclimatic zone. The light tint represents other macrotopes with records for the type.

S A Wallace

Distribution

The most widely distributed of the site types, it nevertheless shows a distinct trend towards the eastern and southern part of the two districts. Its prevalence in Caithness perhaps underlines the somewhat drier nature of the climate and links the type with the *Eriophorum vaginatum* mires of more southern blanket mires.

Site type 6: *Molinia–Sphagnum–Menyanthes* blanket bog (see Figure 56)

General appearance

Typically occurring as gentle valleyside flows or saddles, the dominance of *Molinia* in the vegetation of this type indicates a certain amount of surface seepage, either from upslope parts of the mire or even perhaps from mineral ground. The large proportion of the surface taken up by free water is perhaps the most striking feature when one walks through the site, with ridges only barely prevailing over open water as the major phase. Both pools and ridges tend to be linear, though the most level ground is dominated by deep, rounded pools. Although quaking ground is not strictly a common feature of this type, the narrow ridges between pools can be distinctly unstable, giving the appearance of quaking mire.

Surface microtopes

The dominant microforms are T2 high ridge and A2 hollows, though these latter give way dramatically to large A3/A4 pools where the ground is almost level. The A2 hollows are linear and abundant in much the same fashion as those found on the hyperoceanic Claish and Kentra Mosses on the Ardnamurchan Peninsula, which also have the same eccentrically sloping morphology. T1 low ridge is abundant, but not dominant, forming a fringe to most areas of transition between ridge and hollow. Hummocks are also common.

Vegetation

Most of the ridge communities are characterised by *Sphagnum*–dwarf shrub types, particularly with *S. rubellum* and *S. papillosum*. However, *S. imbricatum* T3 hummocks are common, and higher hummocks are dominated by the eastern community of hypnoid mosses–*Empetrum*. The abundance of *Molinia–Sphagnum* and *Racomitrium–Molinia–Pleurozia purpurea* distinguishes the type. The large extent of aquatic communities is another characteristic of this type, however, with A1 hollows of 'typical'

S. cuspidatum, S. cuspidatum–Eleocharis multicaulis and the transition *S. cuspidatum–S. papillosum.* In the A2 hollows and A3/A4 pools, *S. auriculatum– S. cuspidatum* is the dominant in shallower areas, whilst typical deep pools have *Menyanthes* or are devoid of vegetation.

Distribution

The type is largely central in distribution, with a distinct western 'tail'. It is concentrated in O2.H2/B2, but is also spread between the hyperoceanic and euoceanic parts of H1/B1.

Site type 7: Hyperoceanic patterned blanket bog (see Figure 57)

General appearance

This is perhaps the closest that any of the Caithness and Sutherland mires come to the extreme patterning of Claish and Kentra Mosses on the Ardnamurchan Peninsula. Patterning is linear, with a marked corrugation of the surface, but much of the ground is extremely soft and quaking (unlike that of the Ardnamurchan mires). With *Molinia* as one of the community dominants, the vegetation has a greener appearance than many of the mires further east. The type supports a nationally rare mire community in the form of *Rhynchospora fusca* A2 hollows, on the extreme west coast.

Surface microtopes

Predominantly T2 and T1 ridges forming narrow ribbons between equally narrow A2 mud-bottom hollows, the type also possesses A3 pools in places. T3 hummocks are abundant but not dominant.

Vegetation

The overall character is one of *Molinia*-dominance and of western communities such as *Carex limosa– S. cuspidatum* A1 hollows, *Rhynchospora alba* in both ridges and hollows, and *Myrica*–hypnoid mosses on drier ridges. *Sphagnum imbricatum* hummocks are abundant, as is mixed *Sphagnum* with dwarf shrubs. *Racomitrium* occurs both as hummocks with *Molinia* and within the ridge level as a mat with *Pleurozia purpurea*. As mentioned above, the most significant single community recorded within this type is the A2 *Rhynchospora fusca* mud-bottom hollow, which is recorded from five other ombrotrophic mire sites in Britain, two of those being Claish and Kentra Mosses.

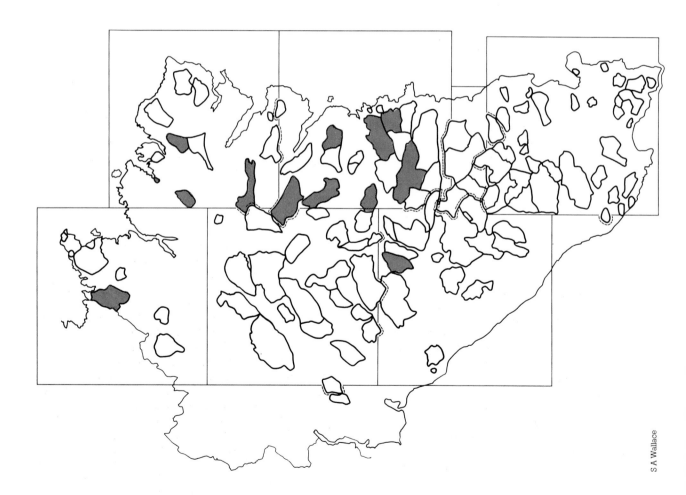

S A Wallace

Figure 57 Distribution of Site type 7 – Hyperoceanic patterned blanket bog. All macrotopes with a record for the type are tinted.

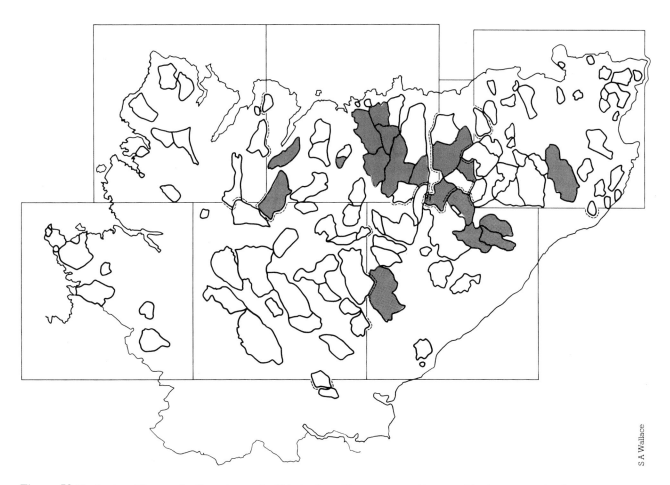

S A Wallace

Figure 58 Distribution of Site type 8 – Central watershed blanket bog. All macrotopes with a record for the type are tinted.

Distribution

Markedly north-western, the type is perhaps best expressed west of the Moine Thrust, but it extends as far east as Strathy.

Site type 8: Central watershed blanket bog
(see Figure 58)

General appearance

This type is one of the western variations on the type which dominates the watersheds in central Caithness. Like the Caithness type, it is characterised by a relative abundance of northern boreal dwarf shrubs and is marked by the complete lack of any more typical western indicators such as *Molinia* or *Potentilla erecta*, but it also has more abundant soft low ridge than typical Caithness watersheds. Although the surface pattern of large, deep pools reveals a close link with eastern watersheds, the soft *Sphagnum* carpets and abundance of *Betula nana* and *Arctostaphylos uva-ursi* also reveal a close affinity to Site type 4: low-relief northern boreal blanket bog.

Surface microtopes

From the air, the pools can be seen to be widely spaced and oval, rather than truly rounded. The dark coloration of the water indicates that they are deep, typically A4. The wide ridges between them have only limited A1 hollows, the majority of these being restricted to the outer edge of the patterning. T1 and T2 ridges predominate, with T3 hummocks dotted regularly across these.

Vegetation

Sphagnum communities dominate the vegetation of this type, with *S. magellanicum* in particular recorded from the T1 level. *S. fuscum* occurs more abundantly in this type than any other, as regular T3 hummocks, and the majority of other *Sphagnum* communities identified in the region are extensively recorded. Particularly significant, however, is the abundance of the *Sphagnum–Betula nana–Arctostaphylos* community. It occurs with T2 high ridges of *Sphagnum papillosum* or *S. fuscum*, but also within T3 hummocks of *Hylocomium splendens* and *Empetrum nigrum*. The A3 and A4 pools tend to have extremely limited vegetation cover. Only the true A2 hollows have extensive *S. auriculatum–S. cuspidatum* communities. The remainder of the water bodies have only *Menyanthes* or are devoid of vegetation.

Distribution

The type is centred on mires within the Halladale and Strathy catchments, but there is something of an eastern trend, with a number of records from the Dubh Lochs of Shielton complex.

Site type 9: 'Eastern' watershed blanket bog
(see Figure 59)

General appearance

This is the great "bog-lake complex" type (see Chapter 1), which is similar in appearance to some tundra systems but which has a much greater depth of peat than is possible under permafrost conditions. The widely spaced *dubh lochain* are often more than 2 m deep, perhaps the deepest encountered being to the south of the main Dubh Lochs of Shielton complex, where the unconsolidated bottom was measured as approximately 3.5 m beneath the water surface. Unfortunately this particular area is now isolated, surrounded by forest ploughing.

Surface microtopes

Obvious features are the A3/A4 pools, the absence of T1 low ridge and the wide, dry expanses of T2 communities which predominate between the large open water bodies. A1 hollows are common around the margins of the pool complexes, but they are not so generally common throughout the mire unit as to be regarded as dominant.

Vegetation

The extent of dry T2 ridge is emphasised by the abundance of the *Empetrum–Aulacomnium palustre–Hylocomium splendens* community, recorded more abundantly from this type than from any other. Within this T2 expanse, the *Sphagnum–Betula nana–Arctostaphylos uva-ursi* community is common, but not as frequent as in the previous type. The presence of extensive A1 *Sphagnum* hollows round the margins of the mire macrotope is indicated by the abundance of 'pure' *S. cuspidatum* carpets, this pure variety being particularly characteristic of Caithness watershed mires. The *S. imbricatum*–dwarf shrub and *S. fuscum*–dwarf shrub communities are also common.

Distribution

Entirely restricted to Caithness, the type is characteristic of the remaining large peat expanses. The type is not found elsewhere in Britain.

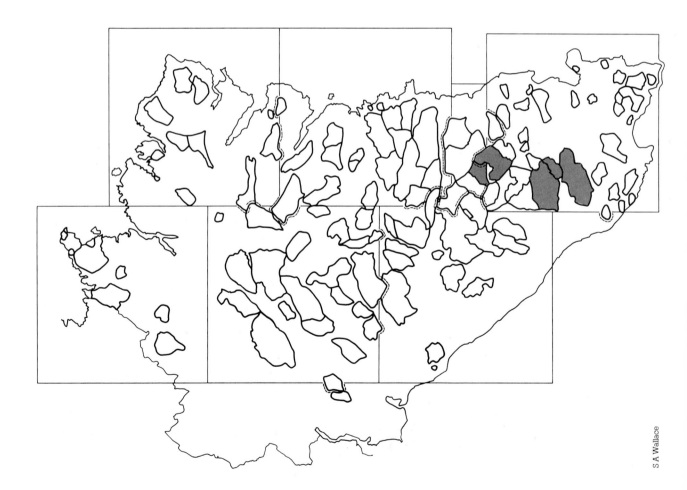

S A Wallace

Figure 59 Distribution of Site type 9 – 'Eastern' watershed blanket bog. All macrotopes with a record for the type are tinted.

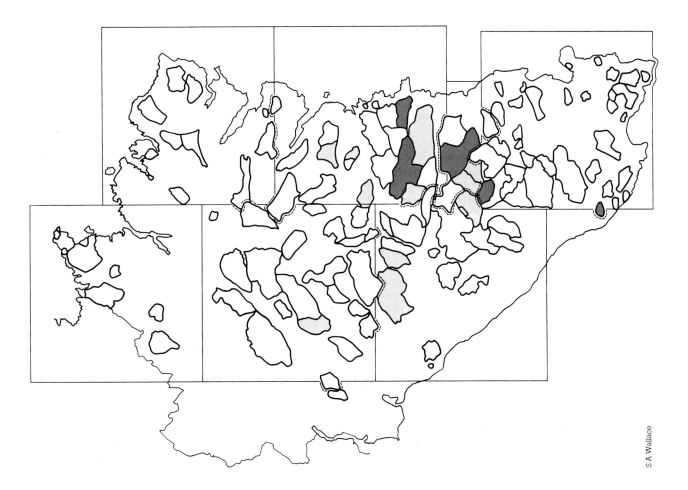

S A Wallace

Figure 60 Distribution of Site type 10 – *Racomitrium* watershed blanket bog. The dark tint represents the macrotope which contains the largest example of the type within each bioclimatic zone. The light tint represents other macrotopes with records for the type.

Site type 10: *Racomitrium* watershed blanket bog (see Figure 60)

General appearance

This type crosses the boundary between undamaged and disturbed sites. Where the bog surface on a watershed is drier than that described for Site type 8, the lower levels of the pattern become dominated by a *Sphagnum–Cladonia* mosaic and the higher levels have increasing amounts of *Racomitrium*, now in a hummock form rather than as a low-lying mat. The impression is of a more irregular surface and all ridge areas are firm, but nowhere is there extensive bare peat. Water is extensive, as oval pools, but the pool edges are sharply defined, often with varying heights of 'peat-cliff'.

Surface microtopes

A3/A4 pools are the dominant feature, with many areas having such closely-spaced oval pools that the solid ridges between can seem quite precarious. The presence of both erosion hags and gullies is generally restricted to the margins of sites, whereas the main expanse of T2 ridge is accompanied by large T3 hummocks, with areas of T1 low ridge and A1/A2 hollows around the fringes of larger pools.

Vegetation

The bulk of the ridge vegetation falls into the *Sphagnum*–dwarf shrub community, but also common are *Sphagnum–Cladina–Pleurozia purpurea* and *S. rubellum–S. tenellum–Cladina*. The type is marked by its much higher frequency of *Trichophorum*–bare peat than in previous types, as well as, of course, the *Racomitrium–Empetrum* and *Racomitrium–Cladina* communities. Hollows and pools have a limited vegetation cover of *S. auriculatum–S. cuspidatum*, with many pools having no vegetation. *S. papillosum–S. cuspidatum* is common as a fringe around otherwise empty pools.

Distribution

The vast majority of this type is restricted to the zone O2. H1/B2, perhaps reflecting a somewhat central and upland tendency.

Site type 11: Damaged northern boreal blanket bog (see Figure 61)

General appearance

This is a type which is characteristic of a small part of Sutherland, being widespread within that restricted

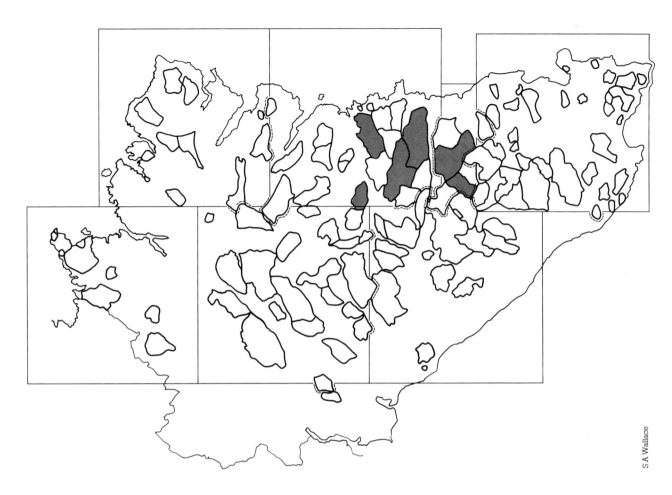

S A Wallace

Figure 61 Distribution of Site type 11 – Damaged northern boreal blanket bog. All macrotopes with a record for the type are tinted.

area. It is almost certainly derived from more *Sphagnum*-rich types by a process of regular burning and trampling and is recognised by the great extent of bare peat at the T1/T2 level. The vegetation, which is most luxuriant on the high T2 ridges and areas of T3 hummocks, consists largely of dwarf shrubs, of which *Betula nana* is a common dominant. Extensive patterning is present, but frequently the pools are half-empty and 'peat-cliffs' are a common feature of pool edges.

Surface microtopes

The most striking difference between the surface topography of this type and of previous types is the wide extent of the erosion gully network through the site. A3 pools are frequent, but many are reduced to expanses of bare peat, and the ridge structures are almost entirely T2 or T3. T1 and A1 are found only as narrow fringes to otherwise dry structures.

Vegetation

The distinctive characteristic of this type is the dominance of *Betula nana* on the T2 ridges, especially over a peat surface possessing only a patchy *Sphagnum* cover. Also typical is the presence of *Calluna*, *Erica tetralix* and *Myrica gale*. *Racomitrium* communities are generally T3 hummock *Racomitrium–Cladina*, though *Racomitrium*–bare peat is also common. *S. fuscum*

and *S. imbricatum* hummocks are frequent, though scattered, whilst the commonest *Sphagnum* community is *S. rubellum–S. papillosum*–dwarf shrubs.

Distribution

As with the softer, undamaged examples of *Betula nana* mire, this is restricted to the Halladale and Strathy catchments and almost entirely to O2.H2/B2.

Site type 12: Microbroken blanket bog
(A distribution map is not included.)

General appearance

The type is recognised by its relatively smooth appearance from a distance, but on closer examination this is shown to resemble a dissected plateau in miniature, with all the raised microbroken hummocks lying no more than 20–30 cm above the bottom of the erosion channel network. Typically, bare peat predominates on the erosion mounds, but the cover of vegetation seems largely to relate to the extent of recent burning.

Surface microtopes

There are only two – the network of shallow erosion channels and the raised, isolated microbroken hags.

106

Vegetation

This varies with the extent of burning, but the characteristic community is the *S. cuspidatum–S. tenellum* mixture which is almost invariably found as the dominant along the bottom of the erosion network. *Trichophorum–S. compactum* may form localised communities.

Distribution

The type is widespread because it covers a large proportion of ground including both entire mire units and much of the intervening thinner peat between major systems. However, because such intervening ground was not usually classed as a mire unit, the locations obtained from the analysis of mire units and quadrats give only a very limited idea of its distribution. A map of its recorded distribution would therefore be highly misleading, indicating only those cases where a recognisable mire unit was recorded as microbroken. It is fair to say that this is one of the most extensive peatland types in the region (and, indeed, elsewhere in Scotland), often covering much of the ground which provides hydrological connections between individual mire units, together forming a mire complex or macrotope.

Site type 13: Regenerating erosion complex
(see Figure 62)

General appearance

Although described as a regenerating system, much of the ground gives the appearance of quite severe erosion, with extensive bare peat, *Racomitrium* and empty pools. However, the characteristic feature of this type is the presence of vigorous mats of *Sphagnum*, generally *S. papillosum* mixed with *S. tenellum* or *S. cuspidatum*, growing out over the bare peat expanses of empty pools and hollows. A most distinctive character is the presence of *Carex pauciflora* within these *Sphagnum* mats.

Surface microtopes

The surface is often extremely uneven, with many hollows and pools completely empty. Ridge communities are thus particularly dry, occurring on the equivalent of T2/T3 levels. T4 erosion hags are also frequent, as are erosion gullies. However, the healthy *Sphagnum* mats are equivalent to a regenerating T1 low ridge.

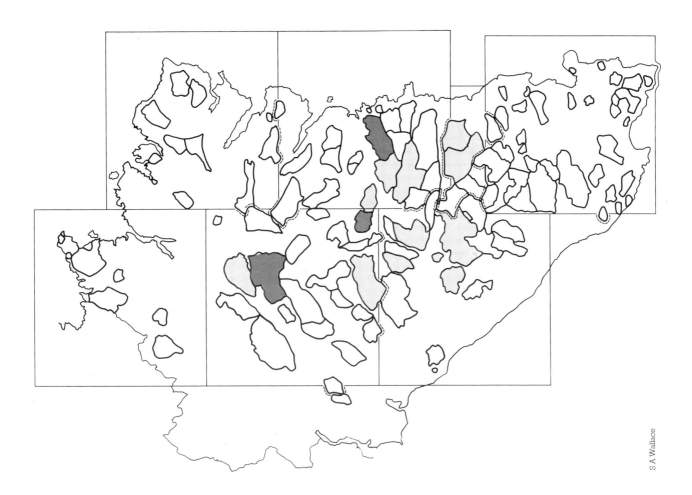

Figure 62 Distribution of Site type 13 – Regenerating erosion complex. The dark tint represents the macrotope which contains the largest example of the type within each bioclimatic zone. The light tint represents other macrotopes with records for the type.

Vegetation

Racomitrium–Cladina–bare peat is one of the most common communities within this type, together with *Trichophorum–Cladina*. Around the margins of empty pools the *Sphagnum*–dwarf shrub communities are extremely patchy, but the most vigorous is the *S. papillosum–Molinia–Carex pauciflora* community.

Distribution

The type is largely restricted to higher altitudes, being shared between O2.H1/B2, H1/B1 and H1/A3. It is found, for example, on Knockfin Heights, the Overscaig ridge and the high-level mires around Ben Armine.

Site type 14: Severely damaged *Trichophorum* blanket bog (see Figure 63)

General appearance

This is the final stage before erosion begins either to create deep gully complexes or to expose the mineral substrate beneath the eroding peat. The surface is typically fairly smooth, all evidence of surface patterning having been destroyed by repeated burning, and the vegetation is best described as sparse. Occasional hummocks break the monotony, and frequently erosion gullies dominate the margins of such sites.

Surface microtopes

Effectively, the ground is a wide expanse of T2 high ridge, with scattered T3 hummocks and occasional depressions which can be variously classed as *Sphagnum* hollows, mud-bottom hollows or pools, depending on the state of vegetation surviving within.

Vegetation

The predominant type is *Trichophorum*–bare peat, with *Trichophorum–Carex panicea* in the wetter parts. Occasional areas of *Sphagnum*–dwarf shrub are usually dominated by *S. tenellum* or *S. rubellum*, whilst T3 hummocks may support *S. imbricatum* or even *S. fuscum. Racomitrium*–bare peat is a frequent hummock- and mat-forming type. *Molinia–Pleurozia purpurea* can be found in occasional wet depressions.

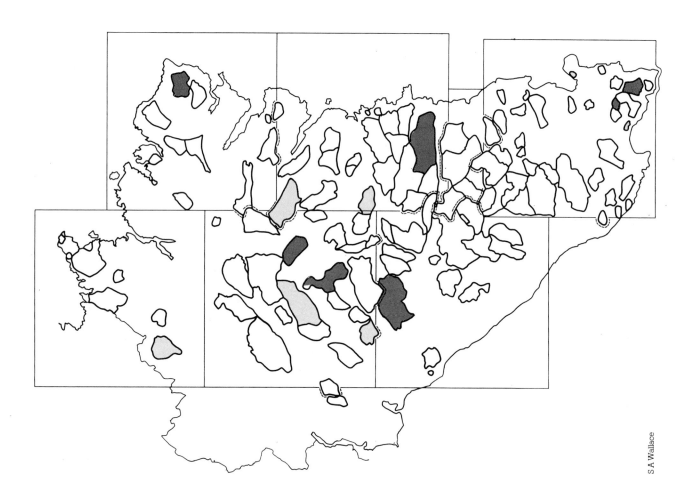

Figure 63 Distribution of Site type 14 – Severely damaged *Trichophorum* blanket bog. The dark tint represents the macrotope which contains the largest example of the type within each bioclimatic zone. The light tint represents other macrotopes with records for the type.

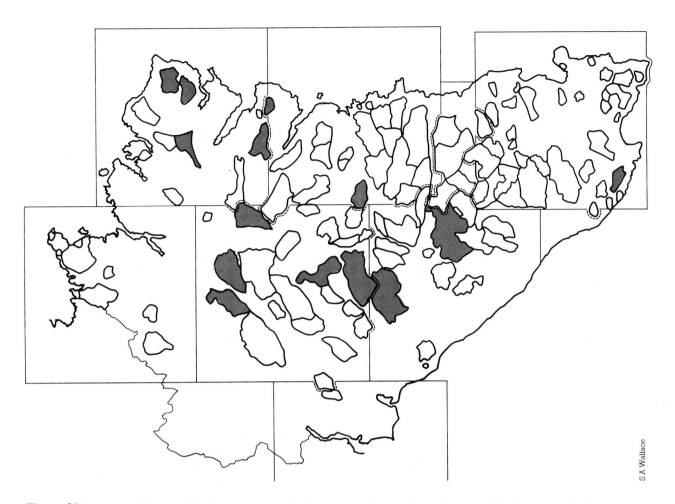

S A Wallace

Figure 64 Distribution of Site type 15 – Plateau erosion, with *Erica cinerea*. All macrotopes with a record for the type are tinted.

Distribution

The type is largely central and western, but it is also recorded from damaged coastal mires in Caithness, particularly in the peatlands around Duncansby Head, where salt spray appears to affect the vegetation types in any case. Like microbroken blanket bog, this is a type which often dominates mire margins and thinner peat. It is therefore relatively widespread, but, because many damaged sites were not surveyed in detail, the mapped extent of the type derived from the analysis is misleading.

Site type 15: Plateau erosion, with *Erica cinerea* (see Figure 64)

General appearance

Knockfin Heights has more than once been described, from the air, as a "moonscape". The large watershed pools which dominate all the high-level plateaux of Caithness and Sutherland are in various stages of erosional decay and, possibly, regeneration. Many areas have deep erosion gullies, as described by Osvald (1949), Goode & Lindsay (1979) and Hulme (1985) for the Outer Hebrides. Other areas have extensive areas of empty watershed pools but few deep erosion gullies. It seems likely that the severity of much of this erosion is a product of burning, because charcoal remains

are never hard to find. However, the extent to which the entire phenomenon is natural or unnatural is discussed in Chapter 5.

Surface microtopes

These are almost entirely erosion features, although within such large areas as Knockfin Heights it is possible to find extensive examples of relatively soft T1/T2 ridge and A2/A3 pools showing little evidence of damage.

Vegetation

The characteristic community is *Racomitrium–Erica cinerea*, which caps many of the higher erosion hags. However, *Campylopus atrovirens*–bare peat, *Molinia–Narthecium–Potentilla erecta* and *Trichophorum*–bare peat are all common components of the vegetation mosaic. In more eastern parts, *Sphagnum–Eriophorum vaginatum–Kurzia pauciflora* is an occasional type. On less damaged areas, *S. imbricatum* and *S. fuscum* hummocks are still found, but the former much less frequently than in most other site types.

Distribution

Markedly western and upland, the type is largely shared between O2.H1/A3 and O1.H1/B1, both climatic zones characteristic of high-level plateaux.

13 The definition of nature conservation requirements

The background purpose of the NCC's survey is to provide a factual basis for a nature conservation programme in the Caithness and Sutherland peatlands, in conjunction with surveys of birds and fresh waters. The information-base reported in the preceding chapters was planned to allow the evaluation of scientific interest in terms of range of variation in peatland hydromorphology, structure, vegetation and flora. The principles and criteria for nature conservation evaluation follow those developed within the NCC for the assessment and selection of important areas (Ratcliffe 1977, 1986a), taking both a Great Britain and an international perspective. One of the crucial aspects of judging the conservation value of the Caithness and Sutherland peatlands is, indeed, that the frame of reference should be knowledge of other peatlands, not only in the rest of this country but across the world.

In the selection of areas of outstanding importance for nature conservation, two major principles have previously been applied. The first is the choice of areas to give an adequate representation of reference points across the whole field of variation in ecosystems, and the second is the identification of a minimum standard of importance, above which every area qualifies for selection. The main criteria used to assess the comparative value of areas of similar ecological character and to define standards of quality are –

- Extent
- Diversity
- Naturalness
- Rarity
- Fragility
- Typicalness
- Position in an ecological/geographical unit

In addition the concept of "non-recreatability" is useful as an integrating measurement of nature conservation value.

Three especially important factors affect the nature conservation assessment of the Caithness and Sutherland peatlands and definition of particular areas within them.

The first factor is that not only is this a very large total expanse, but also much of it is continuous and of such a character that, over extensive areas, natural discontinuities which can be used in the delineation of particular blocks are often few in number. This means that in many places the boundaries between particular mire complexes are somewhat subjective, in as much as a moderate slope or a line of rock outcrops or a road may suggest that a boundary could reasonably be drawn along such a feature, but absolute confidence in such a boundary would depend on a more detailed study of peat depth and water movement.

The second factor is that this is not only one of the most extensive mosaics of natural and semi-natural ecosystems remaining in Britain, but also a globally rare type with high international importance (Chapter 3).

The third factor is that 17% of the total extent, including many important individual mire units, has already been lost (or is programmed to be lost) through afforestation and that this activity has affected 33 out of the 41 major river catchments (Stroud *et al.* 1987).

Evaluation and selection procedure

Previous attempts to assess the range and quality of peatland sites across a geographical region or province have often used various attribute-scoring methods to make overall comparisons between sites. Table 5 presents a synopsis of the factors regarded as important by a number of authors in the assessment of peatlands in various parts of the UK.

Not all the factors in Table 5 are applicable to blanket bog evaluation. For example, Leach & Corbett (1987) were concerned solely with raised mires in Northern Ireland, in which the presence of a lagg fen and the extent of undamaged dome are both factors of considerable importance, but these seldom occur in blanket bogs. A feature of Greig's (1975) and Charter's (1985a, 1985b) surveys is the use of formal scoring methods to evaluate the quality of individual mire units. This method is attractive in that the final ordered table enables priorities to be placed on subsequent action programmes, but the system assumes that attributes are additive, that the arbitrary 'weighting' of their value is appropriate and that an accumulation of factors represents an increasing level of nature conservation interest.

Penford (1985) reviews the problems of drawing up a ranked evaluation table, pointing out the large degree of subjective variability which is inherent in assigning scores to features which cannot practicably be quantified. Although some sites were clearly highlighted by the use of such a scoring system in her study, she concludes that "it would be unwise to base site selection on an evaluation such as this". Her two main objections are, first, that the cumulative scoring has the effect of compounding subjective errors, thereby inviting criticism of the final scoring, and, secondly, that sites not possessing

Factor	Charter (1984)	Leach & Corbett (1987)	Greig (1975)
Sphagnum cover	■	■	■
Structural elements	■		
Other "bog typics"	■	■	■
Size of site	■		
Presence of surface patterning	■	■	
Position of the water table	■		
Damage	■	■	■
• burning	■		
• drainage	■		
• afforestation	■		
• trampling	■		
• erosion	■		
Other notable features			
• mire morphology	■		
• extent of lagg fen		■	
• % size of remaining dome		■	

Table 5

Synopsis of the factors regarded as important in the assessment of peatlands in studies carried out in various parts of the United Kingdom.

all the features in abundance do not score highly, yet they may have particular features which are, of themselves, sufficient to warrant complete protection. In addition, she points out that such an evaluation does not cater for areas where a large proportion of the sites may be of high quality in a wider geographical context. The system tends to encourage an assumption that attention should be focused on, say, the top 25% of sites in the evaluation table, but in a wider context perhaps 75% would be regarded as essential to a conservation programme.

Both criticisms are particularly relevant to the Caithness and Sutherland survey, the former because of the varied sources of survey information used in the analysis. The latter point is perhaps best illustrated by the example of ladder fens, which do not possess many of the usual criteria for "high quality mire" but are of considerable importance in a national and even international context. In a ranked evaluation table, such sites would almost certainly not fall within the top 25%. Moreover, a ranking system based on detailed samples taken only from the two Districts would highlight the gradient of quality within the Flow Country but could not be used to evaluate the difference in quality between the peatlands of Caithness and Sutherland and of other parts of Britain.

While scoring procedures are useful in ranking similar sites in order of value, they do not measure the degree of difference between sites or give an absolute value. They therefore give little help in the crucial decisions about site selection, whether in choice of a representative series or in definition of minimum standards.

These various weaknesses of a numerical approach suggested that a less elaborate method of evaluation should be applied to the data from Caithness and Sutherland, particularly as a number of consistently recorded and essentially simple features were readily identifiable throughout. These are itemised later in this chapter.

The NCC's approach

The method adopted was a semi-quantitative one based on the analysis of site types described in Chapter 12. The 15 site types and the bioclimatic zones (Chapter 4) provide a computer-based matrix for the field of ecological variation in Caithness and Sutherland peatlands which has to be represented in the selection of sites (Table 6). This particular approach and the survey as a whole have produced information directly comparable with that obtained by the NCC's surveys of peatlands elsewhere in Britain, so that valid comparisons between the Flow Country and other regions can be made.

Although the site types described in Chapter 12 are all fairly distinctive, considerable variation exists within each type as a result of topographic and climatic factors. Thus western examples of northern boreal types have significantly greater quantities of *Molinia* or *Myrica*, for example. On the other hand, it is clear that most types have a fairly well-defined centre of distribution, within which the largest

Site type

Table 6 — Bioclimatic zones (part 1)

	O1H1A3	O1H1B1	O1H1B2	O1H1B3	O1H2B1	O1H2B2	O1H2B3	O1H3B1	O1H3B2	O1H3B3	PB1	PA3	PA2	PA1	Totals
Type 1	Ladder fens														313
Type 2	Flushed bog														657
Type 3	Low-relief 'western' bog			13		147		5							255
Type 4	Low-relief northern boreal bog			115	15	41	19	29			165				1668
Type 5	*Eriophorum vaginatum* 'eastern' bog	40		66		20	505	15	26	129	637				5065
Type 6	*Molinia–Sphagnum–Menyanthes* bog		197	12	16		19								1086
Type 7	Hyperoceanic patterned bog		302		23		46								651
Type 8	Central watershed bog														1429
Type 9	'Eastern' watershed bog														3140
Type 10	*Racomitrium* watershed bog						202			46					2129
Type 11	Damaged northern boreal bog														737
Type 12	Microbroken bog								19						32
Type 13	Regenerating erosion complex														2226
Type 14	Severely damaged *Trichophorum* bog		206	96	156					166	161				1276
Type 15	Plateau erosion, with *Erica cinerea*														9331
		40	2799	289	223	61	938	44	50	341	963				29995

Site type

Table 6 — Bioclimatic zones (part 2)

	O2H1A3	O2H1B1	O2H1B2	O2H1B3	O2H2B1	O2H2B2	O2H2B3	O2H3B2	O2H3B3	02PA3	02PA2	02PB3	02PB2
Type 1	Ladder fens	140		286			27							
Type 2	Flushed bog		23	252			42	35						
Type 3	Low-relief 'western' bog			77										
Type 4	Low-relief northern boreal bog		36	341			434		80					
Type 5	*Eriophorum vaginatum* 'eastern' bog	497	900	826			1299		645					
Type 6	*Molinia–Sphagnum–Menyanthes* bog		158	178	32		447	12						
Type 7	Hyperoceanic patterned bog			238			60							
Type 8	Central watershed bog	146	145	471			470	35		162				28
Type 9	'Eastern' watershed bog						2540		600					
Type 10	*Racomitrium* watershed bog			1232		61	588							
Type 11	Damaged northern boreal bog	56		40			641							
Type 12	Microbroken bog						13							
Type 13	Regenerating erosion complex	352	837	944			93							
Type 14	Severely damaged *Trichophorum* bog	61	174	244			264							
Type 15	Plateau erosion, with *Erica cinerea*	5382	628	40							230			
		6634	2901	5169	32	61	6918	82	1325	162	230			28

Table 6

Total areas (ha x 100) of site types within each bioclimatic zone.

number of 'typical' examples can be expected. Table 6 shows the scatter of site types across the range of bioclimatic zones for the region. In particular, it highlights the major zones for any given site type, as well as indicating the site types which best characterise each of the bioclimatic zones. Within the hyperoceanic region, the zones H1/B1, H1/B2 and H2/B2 represent major centres of distribution for particular site types, whilst H1/A3, H1/B2 and H2/B2 are important centres for site types within the euoceanic region.

The approach most appropriate to the selection of exemplary areas of any peatland type involves the selection of a single example from each bioclimatic zone containing that site type. Where a bioclimatic zone contained many examples, the largest site, was selected. Figures 51–64 illustrate the distribution of each site type, with emphasis on the largest examples in each bioclimatic zone. This approach has the advantage that the complete geographical/climatic gradient of each site type can be represented and the selection process is evenly spread throughout the region instead of focusing on particular parts. A fairly high proportion of ground so identified is already recognised as being of high quality for nature conservation, having been described in *A Nature Conservation Review* (Ratcliffe 1977) as "key" national sites or subsequently recognised as having SSSI quality.

In addition, some of the blanket bog features are of sufficient importance for all examples to require protection. This expresses the selection principle of *minimum standards*, above which all examples qualify, and is used as a necessary second approach to complement the series of *exemplary sites*. The criteria of rarity, naturalness and fragility together identify certain general attributes as highly localised, declining and endangered as British habitats. In most cases, their present occurrence represents a much reduced remnant of former distribution and extent. These features are quaking mire, *Sphagnum* cover, rare species and combinations of other species indicating lack of disturbance; they are not peculiar to any one site type and so may elevate the value of any example based on the criterion of size already applied. Site types 1, 2, 3, 4, 7, 8, 9, 11 and 15 qualify under these criteria for selection in their entirety.

There follows a synopsis of the nature conservation value and the selection requirements for all 15 site types. A further section spells out in greater detail the special features within the field of mire variation that require complete protection.

Conservation value and need, according to site types

Site type 1: Ladder fens (see Figure 51)

Conservation status

Maximum protection of all examples. The type has been identified as internationally important by the International Mire Conservation Group.

Site type 2: Flushed bog and valley mire transition (see Figure 52)

Conservation status

Very high. All undamaged examples should be protected. This is a rich mire type characterised by several important conservation features. First, it is frequently associated with quaking mire. Secondly, it is one of the major types within which *Vaccinium oxycoccos* occurs. It also reveals a number of relationships between ladder fens, valley mires and ombrotrophic patterns.

Site type 3: Low-relief 'western' blanket bog (see Figure 53)

Conservation status

High. All examples should be protected. A very small number of sites were recorded. All these would need to be protected to meet normal site selection criteria. In addition, the association of this type with quaking mire and the richness of its vegetation, which forms important links with the Inner and Outer Isles, make the type particularly significant.

Site type 4: Low-relief northern boreal blanket bog (see Figure 54)

Conservation status

Maximum protection for all examples. Although the type cannot be described as rich, it represents one of the rarest mire communities in Britain, provides a phytogeographical link with continental mires and is an important source of undamaged quaking mire. Its concentration within the main area of forestry activity is obviously a major source of concern, and the possible loss already of one of the most easterly outliers simply serves to highlight the problem.

Site type 5: *Eriophorum vaginatum* 'eastern' blanket bog (see Figure 55)

Conservation status

Representative, except for examples of *Sphagnum pulchrum* mire, which require maximum protection. As this is the major type within the region, as well as an important link with mire types further south, it is necessary to ensure that sufficient examples are protected to maintain the range of variation.

Site type 6: *Molinia–Sphagnum– Menyanthes* blanket bog (see Figure 56)

Conservation status

High/representative. Although this type is not striking in its floristics, the combination of vegetation and surface pattern is one which is relatively infrequent outside Sutherland. Sufficient examples should certainly be protected to ensure that its full range of forms is maintained, but there is an argument on national and international grounds for ensuring that a rather larger range of examples is protected.

Site type 7: Hyperoceanic patterned blanket bog (see Figure 57)

Conservation status

Maximum protection required. There are few examples, not only in Caithness and Sutherland but throughout the rest of Britain.

Site type 8: Central watershed blanket bog (see Figure 58)

Conservation status

Maximum protection required. This is one of three major types which characterise the Caithness and Sutherland peatlands and are found, almost certainly, nowhere else in Europe (and therefore, probably, the world). The other two are Site types 4 and 9.

Site type 9: 'Eastern' watershed blanket bog (see Figure 59)

Conservation status

Maximum protection required. All examples (the few remaining) require complete protection because they represent the only known examples of the type.

Site type 10: *Racomitrium* watershed blanket bog (see Figure 60)

Conservation status

High/representative. The type does not support any vegetation communities which are unique to Caithness and Sutherland. However, it is important for the patterns adopted by its microtopes, which show an extreme form of watershed pool development. Such patterns have an extremely localised distribution in Britain. In terms of mire hydromorphology, therefore, a wide range of examples should be protected.

Site type 11: Damaged northern boreal blanket bog (see Figure 61)

Conservation status

High. Although damaged, the type is important for the light it sheds on the distribution of *Betula nana* on British mire systems. In addition, many of these sites have every likelihood of recovery if burning and trampling are reduced. They therefore represent an important additional component within the whole distribution of Caithness and Sutherland northern boreal blanket bog.

Site type 12: Microbroken blanket bog (A distribution map is not included.)

Conservation status

Microbroken ground has little intrinsic value. However, it plays a significant part in maintaining the hydrology of more important mire systems when it forms an adjoining unit.

Site type 13: Regenerating erosion complex (see Figure 62)

Conservation status

Representative. The widespread nature of this type in high-level mires means that sufficient examples should be protected to maintain the range of geographical variation displayed within the two Districts.

Site type 14: Severely damaged *Trichophorum* blanket bog (see Figure 63)

Conservation status

Representative. Like microbroken mire, the type is generally only important as 'connective' land between other more important areas. However, the type is somewhat different in coastal Caithness and this is probably of value as a geographical variant which should be represented in the programme of protection.

Site type 15: Plateau erosion, with *Erica cinerea* (see Figure 64)

Conservation status

High. The status of erosion, in terms of its natural or anthropogenic origins, has yet to be determined (see Chapter 5). Clearly erosion is often made more severe by human agency, but all high-level plateaux are characterised by this type and it is likely that some of the closest links with Scandinavian northern boreal mires are to be found here. It is therefore essential that as wide a range of this type as possible should be protected, particularly as these areas are likely to be of greatest value for research into erosion and its origins.

Conservation value and need, according to special features

Quaking mire

Quaking mire is the very softest type of ground, where the normally solid ridges feel extremely unstable and large areas of the surface may quake under a person's body-weight. Whilst the high water content of any peat means that it is normally possible to make the ground shake slightly, quaking mire literally quakes with every footfall, and the ridges are so soft that crossing such an area is hazardous. The surface layers are typically almost completely unhumified, often to depths of 20-30 cm, and the catotelm as a whole is close to the liquid limit in water content of the peat (Hobbs 1986). This phenomenon is usually associated with an abundance of the *Sphagna* typical of a low-relief microtopography. It seems to be associated with the least damaged mires or parts of mires. Such areas can therefore be taken to display a high degree of "naturalness".

It is important to distinguish here between whole blanket bog units and individual elements of microtopography or certain minerotrophic basin mires. A1 hollows typically quake, but, though generally indicating high quality, they do not represent a quaking mire unit or mesotope. Many mires have certain elements which are extremely soft, but these are usually only individual hollows or pools. "Quaking mire" refers to sites which have large areas of uninterrupted quaking, ombrotrophic surface, so that the whole or most of the catotelm is in an almost liquid state. Whilst the surface of some basin mires can also be extremely hazardous, this is usually a result of their basic structure, where a thin skin of vegetation floats on an underlying lens of water – the *Schwingmoore* typical of such sites as the kettle-hole mires of the north-west Midlands (e.g. Moore & Bellamy 1974).

On a national scale quaking mire is rare, especially in blanket bogs, and has been regarded as an important attribute for the selection of SSSIs on the criterion of "rarity". Only 19 current SSSIs possess examples of quaking mire, although a number of early accounts of peatland systems attest to its former widespread occurrence (Cromertie 1711; Gorham 1953b). There are 43 recorded examples in Sutherland and Caithness, and the region holds a large percentage of the British total of this rare habitat. Figure 65 shows the distribution of quaking mire in the region.

Sphagnum cover

Sphagnum is a sensitive genus, being especially adversely affected by fire, lowering of the water table (Ivanov 1981; Clymo & Hayward 1982), trampling by livestock or humans (Slater & Agnew 1977) and pollution (Ferguson *et al.*). Agricultural reclamation, afforestation and pollution have

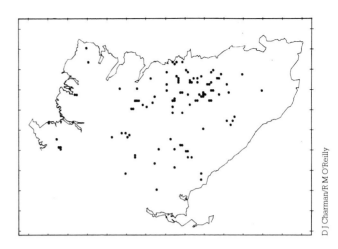

Figure 65 Surveyed peatland sites which were found to contain substantial areas of quaking mire.

removed *Sphagnum* from large parts of its former range in Britain. This means that its occurrence and abundance are a good indication of "naturalness". Abundant, healthy *Sphagnum* over a high proportion of the surface is a sign that the mire is still in an actively growing, rather than moribund, state and that its nature conservation interest is likely to be maintained over the foreseeable future, if it is not disturbed. It is a feature also rating highly under the criterion of "fragility", since it is so easily damaged by human interference. The species associated with active bog growth are *Sphagnum papillosum, S. magellanicum, S. rubellum, S. subnitens, S. cuspidatum* and *S. auriculatum.* Some others, notably *S. recurvum, S. tenellum* and *S. compactum* are often indicators of disturbance or drying, especially when present in abundance.

This is another factor which has been used in the past as an indicator of sites of SSSI quality, increasingly so because the number of *Sphagnum*-rich mires in Britain has declined rapidly since the turn of the century (e.g. Nature Conservancy Council 1982, pp. 8–9).

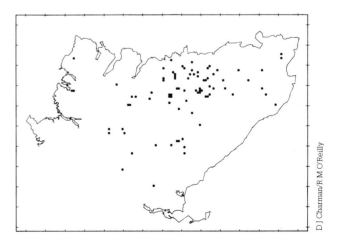

Figure 66 Surveyed peatland sites which were found to possess a high cover of *Sphagnum*.

Caithness and Sutherland hold peatland of considerable value in terms of *Sphagnum* cover, with large proportions of the area possessing high-scoring sites. The region probably contains the bulk of the *Sphagnum*-dominated bogs remaining in Britain. Figure 66 shows the distribution of *Sphagnum*-dominated bogs within Caithness and Sutherland. The scale of the map means that sites which are closer together than 1 km are plotted as a single point.

It is worth stressing that low cover of *Sphagnum* does not always indicate drying and disturbance of the bog surface. Some studies (Moore 1977; Walker 1961) of stratigraphy of Highland and Irish blanket bogs reveal a low content of *Sphagnum* in the peat down to a considerable depth, showing that it may sometimes, and quite naturally, be only a minor component of the active bog surface. This has to be allowed for in evaluation of peatland interest.

Indicator species

The use of particular species for site assessment is well established (e.g. Greig 1975; Charter 1985a, 1985b), either indirectly as indicators of presence or absence of damage or directly for their value in their own right (e.g. as rare species). The species used here are selected for both reasons. Their national and regional importance and distribution are discussed in Chapter 11.

Sphagna

Sphagnum imbricatum and *S. fuscum* are the two species regarded as most characteristic of mires in good condition in western and northern Britain. *S. imbricatum* features prominently in plant remains in sub-surface peat and was much more widespread in the past. The reasons for this decline are not known fully (Tallis 1964c). Both species are conspicuous dry hummock formers on mire surfaces and may therefore be susceptible to fire (McVean & Lockie 1969; Slater & Slater 1978). Frequently they are in a degenerate state, and the possibility that atmospheric pollution is a factor in *Sphagnum* decline has stimulated considerable recent research (e.g. Lee 1981; see also Chapter 5).

S. pulchrum is a national rarity and, while the reasons for its restricted distribution are not known, its continuing decline is a direct result of straightforward habitat destruction, particularly of lowland raised and blanket mires in western Britain. Its Wigtownshire stations on Moss of Cree and Kilquhockadale Flow have been destroyed by afforestation.

The total number of *Sphagnum* species present has been used in some other studies for quality assessment, on the assumption that more diverse sites are more valuable than uniform sites. However, only those species characteristic of intact ombrotrophic mire should be used, as adjacent fen systems and damage features may contain species which should be excluded from additive scoring of this kind.

Other bryophytes

The presence of the rare moss *Dicranum bergeri* is regarded as an important indication of lack of damage to mire surfaces.

Higher plants

Higher plants which can be positively scored to measure mesotope value, on the basis of their restricted distributions, at least as bog plants are *Vaccinium oxycoccos* and *V. microcarpum*, *Rhynchospora fusca* and *R. alba*, *Arctostaphylos uva-ursi*, *Betula nana*, *Carex limosa* and *C. pauciflora*, *Sparganium angustifolium*, *Drosera intermedia* and *D. anglica*. However, the majority of these species are associated with high *Sphagnum* cover and are relatively common within the region, so they were not used in the final selection of mire complexes.

Only *Rhynchospora fusca* and *Sphagnum pulchrum* were considered to be sufficiently rare, both nationally and within the region, to merit their use as selection criteria for particular blanket bog complexes. The remainder of the species were used to evaluate sites, but were not themselves used as selection criteria.

The quite extraordinary aspect of Caithness and Sutherland is the large extent of ground which meets the various criteria listed above. In other parts of Britain such selection standards would tend to identify small units within an otherwise lower-quality matrix of peatland habitat.

The cumulative selection of conservation areas

The combined distribution of mire complexes identified for protection from the site type/bioclimatic zone matrix is shown in Figure 67. This area (189,104 ha) represents the range of best examples for each site type, together with those site types of which all examples should be protected on grounds of national rarity, but also includes areas already lost to forestry. Many mire complexes are shown to contain both exemplary and rare site types.

This selection is based on an assessment, by computer analysis, of those mire complexes for which there is quadrat information. Supplementary information on the occurrence of quaking mire, *Sphagnum* cover and the presence of rare species is available for all sites covered by the survey, so that a list of individual mire units (as distinct from site types) with these attributes is easily accessible through the survey data-base. These were plotted onto 1:50,000 maps, together with their supporting hydrological boundaries. This results in a larger area of rare mire types being shown than in Figure 67. However, some of the highly rated sites have been

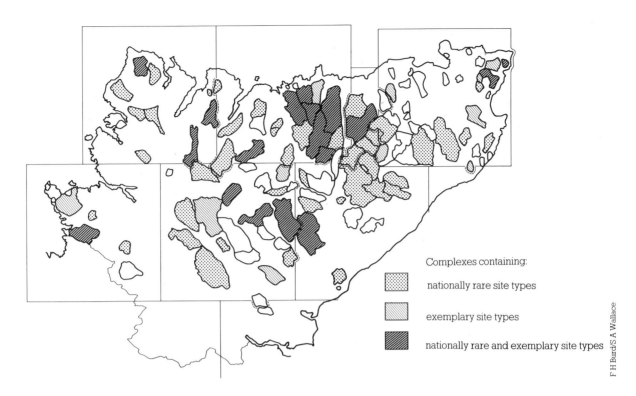

F H Burd/S A Wallace

Figure 67 Distribution of mire complexes identified for protection because they contain exemplary and/or nationally rare site types. Some of the areas have been afforested since they were surveyed or are currently programmed for afforestation.

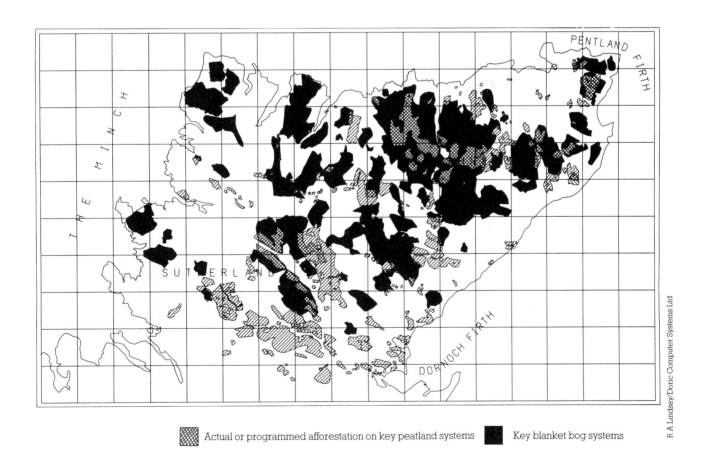

R A Lindsay/Doric Computer Systems Ltd

▨ Actual or programmed afforestation on key peatland systems   ■ Key blanket bog systems

Figure 68 Distribution of "key" (Nature Conservation Review status) peatland systems identified for protection either because they contain exemplary or nationally rare site types or because they support bog vegetation exceeding the criterion of quality which requires all examples to be protected. Existing or proposed peatland SSSIs are also included within this distribution. Key peatland areas which have been afforested since they were surveyed or are now programmed for afforestation are shown cross-hatched; other forestry is shown single-hatched.

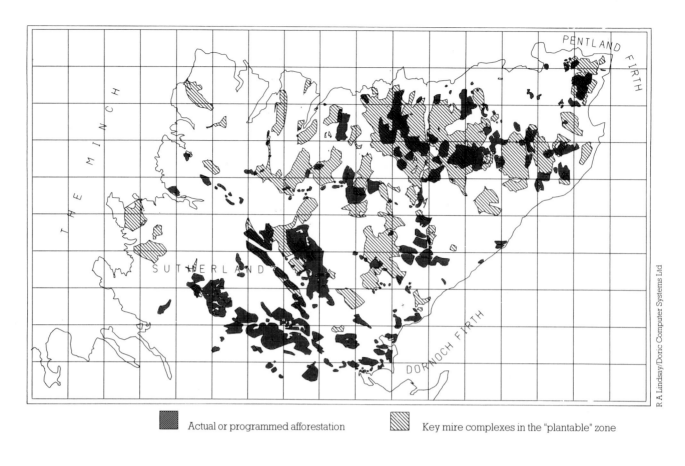

Actual or programmed afforestation

Key mire complexes in the "plantable" zone

R A Lindsay/Doric Computer Systems Ltd

Figure 69 The extent of "key" blanket bog systems which lie within the "plantable" zone. Land which is classed as "unplantable" by the Forestry Commission has been removed. Land shown with single-hatching is therefore key peatland habitat within which further losses through afforestation may occur.

lost since they were surveyed and require substitutes for representation. The combined area of key mire systems, including peatland SSSIs, is shown in Figure 68 (with afforested areas and those programmed for planting superimposed). The total area of important surveyed peatland vegetation remaining outside afforested areas is 195,063 ha. Not all of this land is in conflict with forestry, however, because some ground is classed as "unplantable" by the Forestry Commission. The total area of important peatland vegetation lying within the area defined as "plantable" by the Forestry Commission is 128,584 ha (see Figure 69).

Finally, the selection requirement has to be assessed against the area of blanket bog in the region already lost to afforestation and the international importance of this peatland class. Apart from the overall reduction in blanket bog extent and the destruction of or damage to high-quality sites, an important aspect of this impact is the way it has fallen widely but haphazardly across the whole peatland area. At least 33 out of the 41 major river catchments within the region now contain at least some afforestation. The effect has been to cause a marked fragmentation of many major blocks of once continuous peatland and to destroy the visual integrity of the total blanket bog landscape in many places. It was this visual character, of a continuous tundra-like physiognomy, that was once so striking

and unique a feature of the main flow areas. In parts of the region where this character of intact peatland landscapes still persists, including the associated range of freshwater systems, it is important that it be maintained as far as possible. Because of the propensity of afforestation for affecting the mechanics and chemistry of peats and waters in parts of a catchment well away from the planted ground, it is also important to maintain the integrity of those catchments which have no forest and to avoid further planting on ground draining into highly valued mire systems.

To take account of this need, five major blocks of still continuous peatland have been identified, based on the occurrence of important exemplary and special feature sites but with the addition of connecting ground which is necessary to their continuity. These blocks, which are an important component of the whole conservation programme, should be regarded as particularly sensitive to any further afforestation within their boundaries because even small plantations can have an impact out of all proportion to their size, particularly in an area which was previously almost completely unafforested.

These blocks are indicated in only a general way in Figure 70 because boundaries of landscape units are less clearly definable than, say, the limits of a hydrological catchment.

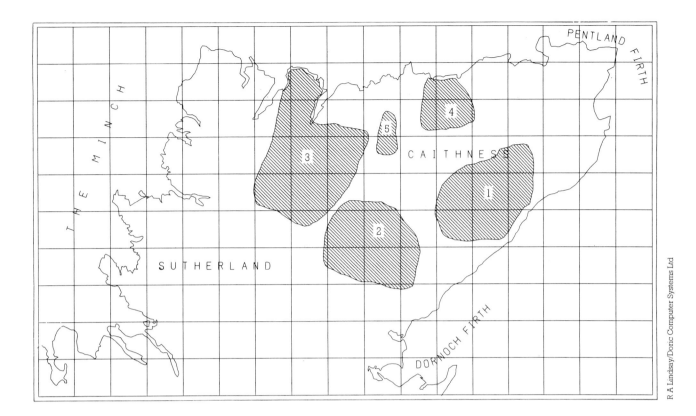

Figure 70 Generalised areas of landscape which are peat-dominated but which currently have a low proportion of afforestation. These landscape units are important as control catchments for fisheries and acid rain research and should therefore be regarded as particularly sensitive to further afforestation.

1 South of the River Thurso – Berriedale – Knockfin

2 Brora – Loch Choire – Borrobol – Black Water

3 A'Mhoine – Ben Loyal – Beinn Stumanadh – Strathnaver – Pole Hill – Ben Klibreck – Ben Hee – Loch Hope

4 Melvich Bay – Trantlemore – Loch Caluim – Reay

5 The catchment of the Allt Lon a'Chuil (between Strathnaver and the Rimsdale Burn)

14   Recent surveys of aquatic flora and fauna

Caithness and Sutherland contain approximately 30,000 ha of open water (Highland Regional Council statistic), comprising many hundreds of lochs and stream systems. Since 1979 botanical surveys have been carried out by the NCC on four rivers – the Forss Water and the Rivers Oykel, Wick and Inver – and over 350 lochs in Caithness and Sutherland. 117 lochs and rivers were surveyed for invertebrates in 1985 by the Caithness Biological Records Centre (Spirit 1987). In 1986 the Freshwater Biological Association was commissioned by the NCC to carry out invertebrate surveys of the River Oykel in Sutherland and the Burn of Latheronwheel and the Forss Water in Caithness. In 1987, 43 sites were surveyed for water beetles by Dr G N Foster, the national recorder for aquatic Coleoptera (Foster 1987). The following information is based mainly on these recent surveys and on records held by the Biological Records Centre at Monks Wood Experimental Station of the Institute of Terrestrial Ecology.

Aquatic vegetation

The NCC has recently produced classifications of the vegetation of rivers (Holmes, 1983) and standing waters (M A Palmer in prep.) throughout Great Britain. Both these classifications reflect the nutrient status of aquatic systems.

Nutrient-poor (oligotrophic) waters are typified by species such as alternate water-milfoil *Myriophyllum alterniflorum*, bulbous rush *Juncus bulbosus*, shoreweed *Littorella uniflora*, water lobelia *Lobelia dortmanna*, floating bur-reed *Sparganium angustifolium*, bog pondweed *Potamogeton polygonifolius* and broad-leaved pondweed *Potamogeton natans*. Nutrient-poor rivers are often dominated by mosses and liverworts rather than higher plants. Lakes and pools floored by peat are usually highly acidic (dystrophic) and often contain few plants apart from *Sphagnum* species, bulbous rush and bogbean *Menyanthes trifoliata*.

Moderately nutrient-rich (mesotrophic) waters typically lack *Potamogeton polygonifolius* and *Sparganium angustifolium*. Mesotrophic lakes are likely to have a more diverse *Potamogeton* flora than oligotrophic sites and often contain perfoliate pondweed *Potamogeton perfoliatus* and various-leaved pondweed *P. gramineus*. Mesotrophic rivers contain proportionally fewer mosses and liverworts and more higher plants than oligotrophic rivers. Mesotrophic and oligotrophic waters occur predominantly in the north and west of Britain.

There are a number of vegetation types typical of nutrient-rich (eutrophic) waters, some dominated by floating plants such as duckweeds *Lemna* species and yellow water-lily *Nuphar lutea*, others by submerged species such as spiked water-milfoil *Myriophyllum spicatum*, fennel pondweed *Potamogeton pectinatus* and (in rivers) the river water-crowfoot *Ranunculus penicillatus* var. *calcareus*. A final category of "mixed" lake has a peculiar and unusual mixture of species typical of oligotrophic and eutrophic conditions, normally occurring as a result of acid inflows to a calcareous basin. Eutrophic systems are found predominantly in lowland Britain, especially in the south and east.

Figures 71 to 73 illustrate the distribution of the various standing water and river types in Caithness and Sutherland, based on botanical survey data collected recently by the NCC and categorised according to its Great Britain classifications. A wide range of vegetation types is represented, but the mesotrophic and eutrophic end of the spectrum is largely confined to areas away from deep peat (Figures 71–72). The two river systems surveyed in Sutherland are relatively uniform throughout their length, whereas those in Caithness show a downstream progression from nutrient-poor to more nutrient-rich conditions. A few lochs in Caithness and on Durness Limestone in north-west Sutherland belong to the nationally rare "mixed" lake type (Figure 72). Most of the lochs examined in the area covered by blanket bog are oligotrophic or dystrophic (Figure 73).

Rare and uncommon plants

Table 7 lists the 10 species of nationally scarce plants which have been recorded in the last four years in water bodies either in the blanket bog of Caithness and Sutherland or in catchments influenced by

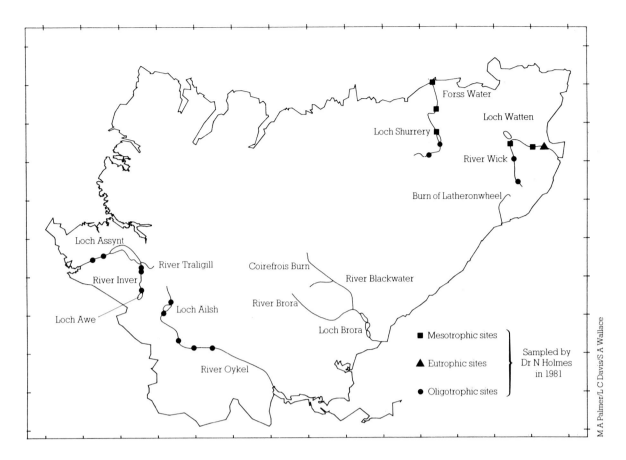

Figure 71 Surveyed river sites in Caithness and Sutherland.

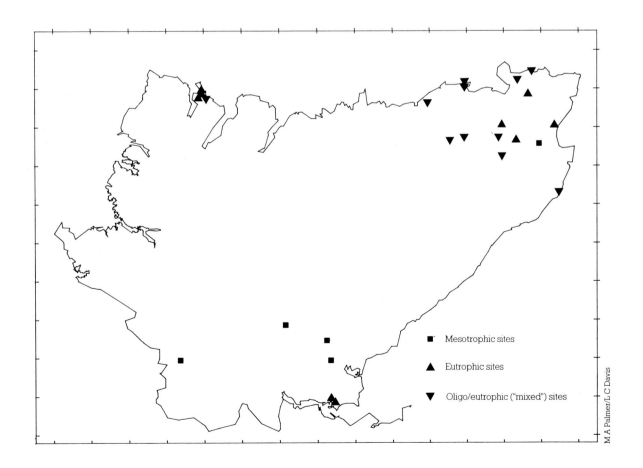

Figure 72 Lochs of richer nutrient status in Caithness and Sutherland.

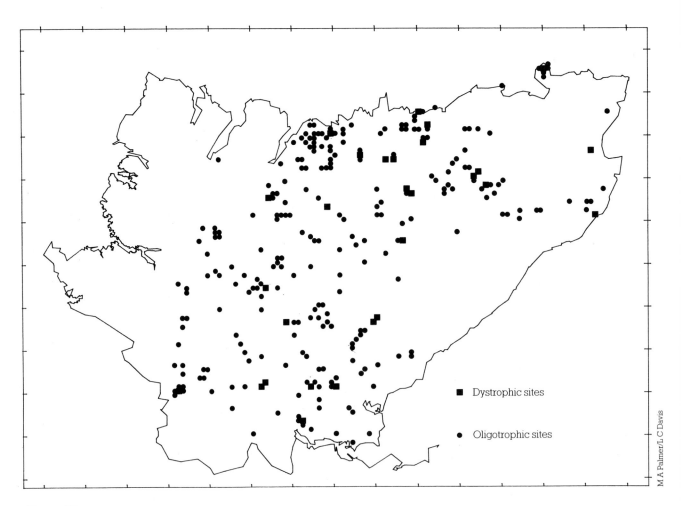

Figure 73 Distribution of nutrient-poor lochs in Caithness and Sutherland.

	No. of 10 km squares in Great Britain*	Records 1984–1987 Caithness	Sutherland	Comments
Callitriche hermaphroditica	80	+	+	
Carex aquatilis	46	+	+	
Deschampsia setacea	41	–	+	
Hammarbya paludosa	67	–	+	
Isoetes setacea	60	–	+	
Lycopodiella inundata	55	–	+	
Nuphar pumila	24	–	+	
Pilularia globulifera	71	–	+	IUCN Red Data Book – vulnerable category
Potamogeton filiformis	48	+	Durness Lochs only	
Potamogeton praelongus	81	+	+	

* 1930 onwards for flowering plants.
  1950 onwards for ferns.
  Includes new sites discovered in 1987.

Table 7

Nationally scarce plant species recorded recently from Caithness and Sutherland waters which are on or influenced by deep peat.

blanket bog. Nationally scarce species occur in between 16 and 100 10 km squares in Great Britain (Palmer & Newbold 1983). Pillwort *Pilularia globulifera*, which occurs in the valley of the River Oykel, is internationally vulnerable (Council of Europe 1983). Least water-lily *Nuphar pumila* is a very uncommon plant (Figure 74), which hybridises with the common yellow water-lily *Nuphar lutea*, itself rare in northern Scotland. Several species in Table 7, notably autumnal water-starwort *Callitriche hermaphroditica*, slender-leaved pondweed *Potamogeton filiformis* and long-stalked pondweed *Potamogeton praelongus*, are more typical of slightly alkaline or neutral waters than of acidic, markedly nutrient-poor sites.

Invertebrates

Whilst the invertebrate communities of waters in northern Scotland are generally less diverse than those of lowland England, they are often of great interest because of their relict arctic-alpine characteristics.

Table 8 lists 21 notable invertebrate species occurring in Caithness and Sutherland waters which are either actually situated on the blanket mire or influenced by it. Not included in the list is the native crayfish *Austropotamobius pallipes*, whose only known Scottish location is a loch near Durness, lying on limestone. The conservation of this species is of great importance since elsewhere in Britain many native crayfish populations are being wiped out by the crayfish plague fungus *Aphanomyces astaci* (Marren 1986).

The most noteworthy of the species in Table 8 are the freshwater pearl mussel *Margaritifera margaritifera*, the blue hawker dragonfly *Aeshna caerulea*, a caddis fly *Nemotaulius punctatolineatus* and a small diving beetle *Oreodytes alpinus*.

The pearl mussel is listed as vulnerable by the IUCN (Wells, Pyle & Collins 1983). Although it occurs in a few rivers in Wales and south-west England, strong populations are restricted to a few cool, fast-flowing, calcium-poor rivers in Scotland. River systems on peat in Caithness and Sutherland with populations of

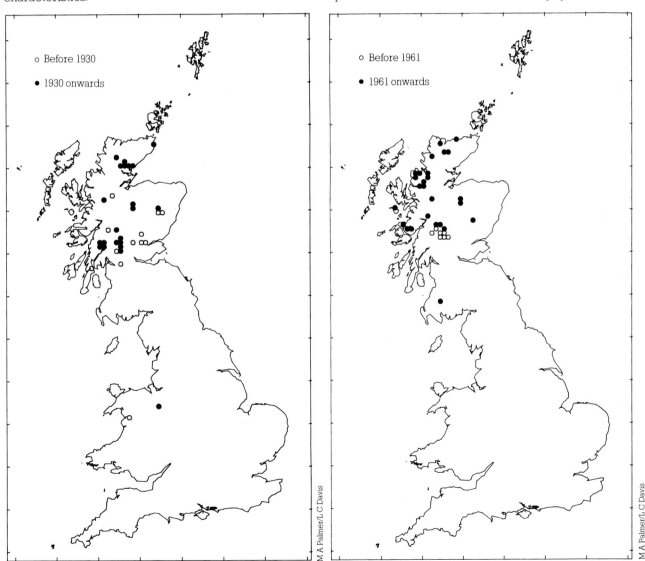

Figure 74 British distribution of least water-lily *Nuphar pumila*.

Figure 75 British distribution of *Aeshna caerulea*.

123

	Caithness	Sutherland	Comments
Molluscs			
Margaritifera margaritifera	+	+	IUCN Red Data Book – vulnerable category
Sphaerium lacustre	+	–	Rare in northern Scotland
Crustaceans			
Gammarus pulex	+	–	Rare in northern Scotland
Stoneflies			
Capnia bifrons	+(Forss)	–	Rare but widespread in Great Britain
Dragonflies			
Aeshna caerulea	–	+	Nationally scarce; confined in Great Britain to north-west Scotland
Cordulegaster boltonii	–	+	Threatened in parts of Europe
Sympetrum nigrescens	+	+	Largely confined in Great Britain to north-west Scotland
Caddisflies			
Nemotaulius punctatolineatus	+	–	British Red Data Book – rare category
Polycentropus kingi	+(Latheronwheel)	–	Uncommon but widespread in Great Britain
Beetles			
Coelambus novemlineatus	+	+	Nationally scarce
Deronectes latus	+	+	Nationally scarce
Dytiscus lapponicus	+	–	Nationally scarce
Gyrinus minutus	+	+	Nationally scarce
Gyrinus opacus	+	+	Scarce in Great Britain and Europe
Hydraena rufipes	+	–	Nationally scarce
Hydroporus longicornis	+	+	Nationally scarce
Ilybius aenescens	+	+	Nationally scarce
Ochthebius bicolon	+(Forss)	–	Nationally scarce
Ochthebius exsculptus	+(Forss)	–	Nationally scarce
Oreodytes alpinus	+	+	British Red Data Book – rare category
Potamonectes griseostriatus	+	+	Nationally scarce

Table 8

Notable invertebrate species recorded recently in Caithness and Sutherland waters which are on or influenced by deep peat.

pearl mussel are listed in Table 9. A recent severe decline in this species has been attributed to pollution, habitat modification and over-fishing for pearls (Young & Williams 1983). The mussel is parasitic in its larval stage on the gills of fish, mainly salmonids, so changes in water quality which make a river unsuitable for these will affect mussel populations. *Margaritifera margaritifera* has recently been recommended by the NCC for addition to

Caithness

Berriedale	Few, small mussels present. Only known site in Caithness.

Sutherland

Borgie	Small numbers of small mussels remain.
Brora	Populations of mussels present.
Helmsdale	Overfishing has reduced the population.
Naver	Mussels common in some places.

Table 9

Catchments on peat with populations of pearl mussel *Margaritifera margaritifera* recorded since 1970.

Schedule 5 of the Wildlife and Countryside Act 1981 and for protection under the Bern Convention (see Chapter 18). At its session of July 1987 the European Parliament adopted a resolution that the habitats of the pearl mussel must be designated as protected sites.

Ten species of dragonfly have recently been recorded from the lochs, pools and streams of the Flow Country. This represents only a quarter of the British dragonfly fauna, a consequence of the natural decline in dragonfly diversity with increasing latitude. *Aeshna caerulea* (Figure 75) is a circumboreal species confined in Britain to acid pools and seepages in Scotland.

The caddisfly *Nemotaulius punctatolineatus* (Figure 76) was discovered breeding in inland *dubh lochain* in Blar nam Faoileag, a peatland SSSI in Caithness, in 1985 (Spirit 1987). This species is included in the Insect Red Data Book (Shirt 1987) and has previously been found in Britain only near Aviemore, in its adult stage.

The beetle *Oreodytes alpinus*, another Red Data Book species (Shirt 1987), was first discovered alive

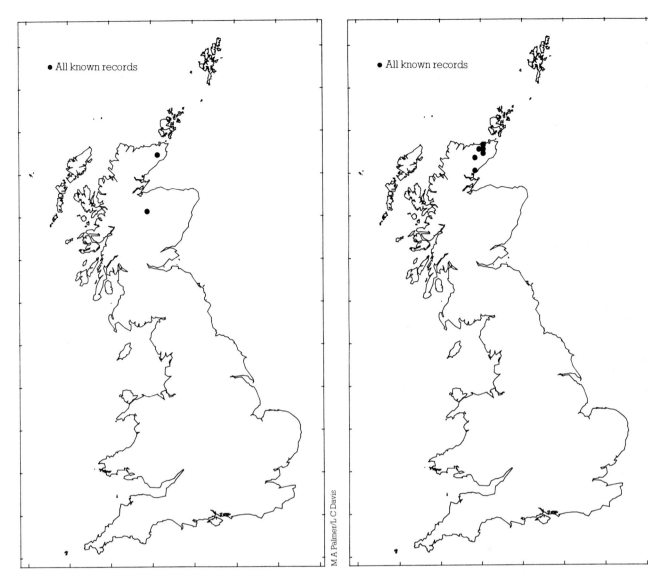

Figure 76 British distribution of *Nemotaulius punctatolineatus.*

Figure 77 British distribution of *Oreodytes alpinus.*

in Britain in 1985 (Foster & Spirit 1986). It was known previously in Britain only as a sub-fossil in glacial deposits. It also occurs in northern Scandinavia and Siberia and has now been recorded from two sandy lochs in Sutherland and several in Caithness (Foster 1987 and Figure 77). On the blanket bog itself, the most favourable type of area for water beetles is a lochan-studded plateau with a range of pools of varying size containing diverse vegetation. Such areas exist at the Flows of Leanas (ND 2648), the Knockfin Heights (NC 9133) and Druim na h-Uamha Moire (NC 2328). The whirligig beetle *Gyrinus*

opacus, which is uncommon in Europe as well as Britain, occurs at these sites. This beetle appears to need highly specialised conditions, preferring eroding lochans without inflows or outflows but with deep water relatively free of loose, floating peaty material (Foster 1987). *Gyrinus opacus* and a scarce diving water beetle, *Dytiscus lapponicus*, which was first found in Caithness in 1985 (Spirit 1987), are also relict arctic-alpine species, confined (apart from one Welsh record for the latter) to Scotland (Figures 78 and 79).

Rivers sampled		BMWP scores			
	Sampling stations	Spring	Summer	Autumn	Seasons combined
Forss Water	1	124	154	181	236
	2	182	117	206	245
Burn of	1	160	121	144	184
Latheronwheel	2	165	112	116	203
River Oykel	1	146	144	70	206
	2	181	120	42	202

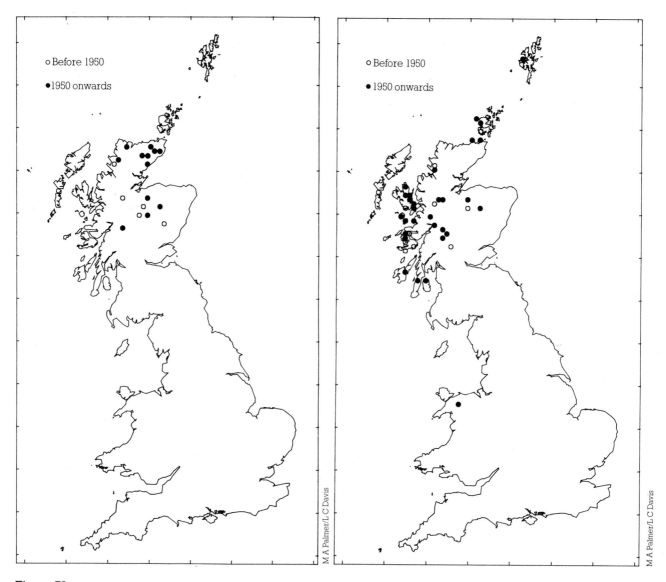

Figure 78 British distribution of *Gyrinus opacus*.

Figure 79 British distribution of *Dytiscus lapponicus.*

A survey of the invertebrate fauna of the Forss Water, Burn of Latheronwheel and River Oykel by the Freshwater Biological Association in 1986 showed that these rivers all contain a diverse fauna, typical of clear, upland rivers. Several uncommon insects were found (Table 8). The Biological Monitoring Working Party (BMWP) scores for sites on these rivers are given on page 125.

The BMWP score is calculated by allotting scores to a range of invertebrate families, according to their sensitivity to pollution, and totalling the scores for the families present in a sample. BMWP scores above

120 are unusual (National Water Council 1981), so it is clear that the rivers surveyed in Caithness and Sutherland are of high quality, especially the Forss Water.

Fisheries

Caithness and Sutherland have important freshwater fisheries, and rivers such as the Helmsdale, Shin, Thurso and Naver are famous for their game fishing. There have however recently been declines in catches on the Helmsdale and other rivers.

15   The impacts of afforestation on freshwater habitats

Afforestation of blanket mire has profound effects on the ecology of associated freshwater systems. The most evident harm occurs when small-scale pool systems are obliterated during ploughing and drainage or natural watercourses are straightened and deepened to form collecting drains. Even where associated freshwater habitat is not destroyed by direct means, it usually suffers fundamental modification. The evidence linking afforestation with changes in aquatic fauna illustrates one aspect of these indirect effects. For instance, Egglishaw, Gardiner & Foster (1986) have demonstrated a close relationship between declines in salmon catches and the afforestation of nursery stream catchments in Scotland.

The most important impacts on freshwater flora and fauna probably result from –

- physical changes (e.g. in run-off timing and quantity; erosion and sedimentation; degree of shading);
- nutrient enrichment (eutrophication);
- acidification;
- pesticide application.

Planting, tree growth and harvesting all have different effects on the hydrology, chemistry and biota of the freshwater system, and each phase can cause profound and destabilising change to the ecosystem.

Physical changes

Run-off

Drainage of peat soils immediately prior to afforestation frequently produces a "flashy" storm response, giving higher flood flows in streams and a reduction in times to peak (Robinson 1980). Later in the cycle, closed canopy forest intercepts much of the rainfall, which can cause a reduction in total run-off of 20–30%, as compared with conditions measured on open moorland (Hornung & Newson 1986), thereby creating prolonged droughts on the forest floor. Many stream invertebrates are adapted to restricted ranges of current velocity and cease to feed or are washed away during extreme spates. Salmonid eggs and fry are also likely to be washed out in such conditions. In streams which dry up or become sluggish, fish will be unable to breed successfully and the invertebrate faunas will be severely reduced or their community structures changed.

Sedimentation

Robinson & Blythe (1982) estimated that a drained peatland catchment suffered an erosion level of 120 tonnes per square kilometre in a five-year period, compared with losses of only 15 tonnes per square kilometre in the five year period prior to draining. Thus, sediment yields in the five years after drainage were equivalent to nearly half a century's natural sediment load. In that Northumberland catchment, draining resulted in an additional level of erosion amounting to 1.05 tonnes per hectare, with concentrations of suspended solids frequently exceeding 500 mg/l in stream water. Battarbee, Appleby, Odell & Flower (1985) reported a marked increase in sediment accumulation in four lakes with partly afforested catchments.

Mills (1980) offered useful guidelines to reduce sedimentation. Unploughed streamside buffer strips were suggested as a means of capturing sediments in an unmodified belt of vegetation and soil. However, research at Llanbrynmair in Wales has shown that the careful implementation of these guidelines failed to prevent a 246% increase in suspended stream sediment loads in one peatland catchment and a 479% increase in another after forestry ploughing (Francis 1987).

Even mature catchments can yield three to five times the volume of stream bed-load discharged from grassland (Newson 1980), probably because herb growth is suppressed and log-jams result in changes to stream-courses. During felling operations significant increases in suspended sediment yields have been measured (Leeks & Roberts 1986). The construction of forestry roads can also exacerbate sedimentation.

Hobbs (1986) points to the phenomenon of "rebound" when a load is removed from a peat body. This arises because the natural shape of the peat mass is distorted by the weight of any load placed on it. Thus, as the timber crop grows, it gains weight and acts as a considerable load, depressing the natural shape of the peat body. The extent of distortion varies with the general degree of humification in the original peat and also, clearly, the weight attained by the trees. When the trees are removed at harvesting, the rebound of the mire surface to something approaching its original shape can be significant and can also occur over a considerable period of time. There is thus the additional problem, at harvesting, of drain 'rejuvenation' caused by small but steady increases in surface gradients further contributing to increased run-off, scouring and sedimentation.

High concentrations of suspended solids limit light

penetration, thus reducing the rate of photosynthesis by aquatic plants. This, together with the settlement of silt on leaves, can kill submerged vegetation in streams and lakes. Blanketing of the stream bed reduces substrate diversity and makes conditions unsuitable for invertebrates adapted to life in stony lakes and gravelly reaches of streams. Filter-feeding molluscs such as the pearl mussel close their shells for prolonged periods in silty water. Their feeding and breathing mechanisms are impaired by heavy silt loads (Ellis 1936).

The gills of fish become inflamed at suspended solids loadings of only 100–270 mg/l (Alabaster & Lloyd 1980). Turbid water may reduce a fish's foraging efficiency. Egg survival is impaired in silt-laden streams because the gravelly spawning sites of salmonid fish become occluded by sediment, which reduces the oxygen supply. Alabaster & Lloyd (1980) have therefore suggested an upper safe limit of 25–80 mg/l suspended solids for salmonid fisheries. Such values are very frequently exceeded in watercourses draining afforested areas.

Shading

Dense shading of coniferous forest streams and pools prevents the growth of marginal vegetation. Reedswamp and shrubs are lost, whereas they would normally tend to stabilise banks, provide niches for invertebrates and give cover for fish. The diversity of both fauna and habitat is therefore reduced. A closed canopy can reduce the light reaching a stream bed to 10% of that in open environments (Smith 1980), an effect which has profound implications for aquatic plants and invertebrate community structures. Although aquatic invertebrate biomass may not be affected by afforestation, diversity can be reduced (Harriman & Morrison 1982). The biomass of invertebrates falling into the water from the surrounding land, another food source for salmonid fish, does, however, appear to be lower in coniferous forest than in deciduous woodland or moorland (S J Ormerod et al. unpublished).

Shading by coniferous forest has a strong moderating influence on stream temperature, and this affects the growth, distribution and life cycles of invertebrates and fish. Welsh stream water in a forested catchment was recorded as on average 2°C cooler in the summer and up to 1°C warmer in the winter than water in moorland catchments (Roberts & James 1972). Simulations of annual growth, based on water temperatures in Wales, have predicted that a 10-gramme fish would attain a weight 15% lower in an afforested than in a moorland stream (Ormerod, Mowle & Edwards 1986).

Nutrient enrichment

Afforestation on nutrient-poor soils is accompanied by the application of fertilisers containing rock phosphate. Often potassium is also applied, and sometimes nitrogen in the form of urea. Quite apart from the effects of fertiliser application, ploughing and felling can cause mobilisation of nutrients and lead to increased concentrations in drainage water.

Harriman (1978) estimated that 15% of the phosphorus in fertiliser applied to an afforested peatland was lost to streamwater. Malcolm & Cuttle (1983) measured nutrient losses to drainwater after fertilising unplanted drained peat. 16% of the phosphorus was lost over three years and they estimated that 25–30% would be lost to drainwater in five or six years. Experience at the Black Esk reservoir in north-east Dumfriesshire suggests that after an aerial application of rock phosphate to the catchment the raw water phosphorus increased from 0.002 mg/l to 0.06 mg/l over a six-month period and stabilised at 0.04 mg/l (Parr 1984). The 30-fold increase in phosphorus concentrations at this reservoir over the first six months following application was possibly due in part to the drift of phosphate directly into watercourses. However, the stabilised figure (a 20-fold increase) seems to reflect a longer-term leaching of fertiliser from soils.

When rock phosphate was applied to forests in the Cree catchment in Galloway during frosty weather, ensuing thaw and rain produced a river load of 321 kg of elemental phosphorus in one day, 25 times the normal level (Coy 1979). Even when fertiliser is applied in warmer conditions, rock phosphate releases phosphorus so slowly that the surface peat may retain a high proportion of this element for a lengthy period. When subsurface layers are frozen or saturated, rain or snow-melt will rapidly transport surface water to drains and natural streams.

Other eutrophication effects may stem from rapid oxidation and mineralisation of peat rather than applied fertiliser. Duxbury & Peverly (1978) reported significant losses of nitrogen after drainage of organic soils. Forest clearance can also affect water quality. In New Hampshire, for two years after clear-felling, nitrate-nitrogen concentrations in streams exceeded the level of 11.3 mg/l recommended by the World Health Organisation for drinking water (Likens, Bormann, Johnson, Fisher & Pierce 1970).

Nutrient enrichment of lakes in afforested catchments has led to blooms of planktonic and filamentous algae, especially nitrogen-fixing blue-green species and diatoms (Richards 1984). Dense algal blooms can lead to suppression of aquatic vegetation, loss of plant and invertebrate species diversity and sometimes fish-kills, owing to algal toxins or deoxygenation. Rivers and streams subject to enrichment will also experience enhanced productivity, which can manifest itself in an increase in epilithon (the film of bacteria, algae and other micro-organisms coating the surface of stones) and in populations of animals such as some mayfly species which graze the epilithon. Leaves decompose rapidly in nutrient-rich waters, so invertebrates which live on fine, decomposing organic matter will benefit. Filter-feeders, including biting blackflies (Simuliidae) which can be serious pests, and detritivores such as worms may increase in numbers, whereas "shredders", such as many of the stoneflies (Plecoptera), which live on coarse organic material, are disadvantaged (Hildrew, Townsend, Francis & Finch 1984). The eutrophication of lakes and streams can therefore cause fundamental changes in their flora and fauna.

Acidification

There is strong evidence that conifer plantations on upland, base-poor soils enhance the acidification of surface waters and increase concentrations of metals such as aluminium. In Wales, for example, streams draining forest blocks have a mean pH (hydrogen ion concentration) which is 0.5 to 1.0 units lower than similar streams draining moorland and aluminium concentrations 0.1 to 0.4 mg/l higher (Stoner, Gee & Wade 1984).

Coniferous tree crops increase the concentration of acidifying sulphur and chlorine compounds in soils and run-off by efficient "scavenging" from oceanic or polluted air (Bergkvist 1986; Reuss & Johnson 1986). Ammonia and compounds of nitrogen and oxygen (NO_x) are also efficiently captured by conifer needles and can contribute to the acidity of run-off, although they do not necessarily accumulate in soils. Further, a considerable proportion of incoming water passes over acidic bark as stem-flow. Enhancement of acidity by coniferous forest is partly related to the level of atmospheric pollution, which is relatively low in Caithness and Sutherland. However, as explained in Chapter 5, the peatlands of Caithness and Sutherland are very sensitive to acid deposition.

Ploughing and drainage cause the oxidation and mineralisation of previously anaerobic organic and inorganic soil components, resulting in the production of further hydrogen ions (Cresser & Edwards 1987). Trees also release hydrogen ions during the uptake of cations such as ammonium. Peats are not well buffered and can be expected to discharge more hydrogen ions than most mineral soils. All these processes may contribute to the increase in acidity of the water draining from afforested areas of blanket bog.

Aluminium is a major component of the mineral ash of peats (Gorham 1953a; Cuttle 1983). This originates both from mineral soil-water in peat and from atmospheric inputs (Peirson, Cawse, Salmon & Cambray 1973). However, such considerations may be almost irrelevant, because ploughing and draining almost always expose some aluminium-rich mineral soil to run-off. Owing to undulations in the bedrock and drifts below the peat, mineral soil is frequently exposed by ploughing as shallow as 45 cm. Drains at either 60 cm or 90 cm will, in the vast majority of cases, connect with patches of mineral soil, especially near mire margins and natural watercourses.

There is a close relationship between water chemistry and the composition of aquatic plant and animal communities. Many of the rarer aquatic plants, for instance *Potamogeton praelongus* and *Callitriche hermaphroditica*, are restricted to waters with a fairly narrow range of pH (Newbold & Palmer 1979). Such species are unlikely to survive in acidified waters. Invertebrate density may be higher in acidic streams draining coniferous forest than in their counterparts draining moorland, but diversity is reduced (Ormerod *et al.* 1986). Crustaceans (e.g. *Gammarus species*), mayflies and some caddisflies are intolerant of pH 5.7 or lower and of aluminium concentrations of more than 0.1 mg/l. These groups are often scarce in forest streams.

Low pH and high aluminium concentrations damage the gills of fish. Data from over 100 sites in upland Wales (Welsh Water Authority unpublished) indicate that salmonid densities are closely correlated with these factors. A review of the effects on fish of acidification associated with conifer forests is contained in *Nature Conservation and Afforestation in Britain* (Nature Conservancy Council 1986). The following examples are cited (pp. 40–41) –

• after afforestation, there has been a reduction in the catches of salmonids in the River Fleet in Galloway (Drakeford 1979, 1982);

• in the upper Tywi, trout are absent from many streams in afforested areas and the number of invertebrate species is less than half that in unafforested areas (Stoner *et al.* 1984);

• after afforestation there has been a decline in salmonids on Plynlimon (Newson 1985);

• salmon eggs and young trout translocated to plantation streams in the Loch Ard (Harriman & Morrison 1982) and upper Tywi areas (Stoner *et al.* 1984) respectively showed much poorer survival than in moorland streams;

• the failure to stock the Rivers Camddwr and Tywi above the Llyn Brianne reservoir with salmon and sea trout has been attributed to afforestation (Stoner & Gee 1985).

Common frog *Rana temporaria* tadpoles, like fish, are sensitive to low pH and high aluminium concentrations (Cummins 1986). Dippers *Cinclus cinclus* have declined since afforestation was carried out along the River Irfon in Wales. This bird is also scarce in other Welsh streams with pH levels below 5.7 and aluminium concentrations above 0.1 mg/l, probably because the invertebrate food is in short supply (Ormerod *et al.* 1986).

Pesticide application

Organophosphorus insecticides such as Fenitrothion have been used in Scotland against pine beauty moth *Panolis flammea* in lodgepole pine forests. After one dose, applied by aerial spraying, concentrations in rivers reached 18–48 μg/l and aquatic invertebrates were affected, as was obvious from the large numbers observed to be drifting downstream (Morrison & Wells 1981). The adult and flying stages of aquatic insects are also susceptible to such pesticides, and the use of these chemicals near the few lochs known to harbour the rare caddisfly *Nemotaulius punctatolineatus* and the rare water beetle *Oreodytes alpinus* could endanger the survival of these species in Britain. Adult dragonflies are especially vulnerable to pesticides because many hunt some way from the water in sheltered situations and are drawn in large numbers to forested areas adjacent to their breeding grounds.

Principles and criteria for selection

The conservation of freshwater habitats requires different emphases, compared with the treatment of terrestrial habitats. Basic to any measures for the protection of rivers and lakes is the need to consider the catchments concerned, for, if adverse changes occur that affect water here, they may nullify attempts to safeguard the confines of the open water bodies. A practical factor is that many of the lochs and rivers in Caithness and Sutherland remain unsurveyed, though it is possible to assign most of these to their broad ecological type by comparison with those for which there is adequate information. The principles of selection are again to give an adequate representation of the range of variation and to ensure that all major examples of rare freshwater types are chosen for protection. The criterion of naturalness is extremely important, in the sense of lack of pollution or disturbance to the hydrological regime. Because oligotrophic and dystrophic water bodies are naturally species-poor, diversity is not necessarily the most significant factor, and the important point is that fresh waters should be assessed according to the characteristics of their type (see Chapter 14).

Oligotrophic and dystrophic lakes and rivers are associated with acidic rock and peat-covered catchments in many parts of Britain and show considerable uniformity. While highly characteristic of the Caithness and Sutherland peatland catchments, they are less notable in their own right either nationally or internationally than the blanket bog systems themselves. They are, nevertheless, important and integral components of the total ecosystem complex, especially as bird habitats (Stroud et al. 1987), and it is essential to ensure that they are well represented within the peatland areas identified as important to nature conservation. This representation should include the full range of bioclimatic zones throughout which the open water habitats occur (see Chapter 4). The particular purpose of the freshwater survey has been to indicate the extra biological interest contained within the freshwater systems incidentally included within the peatland conservation areas and to identify further nationally important examples which need protection in addition, especially on grounds of catchment safeguard.

Choice of nationally important freshwater sites

Morgan & Britton, in A Nature Conservation Review (Ratcliffe 1977), list a series of freshwater sites throughout Great Britain which are nationally important for wildlife conservation. The following five are in Caithness and Sutherland –

Caithness:

Burn of Latheronwheel – eutrophic stream on sandstone
Loch Watten – eutrophic loch on sandstone

Sutherland:

Durness Lochs – four lochs on limestone
Loch Stack and River Laxford – oligotrophic waters, within an acidic rock and peat catchment
Loch Mhaolach-Coire and River Traligill – eutrophic loch and limestone river, with some blanket bog in the catchment.

Figure 80 shows lochs in Caithness and Sutherland notified for their intrinsic value, as distinct from their incidental occurrence as 'bonus' features in association with blanket bog. Apart from the NCR lochs listed above, there are only four lochs notified specifically for freshwater interest. These are three eutrophic lochs – Loch Scarmclate, Loch Heilen and Loch of Wester – and the oligotrophic Loch Glutt, all of them in Caithness.

The recent surveys of rivers and lochs have indicated that three other areas qualify as nationally important (NCR quality) freshwater sites. These are the Forss Water in Caithness, a cluster of three small lochs – Lochs Dola, Craggie and Tigh na Creige – in south-east Sutherland and Loch Brora, also in Sutherland.

The Forss Water is an outstanding example of an unspoilt river showing a transition from oligotrophy to mesotrophy. At the transition lies Loch Shurrery, which is a Site of Special Scientific Interest because of its fen habitat and birds. Several lochs in the catchment contain the rare relict water beetle Oreodytes alpinus.

Data from 1124 recently surveyed standing water sites throughout Britain are now held on computer by the NCC. Only 17 (1.5%) of these sites have 20 or more species of submerged and floating aquatic plants. Loch Dola, one of the few mesotrophic lochs in northern Scotland, is the fourth richest site in the data-base and the richest in Caithness and Sutherland, with 24 species. Seven additional species are present in the nearby oligotrophic waters Lochs Craggie and Tigh na Creige. These three lochs also contain the nationally scarce Callitriche hermaphroditica and Potamogeton praelongus. If emergent aquatic plants as well as floating and submerged species are included in the

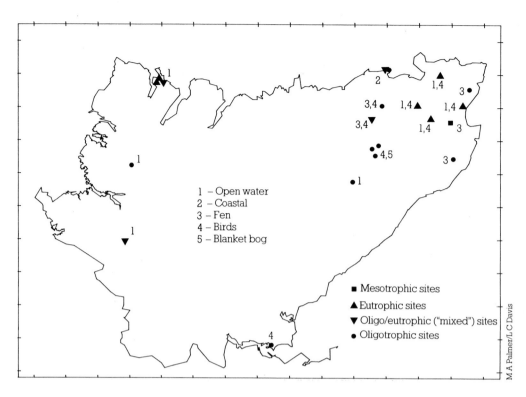

Figure 80 Existing SSSIs which are selected primarily or partly for their freshwater interest.

analysis, Loch Dola is the 13th richest site known to the NCC in Britain.

Loch Brora, despite its oligotrophic nature, has 21 species of open water plants and is the 16th richest of the 1124 sites for submerged and floating species. However, because of its interesting margins, Loch Brora is the 12th richest site in the national data-base if emergent plants are also considered. The loch contains two nationally scarce species, water sedge *Carex aquatilis* and least water-lily *Nuphar pumila*. *Oreodytes alpinus* is also abundant in Loch Brora. The unspoilt oligotrophic rivers upstream of the loch contain healthy populations of the pearl mussel; therefore there is considerable intrinsic interest in the catchment as well as in the loch itself.

Figure 81 shows the extent of the catchments of the existing NCR sites and of the three recently discovered sites which qualify for NCR status because of their freshwater interest. The figure shows that most of the land in the two largest catchments is of national importance either for peatland habitat or for wading birds (Stroud *et al.* 1987), and this combination of interests adds to its importance for wildlife.

Protection of nationally important freshwater sites

To give full protection to these eight nationally important sites, no further afforestation should be carried out in their catchments. This is particularly important in the areas most sensitive to acidification, which are the headwaters of the Forss Water, the

Brora catchment and Loch Stack and its outflow.

Since 1980, at least 90 km of the upper reaches of rivers in Wales have been downgraded in the river quality classification scheme because acidification has made them unsuitable for salmonid fish (Welsh Water Authority pers. comm.). In order to safeguard fisheries, the Welsh Water Authority has drawn up interim guidelines for acceptable levels of afforestation in river catchments lying in areas sensitive to acidification (Welsh Water Authority 1987). The guidelines recommend that, where the mean annual water hardness is less than 12 mg/l $CaCO_3$, plantations should not exceed 10% of the total river catchment subject to acidification (i.e. the catchment upstream of the point on the river having a mean annual hardness of 15 mg/l). Planting should be confined to small catchments drained by first-order streams having a negligible effect on the receiving watercourse. Wet deposited acidity over most of Wales is 0.03 g H^+/m^2/year or less, as it is in Caithness and Sutherland (United Kingdom Review Group on Acid Rain 1987; Warren Spring Laboratory 1987), so extrapolation of these guidelines to northern Scotland seems appropriate.

Data for total hardness of the Forss Water upstream of Loch Shurrery and for the River Brora above Loch Brora are not available. However, the Highland River Purification Board has measured hardness on the Lower Oykel, a river similar to the Brora. The mean hardness for 1986/87 on the River Oykel (at NC 4101) was 11.6 mg/l. Water analyses carried out in 1987, in connection with the NCC's loch survey, showed hardness in Loch Brora to be 11.76 mg/l and that of Glas Loch Beag, in the headwaters of the River

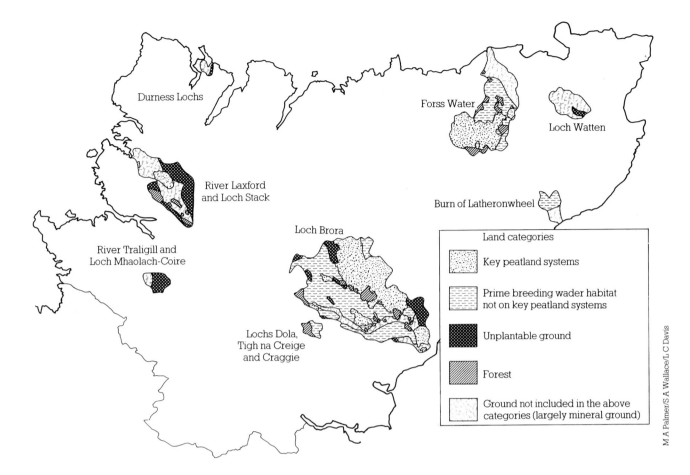

Figure 81 Catchments of nationally important freshwater sites.

Brora, to be 6.32 mg/l. Loch nan Clach Geala, near the headwaters of the Forss Water, had a hardness of only 5.94 mg/l.

Existing plantings are approaching 10% of the catchments of Loch Stack, the Brora and the Forss Water. Much of the catchment of Lochs Dola, Craggie and Tigh na Creige has already been afforested or is planned for planting. Hardness of these loch waters ranged from 15.9 to 18.56 mg/l in

1987, so they are better buffered than Loch Brora. However, effects such as eutrophication and increased sedimentation could be extremely damaging in this catchment, even if acidification is less of a threat. The potential degradation of one of the richest aquatic plant communities in Britain lends urgency to the need for tight protection in the River Brora catchment, as this is still relatively free of afforestation.

Part IV

17   The ornithological importance of the Caithness and Sutherland blanket bogs

This report has described the peatlands of Caithness and Sutherland principally in structural, hydrological and botanical terms. The blanket bogs are also of great ornithological importance, both nationally and internationally. This ornithological interest is fully described in the NCC's publication *Birds, Bogs and Forestry* (Stroud *et al.* 1987). So that the patterns of ornithological importance can be related to other features of conservation interest, this chapter summarises the main findings of that report.

General characteristics of the avifauna

The Caithness and Sutherland blanket bogs support a particularly varied northern type of bird fauna not found in identical composition elsewhere in the world. This includes several taxonomic/ecological groups – waders, other waterfowl, raptors and scavengers, passerines and a miscellany of other types.

There are particularly important breeding populations of golden plover, dunlin, greenshank and arctic skua. The lochs and smaller *dubh lochain* support breeding red-throated and black-throated divers, greylag geese, wigeon, teal, common scoters and red-breasted mergansers. Common and black-headed gulls nest in small colonies. Rare breeding waders include Temminck's stint, ruff, wood sandpiper and red-necked phalarope. Raptors such as hen harrier, golden eagle, merlin, peregrine and short-eared owl also use the bogs as breeding or feeding areas. Many of these species have their main distribution in sub-arctic and arctic areas, and the peatlands of Caithness and Sutherland have considerable ecological affinities with the arctic tundras.

Considerable bird populations are present (Table 10), although densities of individual species are often low. As described below, Stroud *et al.* (1987) estimated that some 4,000 pairs of golden plover, 3,800 pairs of dunlin and 630 pairs of greenshank breed on these peatlands.

The NCC's Moorland Bird Surveys

In 1979, the NCC launched a programme of breeding bird surveys of moorlands likely to be affected by afforestation. This particularly concentrated on Caithness and Sutherland (Stroud *et al.* 1987), where its aims were fivefold –

1 to identify, from sites surveyed, breeding bird assemblages of high nature conservation interest in terms of species diversity and population density;

2 to collect data to assess and identify habitat features important to the breeding birds and from these associations to predict the location of other areas of high ornithological interest;

3 to estimate the size of the populations of breeding birds (especially waders) dependent on the peat flows of Caithness and Sutherland;

4 to understand the effects that rapid changes – especially those resulting from afforestation – would have on these birds;

5 to make recommendations for the conservation of the bird assemblages of the Caithness and Sutherland peatlands.

To these ends, sample areas were surveyed in Caithness in 1979, 1980 and 1984 and in Sutherland from 1980 to 1986. Additionally to the NCC's survey work, the Royal Society for the Protection of Birds carried out other surveys in the same region between 1980 and 1986. In total, the NCC and RSPB surveyed waders on 77 sites (sample areas) in Caithness and Sutherland. The sites were chosen to include many examples of all the major peatland habitats within the total range of types occurring within Caithness and Sutherland. Full details of the methodology employed by the surveys are given by Stroud *et al.* (1987).

The results of these surveys demonstrated that the waders are outstanding in overall numbers and diversity, and the occurrence of at least 15 breeding species reflects the variety of peatland and open

Species	Arctic breeding species (Sage 1986)	Annex 1 species of EEC Birds Directive	Schedule 1 species of W & C Act 1981	Appendix 1 species of 'Bern' Convention	Estimated Caithness/Sutherland peatlands population (pairs)	Estimated British population (pairs)[1,2]	Percentage of British population in Caithness/Sutherland	Status elsewhere in EC	Percentage of EC population in Caithness/Sutherland	World distribution
Red-throated diver	★	★	★	★	150	1,000-1,200	14%	Absent	14%	Boreal—high arctic
Black-throated diver	★	★	★	★	30	150	20%	Absent	20%	Boreal—mid arctic
Greenland white-fronted goose	★	★			c. 200[3]	c. 9,500[3]	2%	9,300[3] (Ireland)	1%	W. Greenland/Britain/Ireland — restricted and localised
Grey heron		+				3,500-8,500		Scattered		Temperate Palaearctic — at N.W. limit of range
Greylag goose		+	★		c. 300	600-800	43%	Scattered	—[4]	Scattered — eastern continental to subarctic
Wigeon	★	+			80	300-500	20%	Absent	20%	Palaearctic
Teal	★	+				3,500-6,000		Widespread		Widespread — continental to low arctic
Mallard	★	+				40,000 +		Widespread		
Common scoter	★	+	★		30 +	75-80	39%	c. 100 (Ireland)	16%	Boreal—low arctic
Goldeneye		+	★			>40				
Red-breasted merganser	★	+				1,000-2,000		North only		Boreal—low arctic
Goosander		+				900-1,300				
Hen harrier	★	★	★		30	600	5%	Scattered	1%	Widespread
Sparrowhawk						15-20,000				
Buzzard						8-10,000		Widespread		Widespread
Golden eagle	★	★	★		30	510	6%	Scattered	<1%[5]	Widespread
Kestrel		+		★		30-40,000		Widespread		Widespread
Merlin	★	★	★	★	30	600	5%	Ireland only	4%	Boreal—low arctic — decreasing in numbers in Britain for reasons attributed to land-use change
Peregrine	★	★	★	★	35	730	5%	Scattered	<1%[6]	Widespread
Red grouse								L. l. scoticus elsewhere only in Ireland		Boreal—low arctic — British/Irish race decreasing throughout range
Black grouse						10-50,000				Northern coastal to low arctic
Oystercatcher	★	+				33-43,000		Mainly northern and coastal		Northern coastal to low arctic
Ringed plover	★	+		★		8,600		Scattered — northern coastal		Northern coastal to mid arctic
Golden plover	★	★			3,980	22,600	18%	<650 prs	17%	Boreal—mid arctic, but several distinct races: most of temperate population breeding in Britain
Lapwing		+			500	181,500	<1%	Scattered		Boreal—continental — Britain holding highest numbers in Europe
Temminck's stint	★	+	★	★	<10	<10	—	Absent	—	Montane boreal—low arctic
Dunlin	★	+		★	3,830	9,900	39%	<1,000 prs	35%	Boreal—mid arctic, but temperate population largely restricted to Britain
Snipe	★	+			c. 500 +	29,600	3%	Widespread but local		Boreal—low arctic arctic
Woodcock		+				8-35,000		Scattered		Boreal—low arctic: Palaearctic to N. India
Ruff	★	★	★		<10	10-12	—	Local in Low Countries: c. 2,000 prs	—	Temperate—boreal—low arctic
Curlew		+			500	33-38,000	1%	<10,000 prs	1%	Mid continental—subarctic
Redshank		+			100	32,100	<1%	Scattered		Widespread — continental, mainly northern
Greenshank		+	★		630	960	66%	Absent	66%	Boreal to edge of low arctic — mainly natural forest bogs in Fenno-Scandia
Wood sandpiper	★	★	★	★	<10	1-12	—	c. 150 prs	—	Boreal to edge of low arctic
Common sandpiper		+		★	500	17-20,000	3%	Scattered		Widespread — continental to low arctic

Species	Arctic breeding species (Sage 1986)	Annex 1 species of EEC Birds Directive[1]	Schedule 1 species of W & C Act 1981	Appendix 1 species of 'Bern' Convention	Estimated Caithness/Sutherland peatlands population (pairs)	Estimated British population (pairs)[2]	Percentage of British population in Caithness/Sutherland	Status elsewhere in EC	Percentage of EC population in Caithness/Sutherland	World distribution
Red-necked phalarope	★	★	★	★	<10	19-24	—	Absent	—	Montane boreal—low arctic
Arctic skua	★	+			60+	2,800+	2%	Absent	2%	Boreal—high arctic
Black-headed gull		+				120-220,000		Widespread but scattered		Continental—boreal
Common gull	★	+			c. 4,000	40,000	10%	Scattered		Northern continental to low arctic
Great black-backed gull		+				22,000		Scattered and localised — Ireland/France/Denmark		Coastal — North Atlantic
Lesser black-backed gull		+				70,000+		Scattered — coastal		Continental coastal to low arctic
Short-eared owl	★	★		★	50	1,000+	5%	Widespread	4%	Widespread
Skylark		+				2 million		Widespread		Widespread
Meadow pipit	★	+				1-1.5 million		Widespread		Widespread—continental—subarctic
Grey wagtail		+		★		15-40,000				
Pied wagtail		+		★		300,000				
Dipper				★		20-25,000		Scattered — subalpine		Widespread — sub-montane— subarctic: declines in highly afforested areas attributed to acid run-off
Whinchat		+		★		15-30,000				
Stonechat		+		★		20-40,000				
Wheatear	★	+		★		60,000		Widespread		Widespread
Ring ouzel		+				6-12,000		Subalpine/alpine		Alpine to boreal—subarctic
Sedge warbler		+		★		200,000				
Hooded crow						1 million				
Raven						4,000				
Twite		+		★		15-30,000				

1 Species marked ★ are listed on Annex 1 of the EEC Directive on the Conservation of Wild Birds as requiring special protection measures, particularly as regards their habitat under Article 4(1). Species marked + are migratory and require similar habitat protection measures under Article 4(2).
2 This excludes the whole of Ireland.
3 Individuals.
4 EC population uncertain owing to unknown proportion of feral birds in other populations. The population in north-west Scotland is the only one thought to be natural, owing to separation from others.
5 Most of the EC population is of the south European race *homeyeri;* Britain holds all of the EC population of the nominate race, 6% of which occur on the Caithness and Sutherland peatlands.
6 Most of the EC population consists of the Mediterranean race *brookei;* Caithness and Sutherland peatlands hold 5% of the EC population of the nominate race.

Table 10

Population and distribution data for birds occurring on the peatlands of Caithness and Sutherland.

water habitats. Golden plover, dunlin, greenshank and curlew occur with high constancy in the sample areas and so have large total populations within the region (see below). Common sandpiper and snipe are also widespread and numerous, but several species are somewhat local – lapwing, oystercatcher, redshank and ringed plover.

The overall density of waders at different sites varied considerably (Figure 82). In Caithness, densities for all breeding waders ranged from 0.9 to 14.0 pairs/km², and in Sutherland from 0.2 to 14.3 pairs/km². The overall mean density of breeding waders was 5.4 pairs/km², but this excluded steep, montane and other areas unsuitable for waders as explained by Stroud *et al.* (1987). The number of breeding waders found on any one site varied between one and ten.

Densities of individual species varied widely according to the differing ecological conditions of the sites. These are summarised and explained in more detail elsewhere (Stroud *et al.* 1987).

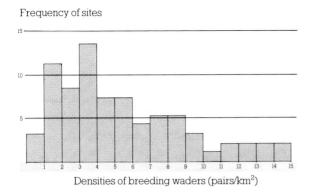

Frequency of sites

Densities of breeding waders (pairs/km²)

Figure 82 The total density of breeding waders on surveyed sites in Caithness and Sutherland.

Overall distribution and numbers of peatland birds in Caithness and Sutherland

Only about one fifth of the peatlands of the region has been surveyed in detail by the standard method employed. Yet the 77 plots surveyed, covering 51,929 ha (Table 11: 19% of the remaining area suitable for breeding waders), required 433 separate visits during 22 man-summers of fieldwork over the period 1979–1986. There are obviously considerable logistical and financial constraints to surveying the remaining 81% of the peatlands to the same standard. A major aim of the analysis in *Birds, Bogs and Forestry* was thus –

- to find out if there were consistent relationships between breeding bird densities and habitat features recognisable on standard Ordnance Survey maps;

- to use any such associations, in combination with information on such habitat features derived from the maps, to predict the ornithological quality of the unsurveyed areas;

- to examine the further possibility of using such associations between breeding densities and map attributes to estimate the total bird populations found in each habitat category and in the total peatland area;

- to enable pre-afforestation maps to be used to assess the previous ornithological quality of land now afforested and, from this, to estimate the reductions in populations, on the same principle as that used for estimating the present populations.

Population estimates and losses of blanket bog waders

Using habitat preferences shown by waders in Caithness and Sutherland (Table 12), Stroud *et al.* (1987) derived four categories of "landform". These landforms combine ecological features of importance to waders and physical features identifiable from map evidence. As such they describe identifiable patterns of structural variation across the peatlands.

Category	Area (ha)	Category as percentage of land area
Total area of Caithness and Sutherland	764,094	100%
Ancient, semi-natural and long-established woodland	12,204	1.60%
Forestry plantations	73,046	9.56%
'Improved' agricultural land and human settlements	104,090	13.62%
Fresh water (minimum area)	25,170	3.29%
Land too steep/high for moorland waders (including some high-altitude blanket bog) and coastal areas	279,484	36.58%
Remaining area of blanket bog currently suitable as breeding habitat for moorland waders*	270,100	35.35%
Total moorland surveyed (included in last category)	51,929	6.80%

* The area of peatland recorded as suitable habitat for breeding waders does not equate to the full extent of blanket bog. There are considerable areas of steep, high-altitude blanket bog that are not considered suitable breeding habitat.

Table 11

Land-use and ornithological survey in Caithness and Sutherland.

	Vegetation type							Vegetation height			Vegetation age			Wetness			
	Trichophorum/Myrica mire	Calluna/Eriophorum mire	Juncus flushes	Dry Trichophorum	Dry Calluna sward	Grass patches	Mosaic of vegetation types	<10cm	10-20cm	>20cm	Young	Medium	Old	Pool/dubh lochan complexes	Bog	Damp	Dry
Golden plover	+	+	●	−	−	●	●	+	+	+	+	●	●	+	+	+	●
Dunlin	+	+	●	−	−	−	●	+	●	−	+	●	●	+	+	●	−
Greenshank	+	●	−	−	●	−	+	+	●	−	+	+	●	+	+	+	+
Curlew	−	−	+	−	−	●	+	+	+	+	+	●	−	−	−	+	●
Snipe	−	−	+	−	−	+	+	+	+	+	+	−	−	−	●	+	−
Redshank	−	−	+	−	−	+	+	+	+	+	+	●	−	−	−	+	−

Key: + preferred
− avoided
● no obvious trend

Habitat preferences of breeding waders on moorlands in Sutherland. Updated from Reed & Langslow (1987). Habitat preferences encompass all the summer activities during the breeding season and include habitats selected for their feeding, nesting and young rearing potential. The surveys did not aim to locate nests, they have tended to record birds in their most visible locations, often at or near feeding places.

The features used in formal identification of categories from maps are given in Table 13, and the following descriptions amplify these in relation to what can be seen on the ground.

Category A comprises the very wettest areas of peat, with numerous pool complexes and extensive *Sphagnum*-dominated flows set in a bog-covered landscape. Maps show high densities of *dubh lochain* clustered into obvious pool complexes, but there are also scattered larger lochans. The ground is either virtually flat or gently sloping, with no steep gradients. There are few, if any, rocky outcrops and no crags are shown on the maps.

Category B consists of sloping blanket bog with pools and is drier. There is a low density of pools, set more or less discretely on gentle slopes, and the ground consists of gentle ridges and watersheds but is not flat. Rocky outcrops and drier morainic features, whilst not numerous, can be evenly spaced across wide areas. There are often numerous larger lochs within the landscape. The blanket bog communities are drier and less *Sphagnum*-dominated than in the previous category, and the surface vegetation is often eroded into gullies. These are either natural or are caused by overgrazing or by severe fires which expose often extensive areas of bare peat.

Category C is that of steeper and more broken ground. Here the gradients are steeper, with no substantial areas of pools or *dubh lochain*. The ground is often highly eroded, with few, if any, wet *Sphagnum*-dominated areas. Rocky outcrops and dry morainic features are abundant. Podsolic and gley soils with shallow peat surface horizons prevail, rather than true blanket peat. The vegetation tends to have *Trichophorum cespitosum*, *Molinia caerulea* or *Calluna vulgaris* dominant and is of the type characterised as 'wet heath' or, in the driest situations, acidic dwarf shrub heath.

Category D is the steepest ground, with screes, outcrops, crags, high montane watersheds and summits with fell-field and shallow montane blanket bog. This was considered to be unsuitable habitat for most moorland waders. Because of the very low wader densities found during preliminary work in these steep moorland and rocky areas, sample plots generally excluded such areas, and it does not form part of the analysis.

Stroud *et al.* (1987) found that each landform

Category	Dubh lochans	Streams	Lochs	Topography	Gradients
A: Pool complexes and wet *Sphagnum* flows	High density of pools and dubh lochans clustered in obvious pool complexes. Usually at least one pool complex or marsh symbol per 1 km². Pool complexes with more than 10 pools per complex.	Few streams, with none issuing from watershed mire pool complexes.	Scattered larger lochs, usually with gently curved edges indicating peaty banks.	Flat, open and obviously boggy.	Gently sloping to flat, with very low gradients. Generally less than five 25-ft contours crossed per 1 km² diagonal at 1:25,000.
B: Sloping blanket bog with pools	Low density of pools set more or less discretely. Pools less than 10 per complex, or less than one complex per 1 km².	More streams, often branched into dendritic drainage systems hillsides.	Larger lochs often numerous and irregular in shape.	Gentle ridges and watersheds.	Generally low gradients, but sloping gently — not flat. Usually from five to 12 25-ft contours crossed per 1 km² diagonal at 1:25,000.
C: Steeper and broken ground	No marsh symbols or dubh lochans marked on 1:25,000 map. Very few, if any pools.	Streams and waterfalls down steep slopes.	Few large lochs, although sometimes surrounded by steep banks.	Hillsides and broken or rough ground indicated on map.	Gradients steeper: more than 13 25-ft contours per 1 km² diagonal at 1:25,000.
D: Montane and other unsuitable areas	None.	Linear, with many waterfalls and streams descending steep slopes.	Small lochs usually in corries, often steeply embanked.	Mountainous, with considerable areas of bare rock/scree shown on map.	Very steep slope, usually more than 25 25-ft contours per 1 km² diagonal at 1:25,000.

Table 13

Features used in categorisation of the Caithness and Sutherland peatlands into four landforms for estimation of breeding wader populations. Landforms were assessed from 1:25,000 maps.

category held differing densities of breeding waders. The validity of using these landform types to estimate numbers and densities of breeding waders was demonstrated in a series of detailed statistical tests, expained more fully in their report. The conclusions drawn from these tests were that –

- the categories of peatland (Table 13) are real and reflect identifiable habitat types;

- it is possible to identify these categories on the basis of map evidence alone.

This has important implications, since it means that the quality of bird habitats of the whole area of blanket bog of Caithness and Sutherland outside survey sites can be assessed.

The total area suitable for breeding waders was divided into three of the four landform categories, as described by Stroud *et al.* (1987). The area of each of the three landform categories was then calculated, and multiplying by the average densities for each category provided population estimates for the peatlands of Caithness and Sutherland. Stroud *et al.* (1987) give the detailed calculation of these totals in their Table 4.5. The distribution of these different areas across the Caithness and Sutherland peatlands is shown in Figure 83.

Golden plover

A total of 3980 pairs of golden plovers is estimated to breed on the remaining unplanted peatlands in Caithness and Sutherland. The total British breeding population is estimated at about 22,600 pairs (data collated for Piersma 1986); thus the Caithness and Sutherland peatlands hold some 18% of British breeding golden plovers and 17% of the breeding population within the European Communities' territories (Table 10).

The breeding distribution shows that golden plovers avoid agricultural land in the extreme north-east of Caithness and have a strong affinity for peatland. Unlike dunlin and greenshank, golden plover densities are often greater on slightly eroded peatlands where there is an even spacing of small hags and hillocks. The highest densities coincide with the area of greatest forestry expansion (Stroud *et al.* 1987), thus giving a potential for further severe losses if afforestation of peatland habitat continues at its current rate.

Dunlin

A total of 3830 pairs of dunlins is estimated to breed in Caithness and Sutherland. Thus Caithness and Sutherland hold about 39% of the British breeding population of 9900 pairs and 35% of the European Communities' breeding population (Table 10). The highest breeding densities in Caithness and Sutherland show close agreement with the extensive wet areas of peatland. This species is thus one which would be directly and significantly affected by loss of further peatland habitat in Caithness and Sutherland.

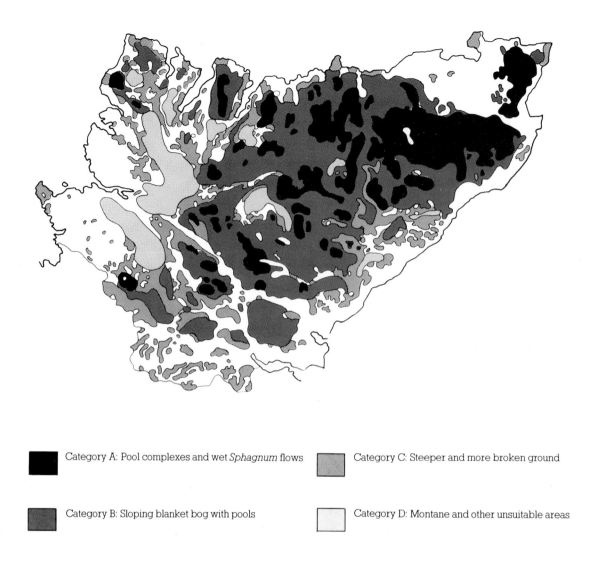

Category A: Pool complexes and wet *Sphagnum* flows

Category C: Steeper and more broken ground

Category B: Sloping blanket bog with pools

Category D: Montane and other unsuitable areas

Figure 83 Extent and quality of habitat for breeding moorland waders on the Caithness and Sutherland peatlands, shown as the landform categories of Table 13.

Greenshank

A total of 630 pairs of greenshanks is estimated to breed in Caithness and Sutherland on landform categories A, B and C. The total British breeding population is currently estimated at 960, with most of the remainder being in Ross and only small numbers breeding elsewhere (Sharrock 1976). Thus Caithness and Sutherland hold about 66% of the British (and therefore the European Communities') breeding population of this species (Table 10).

Although greenshanks are widespread in the extreme west of Sutherland (Nethersole-Thompson, D. & M. 1979), the habitat here is fragmented and discontinuous because of interruption by unsuitable high mountains. In Caithness and east Sutherland the breeding habitat is much more continuous. Greenshanks avoid the agriculturally modified land in the north and east of Caithness and are strongly associated with peatlands throughout both Districts.

Losses of peatland birds

The methods used to estimate the quality of breeding habitat and hence the overall numbers of breeding waders on existing moorland can also be used to estimate the losses of these on areas recently afforested. The areas of recent planting and land released for planting were superimposed on earlier, pre-afforestation Ordnance Survey maps and the quality of lost peatland habitats assessed according to the four landform categories of Table 13. It was then calculated that 912 pairs of golden plovers, 791 pairs of dunlins and 130 pairs of greenshanks once used moorland occupied or planned to be occupied by plantations (see Figure 26). On this basis, the original, pre-afforestation populations for the Caithness and Sutherland peatlands can be calculated to have been 4900 pairs of golden plovers, 4620 pairs of dunlins and 760 pairs of greenshanks. There has thus been an actual or predictable loss of 19% of golden plovers, 17% of dunlins and 17% of greenshanks as a direct effect of afforestation. It has not been possible yet to estimate the losses of other breeding bird species, but many can be presumed to have been affected.

Some of the Caithness and Sutherland peatland birds which occur widely in the British uplands have already lost a good deal of ground elsewhere, through the widespread afforestation of their habitats on both blanket bog and drier moorland. These losses are almost certain to continue through still further afforestation, so that the Caithness and Sutherland populations of affected species will become an increasing proportion of the British totals – unless afforestation continues here, too, at the present rate.

The numbers of other peatland breeding birds

The previous section has shown that it is possible to estimate numbers of golden plover, dunlin and greenshank based on their characteristic association with certain habitat and landform types. For the other peatland birds there are varying difficulties in estimating total population size, previous losses to afforestation or areas which are especially important. For some of the rare species and those favouring localised habitats which are shown on, and therefore easily located from, detailed maps (e.g. pool systems, larger lochs or crags), there are already counts of a large proportion of the total population. Special surveys of arctic skua, black-throated diver, peregrine and golden eagle have given good census information about total breeding numbers.

Other species are patchily distributed according to the occurrence of specialised habitats which are not readily identifiable from maps (e.g. snipe, ringed plover and redshank), and yet others are evidently widespread but elusive (e.g. merlin and short-eared owl). The rarest species, especially of waders, are extremely difficult to find, and in such a large area it is unlikely that all breeding pairs have been discovered. The 77 surveyed sites may give a reasonable sample from which the total numbers of some of these other species could be estimated within broad limits, but there is no means yet of testing such an assumption.

Summary of the ornithological interest

The outstanding features of the ornithological interest of the Caithness and Sutherland peatlands are the high species diversity and the large populations of breeding waders. No fewer than 15 species of waders are known to nest in the region and these include 66%, 39% and 18% of the total British breeding populations of greenshank, dunlin and golden plover respectively. There is a wider ecological spectrum of breeding birds, including waterfowl, raptors and passerines, than for any other moorland area in Britain. Important fractions of the total British breeding populations of other species are as follows – red-throated diver (14%), black-throated diver (20%), greylag goose (wild stock – 43%), wigeon (20%), common scoter (39%), hen harrier (5%), golden eagle (6%), merlin (5%), peregrine (5%), common gull (10%) and short-eared owl (5%).

Rare and local species are well represented, there being three species (Temminck's stint, ruff and wood sandpiper) each with 1–10 pairs nesting in Britain, two species (common scoter and red-necked phalarope) with 10–100 pairs nesting in Britain and seven species (black-throated diver, greylag goose, wigeon, hen harrier, golden eagle, merlin and peregrine) with 100–1000 pairs nesting in Britain.

For 11 species, the area contains significant fractions of the total EC breeding populations, as follows – red-throated diver (14%), black-throated diver (20%), wigeon (20%), common scoter (16%), hen harrier (1%), merlin (4%), golden plover (17%), dunlin (35%), greenshank (66%), arctic skua (2%) and short-eared owl (4%).

Several species have declined and/or are still declining elsewhere in Britain – wigeon, buzzard, golden eagle, merlin, red grouse, golden plover, dunlin, snipe, curlew, greenshank, red-necked phalarope and raven. Some of these have already been reduced in numbers through afforestation in other districts as well as in Caithness and Sutherland.

Many of the above species are mainly or wholly northern European (boreal–arctic) in distribution and depend in the rest of their range on naturally treeless open wetlands and tundras. Britain supports the southernmost populations of these birds because of the large extent of open moorland resembling these more northern habitats. Caithness and Sutherland are an especially favourable area for this bird assemblage because the conjunction of climate and topography have given large areas of wet blanket bog, with a wide variety of associated open water habitats which simulate tundra. Some of the characteristic breeding birds of northern tundra are different, however, the goose tribe being represented in Caithness and Sutherland only by the greylag and the whimbrel being replaced by the curlew, so that the precise combination of species is not exactly replicated anywhere else in the world.

In the winter the region remains important for several scarce or local bird species. The peatlands are used as feeding habitat and roosting sites by internationally significant numbers of Greenland white-fronted geese. Golden eagles and hen harriers stay to hunt the moors, and the red grouse population is resident.

Part V

18 The amalgamation of different conservation interests in the Caithness and Sutherland peatlands

by Dr D A Ratcliffe, Chief Scientist

The overlap of different interests and relevance of the ecosystem concept

The high degree of interest and, hence, the requirements for conservation of blanket bog, open waters and birds in the region overlap considerably and so are mutually reinforcing. Many parts of the peatlands have high combined interest, but this is not always so. While there is a general correlation in quality between certain structural/vegetational and ornithological features, an overall conservation case based on the one would fail to take adequate account of the other. There should not, moreover, be any presumption that an area rating highly for only one interest provides an insufficiently strong case for conservation action.

While survey and evaluation have been approached in a compartmental way, dealing with different interests separately, this is an artificial procedure adopted for pragmatic reasons. A reductionist approach to conservation is usually unsatisfactory, because the ecosystem is more than the sum of its parts. The ecosystem represents the totality of nature, in the functional interdependence of the many physical and biological components and the complexity of their relationships. The ecosystem should thus be the basis of conservation concern.

Unless some attempt is made to define its physical limits in a real situation, the "ecosystem" nevertheless remains an abstraction. In the case of the Caithness and Sutherland peatlands, the central habitat type, blanket bog, is inseparable from open water habitats, varying from pools to lochs and from rills to rivers. The association with other mire types (especially soligenous and valley mires), wet heaths and dry, often rocky heaths is also close and usually lacking in clear boundaries. We are dealing with a moorland ecosystem complex as an entity which equates with a geographer's concept of "landscape"

Conservation practice should, as a principle, aim to maintain the wholeness of such an ecosystem complex. In upland areas generally, conservation should attempt as far as possible to safeguard topographic units consisting of all the catchments which drain from a main watershed, down to the limits of enclosed farmland below. On low moorlands, with mainly gentle relief, it is usually more difficult to define topographic units than in high mountain country, and the areas involved are sometimes large.

The present impact and future portents of afforestation

By 1987, 67,000 ha (17%) of the original peatland area had been planted or programmed for planting, causing a direct loss of habitat through the ecological transformation involved. This overall figure does not convey how afforestation has fallen extra heavily on some of the best flow areas for peatland and ornithological interest. Beyond this direct impact, plantations can create severe and unnatural breaches of the topographic and ecosystem integrity mentioned above (e.g. Stroud *et al.* 1987, pp. 7, 80 and 88). The direct competition between conservation and recent afforestation has meant that areas of high peatland interest now frequently adjoin plantations and in some cases have even been lost since they were surveyed. Figure 84 indicates the distribution of surviving sites of national significance in relation to established or approved planting schemes. The more haphazard and unplanned the location of planting, in regard to non-forestry considerations, the more disruptive it tends to be in conservation impact. Most of the main peat-dominated river catchments in Caithness and Sutherland now contain some plantation forest (33 out of 41 in 1987). There are extremely worrying portents for overspill effects beyond the forest edge, adversely affecting peat structure and chemistry, hydrology and water chemistry, vegetation composition, breeding performance of birds and invertebrate populations (Chapters 6, 15 and 17; see also Stroud *et al.* 1987). Both the direct and the indirect impacts of afforestation (including overspill and edge effects) need a good deal more research

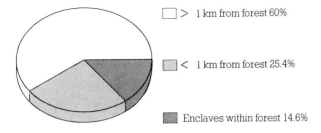

> 1 km from forest 60%

< 1 km from forest 25.4%

Enclaves within forest 14.6%

Figure 84 Sites identified as valuable for nature conservation by the NCC's Peatland Survey, classified according to their location relative to existing or programmed plantations.

before they can be fully understood and taken into account.

In March 1987 the Government confirmed and, indeed, extended its policy and provisions in support of an expansion of upland afforestation in Britain, though accepting that environmental considerations must be taken into account. It therefore has to be supposed that all plantable land within the Caithness and Sutherland peatlands is vulnerable to afforestation unless it is specifically protected to maintain the existing nature conservation interest (see Ogilvie 1986). Even where present landowners do not favour forestry, there is no guarantee against such land-use change in the longer term. From present practice, it can also be assumed that planting would mostly occur up to the exact boundary of any conservation areas and that its methods – and therefore its effects – would be substantially the same as those currently used. Even where a conservation designation is applied to open peatland, maintenance of existing nature conservation interest on areas adjoining forest cannot thus be assured.

National and international value

These may be summarised as follows –

National value:

● the large area and diversity of blanket bog as a physiographic/vegetation feature and the relative lack of disturbance in many places, giving the greatest extent of actively growing mire in Britain and one of the few areas of extensive natural terrestrial vegetation now remaining;

● the extensive development of patterned mire as a feature rare in British bogs elsewhere, and the great variety shown by these pool and hummock systems;

● the wide range of mire plant communities and their relationship to fields of variation in bioclimate, edaphic conditions and land-use influences;

● the abundance of certain rare or local bog plant species;

● the greater diversity of the breeding bird assemblage than that of moorland and bog elsewhere in Britain;

● the large total numbers of many bird species, treated as percentages of their total British populations (Table 10), and the consideration that some of these species are declining elsewhere and will continue to do so, especially as a result of afforestation;

● the presence of several nationally rare breeding bird species;

● the predicted equivalence of interest relating to habitats (mainly open waters) and groups (especially invertebrates) not yet fully surveyed.

International value:

● one of the largest and most intact known areas of blanket bog (a globally rare ecosystem type) in the world;

● a northern tundra-type ecosystem in a relatively southerly geographical and climatic location, by reason of the extreme oceanicity of the northern Scottish climate;

● development of unusually diverse systems of patterned surfaces on blanket bog, whereas elsewhere in the world, though analogous patterns occur, they are on different forms of mire;

● a floristic composition of blanket bog and associated wet heath vegetation unique in the world and representing a highly Atlantic influence on plant distribution and vegetation development;

● a tundra-type breeding bird assemblage showing general similarity to, but specific differences from, that occurring on arctic–sub-arctic tundras;

● significant fractions of the total breeding populations of certain bird species in Europe and particularly in the territories of the European Communities (Table 10);

● insular ecological and other adaptations by several bird species which may represent incipient evolutionary divergence in Britain.

In essence, the outstanding importance of these peatlands, both nationally and internationally, lies in their total extent, continuity and diversity as mire forms and vegetation complexes and in the total size and range of species composition of their bird populations.

The total peatland area which should be conserved

The crucial question remaining is about how much of the total peatland area now left in Caithness and Sutherland is of national and international conservation importance. The needs for conservation of peatland hydromorphological and vegetation interest have been presented in Part II, those for freshwater interest in Part III and those for ornithological interest summarised in Part IV. The factors considered above underline the great difficulty in trying to delineate isolated units of peatland of high quality which will satisfy the need to represent adequately the total field of interest and at the same time ensuring that the units will be individually viable and secure from gradual loss of interest. Because the Caithness and Sutherland peatlands are a *continuity* of subtle variation on a scale unique in Britain and indeed in the world, such a quest for a representative series of exemplary sites (see Chapter 13) would miss the essential point. This selective approach, adopted in *A Nature Conservation Review* and in the normal process of choice of sites for designation as Sites of Special Scientific Interest, is not appropriate, given the particular circumstances of the region as recorded by full survey information, knowledge of the international dimension and an evaluation of the losses that have already occurred through afforestation.

While there is still a premium on the protection of topographic/landscape units and catchments which have little or no forest, this also would be insufficient to meet the overall need for conservation of all interests within this ecosystem complex. This is because such catchments alone have only a small fraction of the total valuable extant peatland and the important bird populations. Some 67,000 ha of this outstanding natural heritage have already been, or will be, lost, and any further losses will represent a continuing depletion of its nature conservation value both to Britain and to the world. To protect its unique diversity and quality and its important bird populations, the whole remaining peatland expanse should be conserved. The recommended area for nature conservation is thus obtained by adding together the three maps, for peatland hydromorphology and vegetation (Figure 68), fresh waters (Figure 81) and ornithology (Figure 83), to give the composite Figure 85, which includes "unplantable" land and totals 365,310 ha. Of this, 73,946 ha of peatland have been notified or are proposed as Sites of Special Scientific Interest. Land already planted or already programmed for planting is not included in these totals. Figure 86 shows the same information, but with "unplantable" land removed to highlight the "plantable" area. This vulnerable area totals 256,534 ha, but, within this, 28,722 ha of peatland have already been notified or are proposed as SSSIs, so that the area of importance which remains undefended against further afforestation is 227,812 ha.

The maintenance of the nature conservation interest over the peatlands is largely compatible with the traditional land-uses, which include crofting, game-management and fishing. Greater regulation of moor-burning and avoidance of further moor-gripping are desirable. Peat-cutting from trenches and baulks in present locations is quite acceptable on its present scale, for it has had little impact on the main peatland areas. More extensive and mechanised peat-cutting could cause problems, but the peat resources of the area are such that, with careful planning and management, some development could take place without appreciably damaging nature conservation interests.

Claims and responsibilities for international designations will be considered briefly. Beyond this, the present report does not discuss the possible formal conservation measures which might be applied as safeguards.

International implications

Stroud *et al.* (1987) have discussed the international importance of the Caithness and Sutherland peatlands in relation to overseas opinion and the requirements which stem from international treaties concerning nature conservation to which the United Kingdom is a party. Only the main points of this discussion will be summarised here.

In September 1986, the International Mire Conservation Group visited the region and concluded that the blanket bogs of northern Scotland were "unique and of global importance", but expressed dismay at the extent and rate of their destruction by afforestation.

The Bern Convention on the Conservation of European Wildlife and Natural Habitats requires the promotion of "national policies for the conservation of wild flora, wild fauna and natural habitats, with particular attention to endangered and vulnerable species . . . and endangered habitats". Article 4 especially concerns conservation of endangered habitats and those important to breeding migratory species. The Caithness and Sutherland peatlands are especially relevant to these provisions.

The Ramsar Convention on Wetlands of International Importance especially as waterfowl habitat requires contracting parties to promote the conservation of listed protected wetlands and gives eight criteria for assessment of international importance of wetlands for listing. The Caithness and Sutherland peatlands are exceptional in meeting all eight of these criteria.

The EEC Directive on the Conservation of Wild Birds requires that Member States give special attention to protection of the habitats of certain listed birds which are rare, vulnerable or otherwise needing particular attention and that similar measures are taken over other regularly occurring migratory species. The Caithness and Sutherland peatlands have 11 of the species listed in Annex 1, and most of the other breeding species of the area require habitat protection because they belong to the second, migratory group.

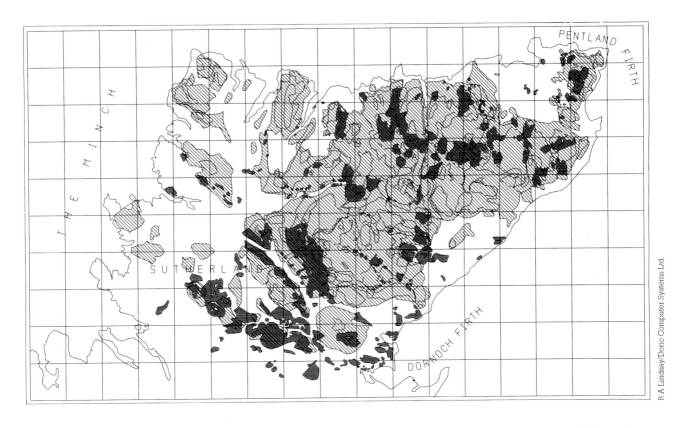

Figure 85 Total area recommended for nature conservation, on the basis of "key" peatland systems and ornithological and freshwater interests. The extent of land already afforested or programmed for planting is shown by dark shading. Freshwater catchments lying entirely off the peat are not shown.

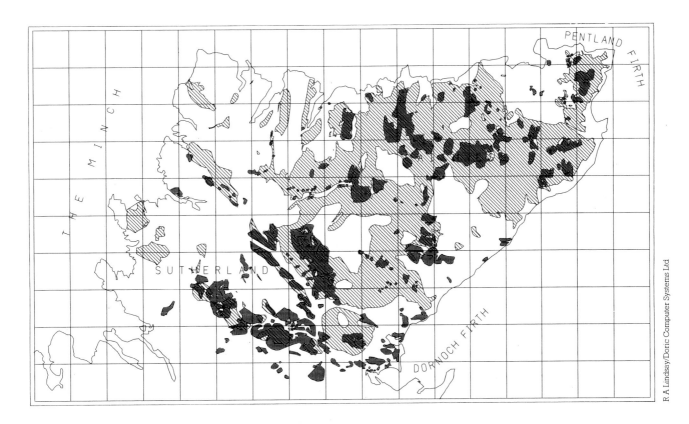

Figure 86 Total recommended area for nature conservation, on the basis of "key" peatland systems and ornithological and freshwater interests, within the "plantable" zone. Land classed as "unplantable" by the Forestry Commission has been excluded. Land already afforested or programmed for planting is shown by dark shading. Freshwater catchments lying entirely off the peat are not shown.

The World Heritage Convention requires each State Party to nominate a list of "cultural and natural properties" which it considers to be of "outstanding universal value" against a set of carefully defined criteria. The peatlands of Caithness and Sutherland meet all three criteria for "natural heritage" and all four of the criteria for a natural heritage property of "outstanding universal value" (Clause 24), as well as fulfilling necessary conditions of integrity. Indeed, of all natural or semi-natural ecosystems occurring in Britain, this one comes closest to uniqueness on the world scale and appears especially well qualified for World Heritage listing.

This makes it clear that the international importance of the Caithness and Sutherland peatlands is lifted beyond mere opinion, in meeting specific criteria defined under all four of these formal international treaties. This is a factor needing careful consideration in reaching a domestic conservation strategy for the area.

A final reflection

During recent years, a great deal of concern has been expressed over the past losses of natural and semi-natural habitat and its wildlife in Britain. Many of these losses took place during earlier periods before nature conservation was conceived – notably the destruction of the great forests and the fenlands before 1800 AD. The post-1940 inroads into the coastlands, chalk grasslands, lowland heaths, moorlands, old hay meadows, marshes and hedges and the pollution of lakes and rivers mostly occurred in response to national need or before effective legislation and adequate knowledge existed. The area of the Caithness and Sutherland peatlands already lost to forestry – most of it since the passing of the Wildlife and Countryside Act 1981 – represents perhaps the most massive single loss of important wildlife habitat since the Second World War. Every effort must be made to prevent further losses.

Annex

1 Vegetation and small-scale patterning

As part of the programme for the NCC's revision of its guidelines for the selection of biological Sites of Special Scientific Interest, a number of sites, taken from the main areas of peatland distribution in Britain, were selected for detailed survey between 1982 and 1985. The survey methods were designed to identify geographical trends in both mire surface pattern and vegetation and to determine whether any relationships existed between these two features. As part of this survey, seven sites in Caithness and Sutherland were examined.

In order to illustrate the range of detailed surface patterning within and between sites across Caithness and Sutherland and the distribution of vegetation types within these, data from five of the sites are presented here. These transect profiles are merely examples of the range of microtopography

	D.1	D.2	D.3	D.4	D.5
Cladonia arbuscula	I				
Cladonia impexa	III*				
Arctostaphylos uva-ursi	IV*			I	
Bare peat	V*	III*	I	I	
Sphagnum tenellum	I		I		
Hypnum cupressiforme	IV*	IV*	I		
Calluna vulgaris	V*	V*	II		
Eriophorum vaginatum	IV		II	I	
Erica tetralix	IV	I	III	I	
Trichophorum cespitosum	I		I	I	
Pleurozium schreberi		II	I		
Sphagnum rubellum	III	I	V*	II	
Eriophorum angustifolium	II	V*	V*	IV*	
Empetrum nigrum		V*	III	I	
Plagiothecium undulatum		I	I		
Narthecium ossifragum	I	I	IV	I	I
Aulacomnium palustre		I	II		
Hypogymnia physodes			I		
Hylocomium splendens			I		
Listera cordata			I		
Rhytidiadelphus loreus			I		
Vaccinium oxycoccos			I		
Acrocladium stramineum			I		
Odontoschisma sphagni			I		
Drosera rotundifolia			I	I	
Drosera anglica			I	I	
Polytrichum commune			I	I	
Sphagnum papillosum			II	IV*	I
Sphagnum cuspidatum			I	V*	
Menyanthes trifoliata			I	II	I
Sphagnum auriculatum			I	I	
Open water					V*
Eleocharis multicaulis			I	II	
Wet bare peat			I		IV*

Table 14a

Synoptic table for Dubh Lochs of Shielton. Constancy values are indicated in Roman numerals. High abundance is indicated by an asterisk.

and vegetation patterning, to show how the two interact and to emphasise the way in which pattern and vegetation change from east to west across the two Districts. The full range of variation is much greater than is shown by these examples and should be a major element in determining the scope of a mire protection programme.

Methods of survey and analysis

Transect lines were used as the standard sampling method on each site in the hope that the scale of pattern for both vegetation and microtopography would emerge from the study, rather than be imposed by the sampling method. Kershaw (1973) stated that transects with contiguous quadrats are most appropriate for sampling within small-scale environmental gradients. The method had been used to some effect by Godwin & Conway (1939) on Cors Tregaron in Wales.

Like Godwin & Conway, the NCC surveyors took 10 cm squares as the basic mapping unit, but these lay contiguously within a transect of 0.5 m x 2 m. Five transects were taken from each site and were placed so as to sample as wide a range of microtopography as possible. The relative abundance of each vegetation type and zone in the microtopography within the transect did not therefore reflect the overall abundance on the site.

Species were recorded on a three-point scale – Dominant, Common, Rare – within each 10 cm square, and the height of each square was noted (± 0.5 cm) relative to an arbitrary datum. Stereo-photographs were taken of each transect. The vegetation records were then analysed by using TWINSPAN (Hill 1979), and the resulting noda were mapped onto a representation of the transect grid. The TWINSPAN noda were recombined up the hierarchy until the distribution of noda on the transect corresponded with any vegetation pattern discernible on the stereo-photographs; i.e. the final noda existed in a recognisable form in the field. The details of the noda for each site were drawn up into a synoptic table with the use of a computer spreadsheet.

The height data for the transects were then plotted on the transect grid. The range of heights for each nodum and its mode were recorded. The location of the average water table, which is the single most important limiting factor within the microtopography, was taken to be represented by the upper limit of vegetation noda characterised by *Sphagnum*

	S.1	S.2	S.3	S.4	S.5	S.6
Sphagnum imbricatum	V*			I		
Arctostaphylos uva-ursi		I				
Cladonia gracilis		I	I	I		
Cladonia impexa		V*	II			
Racomitrium lanuginosum		I	I			
Pleurozium schreberi			III			
Aulacomnium palustre			I			
Cladonia uncialis			I			
Bare peat	IV*	III	I	II	I	
Calluna vulgaris	V*	V*	V*	III	I	I
Sphagnum rubellum	V*	I	IV*	III	I	
Erica tetralix	II	III	IV*	II	I	
Drosera rotundifolia	III	I	II	II	I	I
Hypnum cupressiforme			I	I		
Menyanthes trifoliata	II		I	I	I	
Mylia anomala			I	I		
Narthecium ossifragum	II	II	III	III	I	I
Trichophorum cespitosum	I	I	I	I	I	
Pleurozia purpurea	I		I	I		
Eriophorum vaginatum	IV*	III	III	II	I	
Betula nana			I	I	I	
Eriophorum angustifolium	II	V*	III	III	III	I
Sphagnum tenellum			II	II	I	I
Sphagnum papillosum	II	I	I	V*	II	
Drosera anglica	I			II	I	I
Sphagnum magellanicum			I	I	I	I
Eleocharis multicaulis			I	I		
Sphagnum cuspidatum	I			III*	V*	IV
Sphagnum auriculatum					I	I
Wet bare peat					I	V*

Table 14b

Synoptic table for Strathy Bog. Constancy values are indicated in Roman numerals. High abundance is indicated by an asterisk.

148

	C.1	C.2	C.3	C.4	C.5	C.6	C.7
Cladonia arbuscula							I
Mylia taylorii	IV	I					
Carex pauciflora	III	II					I
Sphagnum rubellum	V*	V*	II	I	V*	I	
Eriophorum vaginatum	III	IV*	II	I	II		I
Carex dioica		I			I		
Pinguicula vulgaris			I				
Cladonia uncialis	I		II		I		
Cladonia impexa	II	I	V*	I	I		
Hypnum cupressiforme			I		I		
Calluna vulgaris	V*	IV*	V*	II	IV*	I	I
Sphagnum magellanicum	III	III			II		I
Drosera rotundifolia	III	II	I	I	IV	I	I
Bare peat	I	I	V*	II	III		
Narthecium ossifragum	IV*	IV	V*	V*	I	II	
Potentilla erecta		I		I			
Racomitrium lanuginosum	I		V*	III*		I	
Sphagnum papillosum	I	V*	I	III*	V*	I	I
Sphagnum tenellum	I	II		I	III		I
Erica tetralix	I	I	II	II	IV	I	I
Pleurozia purpurea			I	III		I	
Trichophorum cespitosum			IV*	III	I	I	I
Molinia caerulea		I	I	V*		I	I
Polygala vulgaris			I	I		I	
Myrica gale			I		II		II
Molinia litter		I		II	I	II	
Drosera anglica		I		I	I	I	I
Drosera intermedia					I		I
Eriophorum angustifolium	I	I	II	II	III	III	IV*
Menyanthes trifoliata				I		I	
Sphagnum auriculatum				I		II	
Carex limosa						III	
Potamogeton polygonifolius						II	
Wet bare peat				I	I	V*	V*
Sphagnum cuspidatum		I			II		III*
Amorphous peat							II

Table 14c

Synoptic table for Loch Bad a'Choille. Constancy values are indicated in Roman numerals. High abundance is indicated by an asterisk.

cuspidatum, a good indicator of the transition from aquatic to terrestrial conditions in British mires. This upper limit for each site was taken as the factor necessary to correct the arbitrary height data to heights relative to the average water table.

Small-scale vegetation and surface patterns in Caithness and Sutherland

Tables 14a–e provide synoptic results for each of the five sites. Figures 87a–j present the data for each transect as a three-dimensional surface plot, generated by PC-Surfplot, and as a graph of ranges and medians for the vegetation noda. By using the combined information obtained from the synoptic tables and surface plots, the noda were provisionally assigned to associations described by Birse (1984) or Dierssen (1982). In the main surface plot in each

figure, the noda or associations are mapped onto the 10 cm squares which make up the transect grid. The smaller surface plot shows the distinction between aquatic and terrestrial conditions within the transect. The graph of ranges and medians combines information from two of the five transects from each site, selected arbitrarily, and distinguishes between the height ranges for any nodum which occurs on both transects. The vertical scale for all such graphs has been standardised for the entire range of transects. The height range of one transect can therefore be compared directly with that of another, though the five height range graphs are also displayed together in Figure 88 to make comparison easier.

Dubh Lochs of Shielton

The most easterly of the sites, this shows a clear northern boreal influence in its vegetation. The

	F.1	F.2	F.3	F.4	F.5	F.6	F.7
Potentilla erecta	I						
Hypnum cupressiforme	IV		I				
Racomitrium lanuginosum	III*		I				
Cladonia impexa	V*	II	I				
Bare peat	III	I	II				
Pleurozium schreberi	I	I					
Calluna vulgaris	V*	IV	IV*	I	I		
Sphagnum rubellum	III*	V*	V*	III	I	I	
Sphagnum subnitens	I	II	I		I		
Myrica gale	II	II	II		I	I	
Erica tetralix	IV*	IV*	III	I	II		I
Odontoschisma sphagni	I	II	I		I		
Eriophorum vaginatum	I	I	I		I		
Drosera rotundifolia	I	IV	II	III	I		
Molinia caerulea	IV	II	III	I	II	I	I
Cladonia uncialis	I	I	I		I		
Sphagnum magellanicum	I	III	V*	IV	III	I	I
Narthecium ossifragum	I	II	V*	I	III	I	
Sphagnum tenellum	I	III	V*	II	IV*	I	
Cephalozia connivens			I		I		
Trichophorum cespitosum	I	I	II	I	II	I	
Pleurozia purpurea	I	I	I		III	I	
Sphagnum papillosum		II	I	V*	IV*	II	
Eriophorum angustifolium	III	III	I	III	IV*	IV*	I
Sphagnum compactum					I	I	
Rhynchospora alba		III	I	IV	IV*	III	I
Menyanthes trifoliata	I	II	II	I	II	I	II
Wet bare peat					I	I	
Drosera anglica		I		I	II	II	I
Sphagnum cuspidatum		I		I	IV*	V*	V*
Sphagnum auriculatum					I	III*	II
Open water					II	V*	
Carex limosa					I	I	II
Amorphous peat				I	I	II	V*
Molinia litter				I	I	IV	
Eleocharis multicaulis							II

Table 14d

Synoptic table for Blar nam Fear Mhora. Constancy values are indicated in Roman numerals. High abundance is indicated by an asterisk.

broad T2 high ridges are dominated by dwarf shrubs, though with a *Sphagnum* understorey, and a range of hypnoid mosses such as *Hylocomium splendens, Rhytidiadelphus loreus* and *Hypnum cupressiforme* can be found within the moss layer. *Arctostaphylos uva-ursi* occurs on high hummocks and across some high ridge areas towards the margin of the site. This species has been taken as an indicator of continental affiliations (Goode & Ratcliffe 1977), but, as it is regarded as a woodland species in Fennoscandia, the relationship is not entirely clear.

The lack of both *Molinia caerulea* and *Racomitrium lanuginosum* is an important feature, as is the presence of *Eleocharis multicaulis* in the A1 hollows and deep A3/A4 pools. The site is one of the few for *Vaccinium microcarpum* in the two Districts.

The extreme height range of the site can be seen in Figures 87a–b, where the wide T2 ridges possess a relatively uniform vegetation cover and the deep watershed pools drop away with very little marginal vegetation.

Strathy River Bog

Described by Pearsall in 1956, this is one of the classic sites of British mire ecology. The small valleyside flow is dominated by crescentic hollows which are much shallower than the deep watershed pools of the Dubh Lochs of Shielton. Figure 87c illustrates a cross-section of such an A2 mud-bottom hollow, in contrast to an A1 *Sphagnum* carpet, whereas Figure 87d demonstrates the gradual transition from T1 low ridge dominated by *Sphagnum papillosum* down to *S. cuspidatum* A1 carpet. A *S. imbricatum* T3 hummock is illustrated in Figure 87c.

Arctostaphylos uva-ursi occurs in small amounts, but it is joined by the characteristic shrub of northern boreal mires, *Betula nana*. Here it is within the central part of its distribution. The site lies near the transition between the Erico-Sphagnetum magellanici and the Pleurozio-Ericetum tetralicis, indicated by the small amounts of *Racomitrium lanuginosum* and *Pleurozia purpurea* in the sward.

	AF.1	AF.2	AF.3	AF.4	AF.5	AF.6	AF.7	AF.8	AF.9
Hylocomium splendens	I								
Sphagnum fuscum	V*								
Pleurozium schreberi	II			I					
Empetrum nigrum	V*	V*	II	V*					
Eriophorum vaginatum	III	I	II	I	I	I			
Drosera rotundifolia	III		II	I	I	II			
Sphagnum subnitens			II						
Rhytidiadelphus loreus	I			II					
Erica tetralix	IV		III	III	III	II		I	
Hypnum cupressiforme	I		I	V*	I				
Racomitrium lanuginosum	I	V*	I	II	IV*	I			
Eriophorum angustifolium	II	I	III	III	III	III		I	
Cladonia uncialis			I		I	I			
Cladonia impexa	I	I	II	II	III	I			
Sphagnum rubellum			V*	II	II	III		I	
Bare peat		I	I	V*	IV*	I			
Calluna vulgaris	II		V*	I	IV*	IV*	I		
Carex pauciflora			I	I	I				
Trichophorum cespitosum	I	I	I	IV*	III	IV	I	IV*	I
Narthecium ossifragum	I	I	IV*	IV	V*	V*	I	III	I
Pleurozia purpurea				I	V*	II			
Sphagnum tenellum			III	I	II	IV		IV*	I
Mylia anomala					I	I			
Sphagnum papillosum			I		II	V*	I	II	
Drosera anglica					I	II	I	III	
Wet bare peat					I	I	V*		
Menyanthes trifoliata						I	I	I	I
Carex limosa						I	IV	I	I
Sphagnum cuspidatum					I	I	II	IV	III
Sphagnum auriculatum						I	III	I	I
Amorphous peat					I	II	V*	V*	
Open water									V*

Table 14e

Synoptic table for Allt an Fhaing. Constancy values are indicated in Roman numerals. High abundance is indicated by an asterisk.

Loch Bad a' Choille

This site is an example of the mire type identified as ladder fen and described in Chapter 9. The hollows are typical mud-bottom ones, with dominant bare peat and a scatter of aquatic *Sphagna*, but the slight minerotrophic element in the site is indicated by the presence of *Potamogeton polygonifolius*. Similarly, the ridges indicate an enhanced level of enrichment by the presence of *Carex dioica* and, to a lesser extent, *C. pauciflora*, *Molinia caerulea* and *Pinguicula vulgaris*.

The relative abundance of *Molinia*, *Pleurozia purpurea* and *Racomitrium lanuginosum* confirms the ridge communities as facies of the Pleurozio-Ericetum tetralicis, though some ladder fen ridges are more closely related to the Campylio-Caricetum dioicae.

The relatively small-scale relief, typically consisting of no more than T2, T1 and A2 (high ridge, low ridge and mud-bottom), is clearly seen on the surface plots and the graphs of height ranges (Figures 87e–f).

Blar nam Fear Mhora

This is the most westerly of the examples, lying within the line of the Moine Thrust mountains and 10 km east of Lochinver, a major west coast fishing port. The small-scale relief of this site is in complete contrast to the microtopography of the Dubh Lochs of Shielton, although the immediate appearance of many of the A2/A3 pools is very similar to that in parts of the Dubh Lochs. The wide, open water pools are in fact relatively shallow, as indicated by Figure 87h. The dense mixture of detritus and *Molinia* litter produces a matrix which, though not capable of supporting the weight of a man, can form a firm base into which species such as *Carex limosa*, *Eleocharis multicaulis* and *Rhynchospora alba* can root. This type of pool bottom is common in hyperoceanic areas, and the influence of accumulated *Molinia* litter within pools on the Silver Flowe is discussed by Goode (1970).

The presence of *Potentilla erecta*, *Molinia caerulea*, *Pleurozia purpurea* and *Rhynchospora alba*, together with hummocks of *Racomitrium*

Figure 87 Surface plots for sites listed in Tables 13a–e indicating – (a) distribution of individual vegetation associations within the 2 m × 50 cm transects, together with (b) the location of the average water table through the transect, and (c) the median and range of heights for each association. Associations which occur in two transects on the same site are indicated as separate records in the graph of heights (c). Surface and water table plots generated by Surfplot.

Figure 87a

Dubh Lochs of Shielton Transect 1

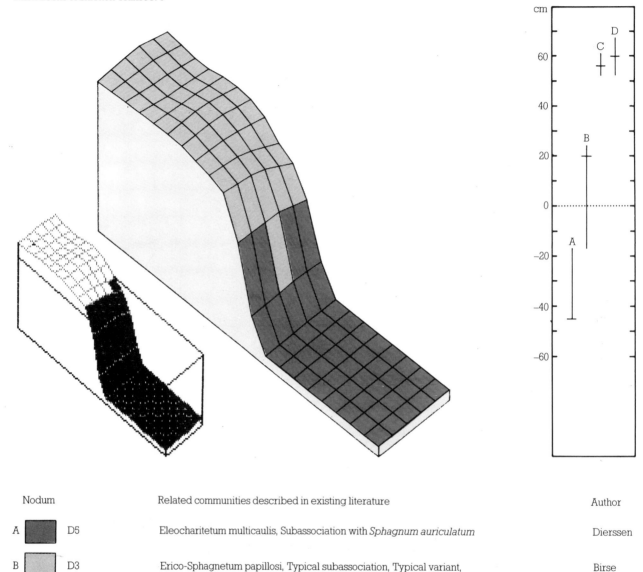

Nodum			Related communities described in existing literature	Author
A		D5	Eleocharitetum multicaulis, Subassociation with *Sphagnum auriculatum*	Dierssen
B		D3	Erico-Sphagnetum papillosi, Typical subassociation, Typical variant, Subvariant with *Empetrum nigrum*	Birse

lanuginosum not linked to erosion or damage, typifies the mire vegetation of western Sutherland, contrasting strongly with that of eastern Caithness. Indeed, the vegetation is more closely related to that found in the Hebrides (Goode & Lindsay 1979; Lindsay *et al.* 1983) or western Ireland (Boatman 1960).

Allt an Fhaing

This site is included to demonstrate some of the effects of damage and erosion on vegetation and microtopography. It lies on the flood plain of the Allt

an Fhaing and has a surface pattern consisting largely of erosion features, though some small areas remain relatively intact.

The highest level in the pattern is occupied by *Sphagnum fuscum* hummocks. Though regarded as important features because *S. fuscum* is fast becoming an endangered species in Britain, such hummocks are typically the slowest part of the original surface pattern to be lost when erosion produces a lowering of the average water table. This is because hummock species are more adapted to long drought periods and can therefore tolerate the effects of drawdown in the water table more easily

152

Figure 87b

Dubh Lochs of Shielton Transect 4

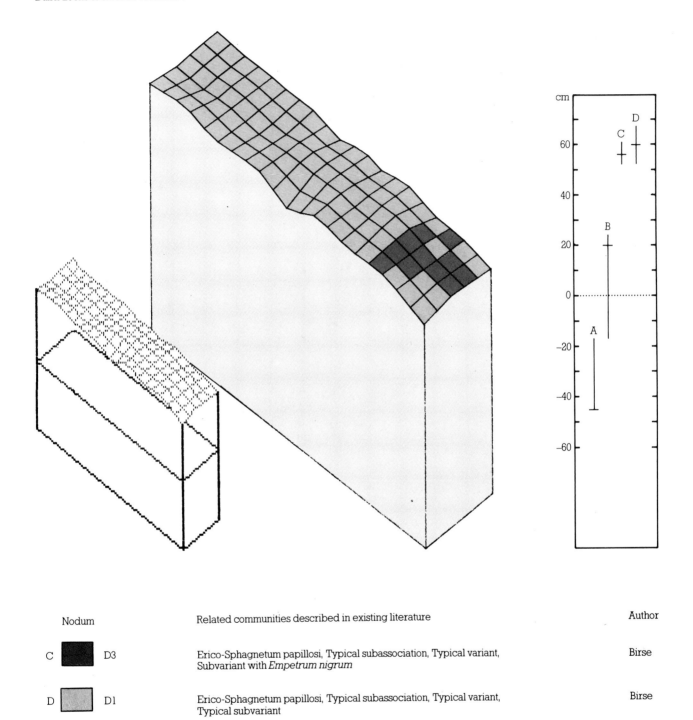

	Nodum		Related communities described in existing literature	Author
C	▨	D3	Erico-Sphagnetum papillosi, Typical subassociation, Typical variant, Subvariant with *Empetrum nigrum*	Birse
D	▨	D1	Erico-Sphagnetum papillosi, Typical subassociation, Typical variant, Typical subvariant	Birse

Figure 87c

Strathy Bog Transect 2

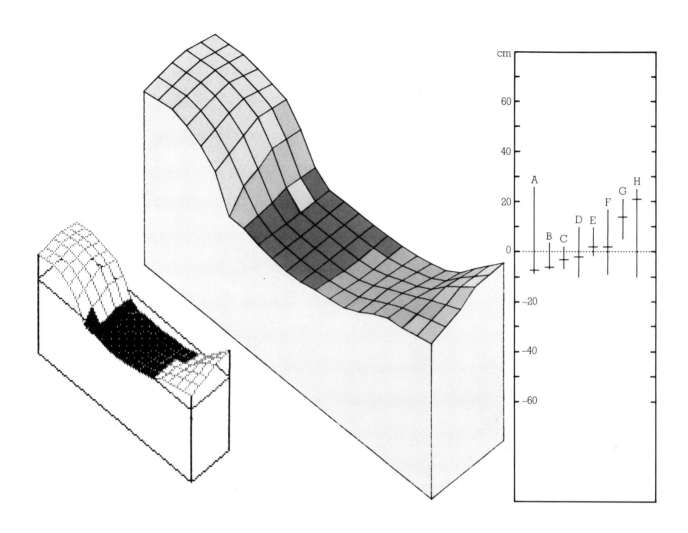

Nodum		Related communities described in existing literature	Author
A	S6	*Eriophorum angustifolium*, Subassociation with *Sphagnum cuspidatum*	Dierssen
D	S5	*Eriophorum angustifolium*, Subassociation with *Sphagnum cuspidatum*	Dierssen
F	S4	*Eriophorum angustifolium*, Subassociation with *Sphagnum cuspidatum*	Dierssen
H	S1	Erico-Sphagnetum magellanici, Typical subassociation, Phase with *Sphagnum imbricatum*, Typical variant	Dierssen

Figure 87d

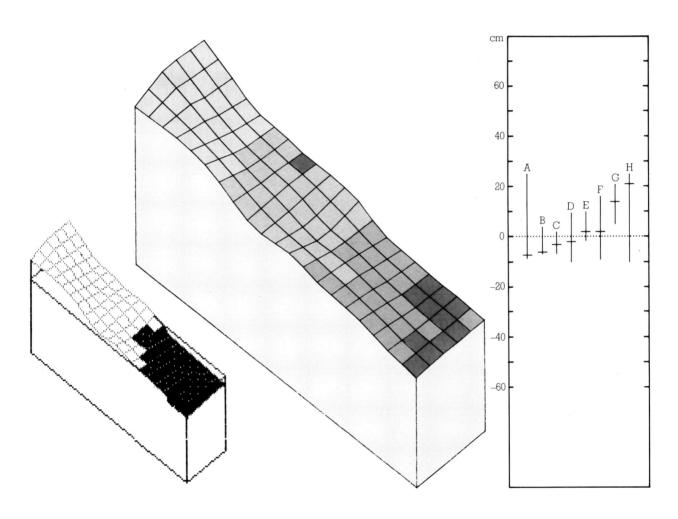

Nodum			Related communities described in existing literature	Author
B		S6	*Eriophorum angustifolium*, Subassociation with *Sphagnum cuspidatum*	Dierssen
C		S5	*Eriophorum angustifolium*, Subassociation with *Sphagnum cuspidatum*	Dierssen
E		S4	*Eriophorum angustifolium*, Subassociation with *Sphagnum cuspidatum*	Dierssen
G		S3	Erico-Sphagnetum magellanici, Subassociation with *Cladonia uncialis*, Typical variant	Dierssen

Figure 87e

Loch Bad a'Choille Transect 1

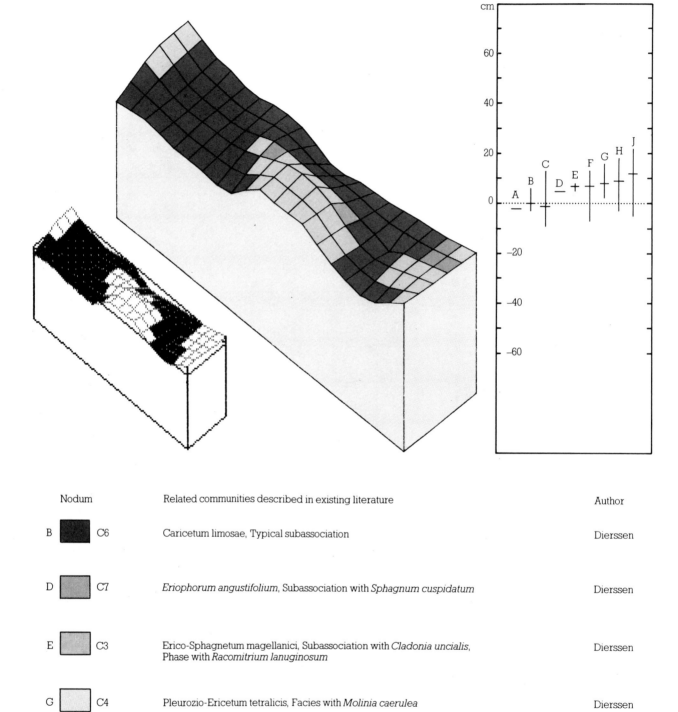

Nodum		Related communities described in existing literature	Author
B	C6	Caricetum limosae, Typical subassociation	Dierssen
D	C7	*Eriophorum angustifolium*, Subassociation with *Sphagnum cuspidatum*	Dierssen
E	C3	Erico-Sphagnetum magellanici, Subassociation with *Cladonia uncialis*, Phase with *Racomitrium lanuginosum*	Dierssen
G	C4	Pleurozio-Ericetum tetralicis, Facies with *Molinia caerulea*	Dierssen

Figure 87f

Loch Bad a'Choille Transect 4

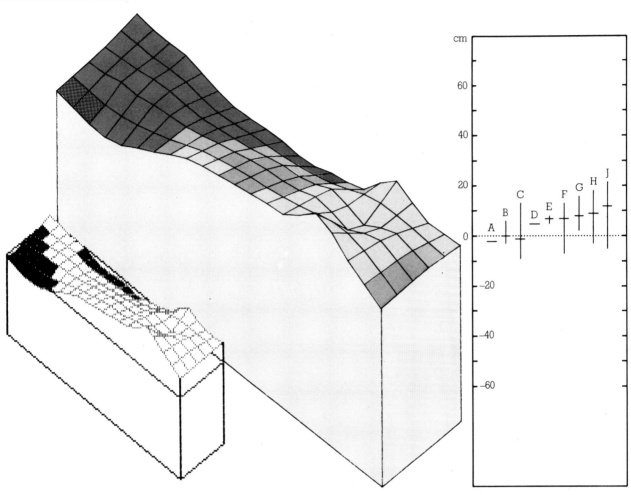

Nodum		Related communities described in existing literature	Author
A	C6	Caricetum limosae, Typical subassociation	Dierssen
C	C7	*Eriophorum angustifolium*, Subassociation with *Sphagnum cuspidatum*	Dierssen
F	C5	Erico-Sphagnetum papillosi, Typical subassociation, Variant with *Molinia caerulea*, Typical subvariant	Birse
H	C2	Erico-Sphagnetum papillosi, Typical subassociation, Variant with *Molinia caerulea*, Typical subvariant	Birse
J	C1	Erico-Sphagnetum papillosi, Typical subassociation, Variant with *Molinia caerulea*, Typical subvariant	Birse

Figure 87g

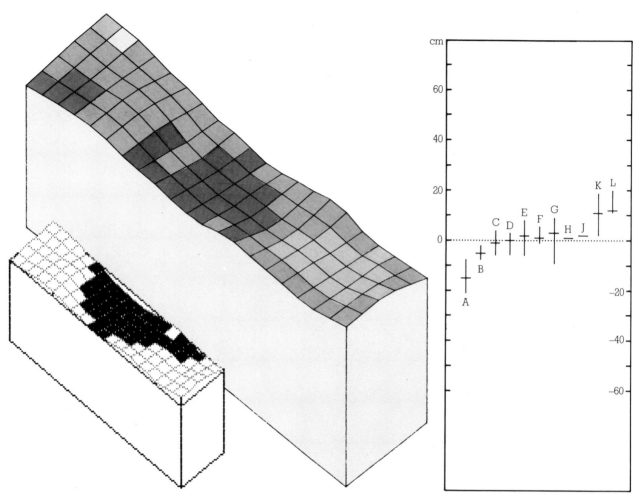

Nodum			Related communities described in existing literature	Author
C		F6	Sphagno tenelli-Rhynchosporetum albae, Subassociation with *Sphagnum auriculatum*, Variant with *Rhynchospora alba*	Dierssen
E		F5	Sphagno tenelli-Rhynchosporetum albae, Subassociation with *Sphagnum tenellum*, Variant with *Sphagnum papillosum*	Dierssen
F		F4	Sphagno tenelli-Rhynchosporetum albae, Subassociation with *Sphagnum tenellum*, Variant with *Sphagnum papillosum*	Dierssen
H		F3	Sphagno tenelli-Rhynchosporetum albae, Subassociation with *Sphagnum tenellum*, Variant with *Sphagnum papillosum*	Dierssen
J		F2	Sphagno tenelli-Rhynchosporetum albae, Subassociation with *Sphagnum papillosum*, Variant with *Sphagnum papillosum*, Facies with *Rhynchospora alba*	Dierssen

Figure 87h

Blar nam Fear Mhora Transect 3

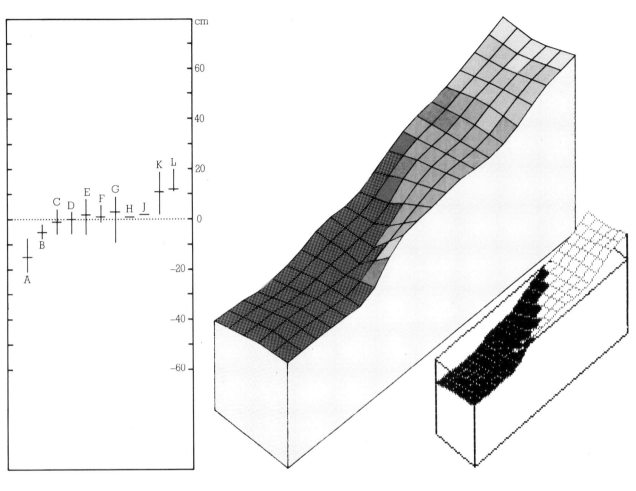

Nodum		Related communities described in existing literature	Author
A	F7	Eleocharitetum multicaulis, Subassociation with *Sphagnum auriculatum*	Dierssen
B	F6	Sphagno tenelli-Rhynchosporetum albae, Subassociation with *Sphagnum auriculatum*, Variant with *Rhynchospora alba*	Dierssen
D	F5	Sphagno tenelli-Rhynchosporetum albae, Subassociation with *Sphagnum tenellum*, Variant with *Sphagnum papillosum*	Dierssen
G	F4	Sphagno tenelli-Rhynchosporetum albae, Subassociation with *Sphagnum tenellum*, Variant with *Sphagnum papillosum*	Dierssen
K	F2	Sphagno tenelli-Rhynchosporetum albae, Subassociation with *Sphagnum papillosum*, Variant with *Sphagnum papillosum*, Facies with *Rhynchospora alba*	Dierssen
L	F1	Pleurozio-Ericetum tetralicis, Subassociation with *Racomitrium lanuginosum*, Facies with *Molinia caerulea*	Dierssen

Figure 87i

Allt an Fhaing Transect 1

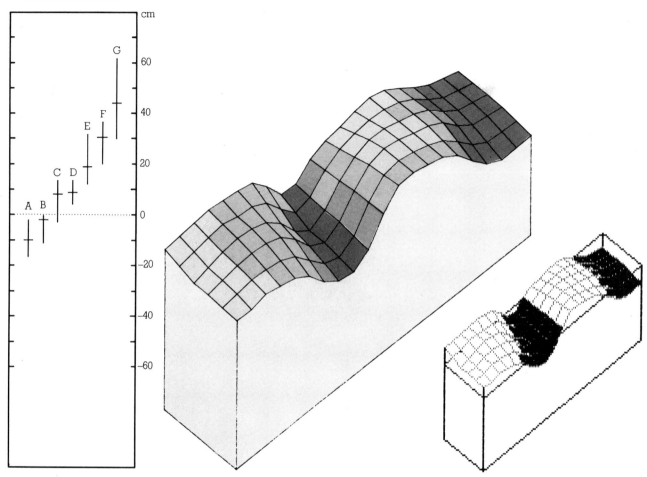

Nodum			Related communities described in existing literature	Author
A		AF9	*Eriophorum angustifolium**, Subassociation with *Sphagnum cuspidatum* (* AF9 lacks *Eriophorum angustifolium*)	Dierssen
B		AF8	Sphagno tenelli-Rhynchosporetum albae*, Subassociation with *Sphagnum tenellum*, Variant with *Sphagnum papillosum* (* AF8 lacks *Rhynchospora alba*)	Dierssen
C		AF6	Narthecia-Sphagnetum papillosi, Typical subassociation, Typical variant	Dierssen
D		AF5	Pleurozio-Ericetum tetralicis, *Molinia caerulea* facies*, Subassociation with *Racomitrium lanuginosum* (*AF5 lacks *Molinia caerulea*)	Dierssen

Allt an Fhaing Transect 4

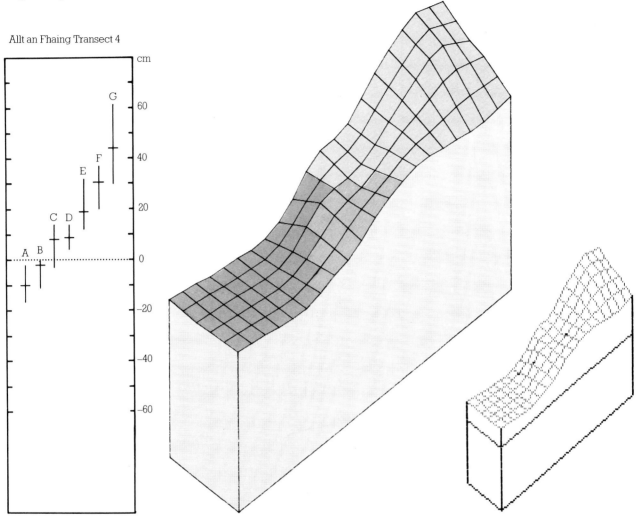

Nodum		Related communities described in existing literature	Author
E	AF4	Empetro-Eriophoretum*, Typical subassociation (*AF4 lacks *Rubus chamaemorus*)	Dierssen
F	AF2	Empetro-Eriophoretum*, Subassociation with *Cladonia arbuscula***, Variant with *Racomitrium lanuginosum* (*AF2 lacks *Rubus chamaemorus*, **AF2 lacks *Cladonia arbuscula*)	Dierssen
G	AF1	Empetro-Sphagnetum fusci, Subassociation with *Sphagnum fuscum*, Typical formation with *Calluna vulgaris*	Dierssen

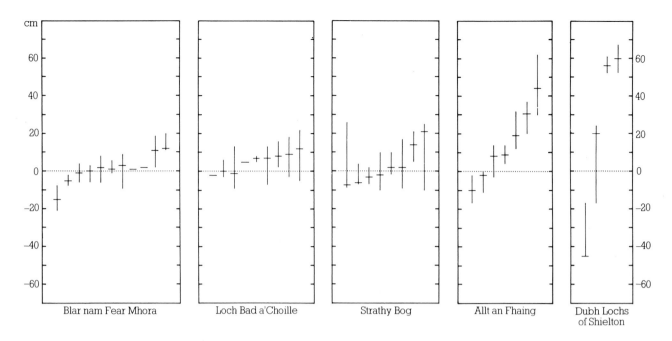

Figure 88 Range of heights and modes displayed by all the noda illustrated in Figures 87a–j, to emphasise the variation in height ranges between sites. Noda which occur in two transects on one site are displayed as separate records for each transect.

than species typical of wetter levels in the microtopography (see Chapter 5). In addition, the extremely fibrous nature of hummocks makes them highly resistant to erosive scouring (Hobbs 1986).

Racomitrium lanuginosum is present as hummocks and within the T1/T2 ridge, but its relative abundance on this site is more an indication of damage than a reflection of climate. Indeed the level of damage can be seen from the extensive occurrence of noda AF1 and AF2 throughout the T2 zone. Once down from the hummocks, the general mire surface is dominated by these two noda, which are characterised by abundant bare peat and *Trichophorum cespitosum*.

The T1 zone (low ridge) is reduced to a small fringe of vegetation dominated by *Sphagnum tenellum* around the margins of eroding hollows and pools. *S. tenellum* is characteristic of damaged areas in the west. It acts as 'scar tissue' on ground which has been burnt or drained and then resoaked (Lindsay unpublished) and forms a distinct association with *S. cuspidatum* on ground which is eroding but has not reached the deep gully stage. This type of ground has been termed "microbroken" during the survey, because it indicates a microtopography which is broken into an anastomosing network enclosing small ridge-islands but which has not developed the deep gullies and hags of the more typical dendritic erosion complex. The channels of such microbroken ground are characteristically dominated by a *Sphagnum tenellum/S. cuspidatum* mixture which is illustrated by noda AF8 and AF9; the form of this microtopography is well illustrated by Figure 87i.

The wide range of heights displayed by the microtopography at Allt an Fhaing is typical of an eroding surface, where the ridge zone is left high above the water table and hummocks become hags.

References

AARIO, L. 1932. Pflanzentopographische und paläogeographische Mooruntersuchungen in N-Satakunta. *Institutum Forestale Fenniae. Communicationes, 17.*

ACADEMY OF SCIENCES OF THE U.S.S.R., & CHIEF DIRECTORATE OF GEODESY AND CARTOGRAPHY, STATE GEOLOGICAL COMMITTEE OF THE U.S.S.R. 1964. *Fiziko-geograficheskii Atlas Mira. [Physico-geographical Atlas of the World]*. Moscow.

ALABASTER, J.S., & LLOYD, R., eds. 1980. *Water Quality Criteria for Freshwater Fish*. London, Butterworth Scientific, for F.A.O.

ALLEN, S.E. 1964. Chemical aspects of heather burning. *Journal of Applied Ecology, 1*, 347–367.

ANGUS, S. 1986. The peatland habitat resource of Sutherland and Caithness in relation to forestry. Inverness, Nature Conservancy Council, North-West Scotland Region (unpublished report).

ARMSTRONG, W., & BOATMAN, D.J. 1966. Some field observations relating the growth of bog plants to conditions of soil aeration. *Journal of Ecology, 55*, 101–110.

AUER, V. 1933. Verschiebungen der Wald- und Steppengebiete Feuerlands in postglazialer Zeit. *Acta Geographica, Helsinki, 5*(2), 1–313.

AUER, V. 1965. The Pleistocene of Fuego-Patagonia. Part IV: Bog profiles. *Annales Academiae Scientiarum Fennicae, A, 80*, 1–160.

BAINBRIDGE, I.P., MINNS, D.W., HOUSDEN, S.D., & LANCE, A.N. 1987. *Forestry in the Flows of Caithness and Sutherland*. Sandy, Royal Society for the Protection of Birds.

BAKKER, E.M. van Z., Sr., WINTERBOTTOM, J.M., & DYER, R.A., eds. 1971. *Marion and Prince Edward Islands; report on the South African Biological and Zoological Expedition, 1965–66*. Cape Town, Balkema.

BANNER, A., POJAR, J., & TROWBRIDGE, R. 1986. *Representative Wetland Types of the Northern Part of the Pacific Oceanic Wetland Region*. Province of British Columbia, Ministry of Forests.

BARBER, K.E. 1981. *Peat Stratigraphy and Climatic Change*. Rotterdam, Balkema.

BATTARBEE, R.W., APPLEBY, P.G., ODELL, K., & FLOWER, R.J. 1985. ^{210}Pb dating of Scottish lake sediments, afforestation and accelerated soil erosion. *Earth Surface Processes and Landforms, 10*, 137–142.

BATTARBEE, R.W., FLOWER, R.J., STEVENSON, A.C., & RIPPEY, B. 1985. Lake acidification in Galloway: a palaeoecological test of competing hypotheses. *Nature, 314*, 350–352.

BELLAMY, D.J. 1968. An ecological approach to the classification of European mires. *In: Proceedings of the Third International Peat Congress, Quebec, 1968*, ed. by C. Lafleur and J. Butler, 74–79.

BELLAMY, D.J., & BELLAMY, R. 1966. An ecological approach to the classification of the lowland mires of Ireland. *Royal Irish Academy. Proceedings, 65B*, 237–251.

BELLAMY, D.J., & PRITCHARD, T. 1973. Project 'Telma': a scientific framework for conserving the world's peatlands. *Biological Conservation, 5*, 33–40.

BERGKVIST, B. 1986. Leaching of metals from a spruce forest soil as influenced by experimental acidification. *Water, Air, and Soil Pollution, 31*, 901–916.

BIBBY, J.S., DOUGLAS, H.A., THOMASSON, A.J., & ROBERTSON, J.S. 1982. *Land Capability Classification for Agriculture*. Aberdeen, Macaulay Institute for Soil Research.

BIRKS, H.H. 1970. Studies in the vegetational history of Scotland. I. A pollen diagram from Abernethy Forest, Inverness-shire. *Journal of Ecology, 58*, 827–846.

BIRKS, H.H. 1972. Studies in the vegetational history of Scotland. II. Two pollen diagrams from the Galloway Hills, Kirkcudbrightshire. *Journal of Ecology, 60*, 183–217.

BIRKS, H.H. 1975. Studies in the vegetational history of Scotland. IV. Pine stumps in Scottish blanket peats. *Royal Society. Philosophical Transactions, B, 270*, 181–226.

BIRKS, H.J.B. 1973. *Past and Present Vegetation of the Isle of Skye – a Palaeoecological Study*. Cambridge, Cambridge University Press.

BIRKS, H.J.B. in press. Long-term change in the British uplands. *In: Ecological Change in the Uplands*, ed. by M. Usher and D.B.A. Thompson. Oxford, Blackwell Scientific.

BIRNIE, J.F. 1984. Trees and shrubs in the Shetland

Islands: evidence for a postglacial climatic optimum? *In: Climatic Changes on a Yearly to Millennial Basis*, ed. by N.A. Morner and W. Karlen, 155–161. Dordrecht, Netherlands, Reidel.

BIRSE, E.L. 1971. *Assessment of Climatic Conditions in Scotland. 3. The Bioclimatic Sub-regions.* Aberdeen, Macaulay Institute for Soil Research.

BIRSE, E.L. 1980. *Plant Communities of Scotland. A Preliminary Phytocoenonia.* Aberdeen, Macaulay Institute for Soil Research (Soil Survey of Scotland Bulletin No. 4).

BIRSE, E.L. 1984. *The Phytocoenonia of Scotland. Additions and Revision.* Aberdeen, Macaulay Institute for Soil Research (Soil Survey of Scotland Bulletin No. 5).

BIRSE, E.L., & DRY, F.T. 1970. *Assessment of Climatic Conditions in Scotland. 1. Based on Accumulated Temperature and Potential Water Deficit.* Aberdeen, Macaulay Institute for Soil Research.

BIRSE, E.L., & ROBERTSON, L. 1970. *Assessment of Climatic Conditions in Scotland. 2. Based on Exposure and Accumulated Frost.* Aberdeen, Macaulay Institute for Soil Research.

BLYTT, A. 1876. *Essay on the Immigration of the Norwegian Flora during alternating Rainy and Dry Periods.* Christiana, Cammermeyer.

BOATMAN, D.J. 1960. The relationships of some bog communities in western Galway. *Royal Irish Academy. Proceedings, 61B*, 141–166.

BOATMAN, D.J. 1983. The Silver Flowe National Nature Reserve, Galloway, Scotland. *Journal of Biogeography, 10*, 163–274.

BOATMAN, D.J., & ARMSTRONG, W. 1968. A bog type in north-west Sutherland. *Journal of Ecology, 56*, 129–141.

BOATMAN, D.J., GOODE, D.A., & HULME, P.D. 1981. The Silver Flowe. III. Pattern development on Long Loch B and Craigeazle mires. *Journal of Ecology, 69*, 897–918.

BOATMAN, D.J., & TOMLINSON, R.W. 1973. The Silver Flowe. I. Some structural and hydrological features of Brishie Bog and their bearing on pool formation. *Journal of Ecology, 61*, 653–666.

BOELTER, D.H. 1972. Water table drawdown around an open ditch in organic soils. *Journal of Hydrology, 15*, 329–340.

BOTCH, M.S., & MASING, V.V. 1983. Mire ecosystems in the U.S.S.R. *In: Mires: Swamp, Bog, Fen and Moor. Regional Studies*, ed. by A.J.P. Gore, 95–152. Amsterdam, Elsevier Scientific (Ecosystems of the World 4B).

BOWER, M.M. 1962. The cause of erosion in blanket peat bogs: a review of recent work in the southern Pennines. *Scottish Geographical Magazine, 78*, 33–43.

BOWLER, M., & BRADSHAW, R. 1985. Recent accumulation and erosion of blanket peat in the Wicklow Mountains, Ireland. *New Phytologist, 101*, 543–550.

BRAGG, O.M. 1982. The acrotelm of Dun Moss. PhD thesis, University of Dundee.

BRIMBLECOMBE, P., DAVIES, T., & TRANTER, M. 1986. Nineteenth-century black Scottish showers. *Atmospheric Environment, 20*, 1053–1057.

BROWN, R.J.E. 1983. Effects of fire on the permafrost ground thermal regime. *In: The Role of Fire in Northern Circumpolar Ecosystems*, ed. by R.W. Wein and D.A. MacLean, 97–110. Chichester, Wiley.

BURKE, W. 1975. Fertiliser and other chemical losses in drainage water from blanket bog. *Irish Journal of Agricultural Research, 14*, 163–178.

CAJANDER, A.K. 1913. Studien über die Moore Finnlands. *Acta Forestalia Fennica, 2*, 1–208.

CAMPBELL, E.O. 1983. Mires of Australasia. *In: Mires: Swamp, Bog, Fen and Moor. Regional Studies*, ed. by A.J.P. Gore, 153–180. Amsterdam, Elsevier Scientific (Ecosystems of the World 4B).

CHAPMAN, S.B. 1964. The ecology of Coom Rigg Moss, Northumberland. I. Stratigraphy and present vegetation. *Journal of Ecology, 52*, 299–313.

CHAPMAN, S.B., & ROSE, R.J. 1986. *An assessment of changes in the vegetation at Coom Rigg Moss National Nature Reserve within the period 1958–86.* Wareham, Institute of Terrestrial Ecology, Furzebrook Experimental Station (contract report to NCC; ITE Project 1092).

CHARMAN, D.J. 1986. The influence of area, habitat diversity and isolation period on species numbers of the Border Mires of Northumberland. BSc thesis, University of Newcastle upon Tyne.

CHARTER, E. 1985a. *A survey of some peatland sites in Sutherland.* Edinburgh, Nature Conservancy Council, Scottish Field Survey Unit (SFSU Report No. S20).

CHARTER, E. 1985b. *A survey of some peatland sites in Caithness.* Edinburgh, Nature Conservancy Council, Scottish Field Survey Unit (SFSU Report No. S24).

CHILDS, E.C. 1969. *An Introduction to the Physical Basis of Soil Water Phenomena.* London, Wiley.

CHISTJAKOV, V.I., KUPRIJANOV, A.I., GORSHKOV, V.V., & ARTSYBASHEV, E.S. 1983. Measures for fire-prevention on peat deposits.

In: The Role of Fire in Northern Circumpolar Ecosystems, ed. by R.W. Wein and D.A. MacLean, 259–271. Chichester, Wiley.

CLAPHAM, A.R., TUTIN, T.G., & WARBURG, E.F. 1962. *Flora of the British Isles.* 2nd ed. Cambridge, Cambridge University Press.

CLYMO, R.S. 1967. Control of cation concentrations, and in particular of pH, in *Sphagnum* dominated communities. *In: Chemical Environment in the Aquatic Habitat*, ed. by H.L. Golterman and R.S. Clymo, 273–284. Amsterdam, North-Holland Publishing Company.

CLYMO, R.S. 1983. Peat. *In: Mires: Swamp, Bog, Fen and Moor. General Studies*, ed. by A.J.P. Gore, 159–224. Amsterdam, Elsevier Scientific (Ecosystems of the World 4A).

CLYMO, R.S. 1984. The limits to peat bog growth. *Royal Society. Philosophical Transactions, B, 303*, 605–654.

CLYMO, R.S., & DUCKETT, J.G. 1986. Regeneration of *Sphagnum. New Phytologist, 102*, 589–614.

CLYMO, R.S., & HAYWARD, P.M. 1982. The ecology of *Sphagnum. In: Bryophyte Ecology*, ed. by A.J.E. Smith, 229–291. Newton Abbot, David and Charles.

CONOLLY, A.P., & DAHL, E. 1970. Maximum summer temperature in relation to the modern and Quaternary distributions of certain arctic-montane species in the British Isles. *In: Studies in the Vegetational History of the British Isles*, ed. by D. Walker and R.G. West, 159–224. London, Cambridge University Press.

CONWAY, V.M. 1949. Ringinglow Bog, near Sheffield. II. The present surface. *Journal of Ecology, 37*, 148–170.

CONWAY, V.M. 1954. Stratigraphy and pollen analysis of southern Pennine blanket peats. *Journal of Ecology, 42*, 117–147.

CONWAY, V.M., & MILLAR, A. 1960. The hydrology of some small peat-covered catchments in the northern Pennines. *Institution of Water Engineers. Journal, 14*, 415–424.

COULSON, J.C., & BUTTERFIELD, J.E. 1978. An investigation of the biotic factors determining the rates of plant decomposition on blanket bog. *Journal of Ecology, 66*, 631–650.

COUNCIL OF EUROPE. 1983. *List of rare, threatened and endemic plants in Europe.* Strasbourg, Council of Europe (Nature and Environment Series, No. 27).

COWARDIN, L.M., CARTER, V., GOLET, F.C., & LaROE, E.T. 1979. *Classification of Wetlands and Deepwater Habitats of the United States.* U.S. Fish and Wildlife Service.

COY, J.S. 1979. Forestry Commission aerial application of fertilisers: effects on water quality. Dumfries, Solway River Purification Board (unpublished report).

CRAMPTON, C.B. 1911. *The Vegetation of Caithness considered in relation to the Geology.* Edinburgh, Committee for the Survey and Study of British Vegetation.

CRESSER, M., & EDWARDS, A. 1987. *Acidification of Fresh Waters.* Cambridge, Cambridge University Press.

CROMERTIE, George, Earl of. 1711. An account of the mosses in Scotland. *Royal Society. Philosophical Transactions, 27*, 296–301.

CUMMINS, C.P. 1986. Effects of aluminium and low pH on growth and development in *Rana temporaria* tadpoles. *Oecologia, 69*, 248–252.

CUTTLE, S.P. 1983. Chemical properties of upland peats influencing the retention of phosphate and potassium. *Journal of Soil Science, 34*, 75–82.

DANIELS, R.E. 1978. Floristic analyses of British mires and mire communities. *Journal of Ecology, 66*, 773–802.

DEPARTMENT OF AGRICULTURE AND FISHERIES FOR SCOTLAND. 1965. *Scottish Peat Surveys. Vol. 2. Western Highlands and Islands.* Edinburgh, H.M.S.O.

DEPARTMENT OF AGRICULTURE AND FISHERIES FOR SCOTLAND. 1968. *Scottish Peat Surveys. Vol. 4. Caithness, Shetland and Orkney.* Edinburgh, H.M.S.O.

DEPARTMENT OF AGRICULTURE AND FISHERIES FOR SCOTLAND. 1977. *A Guide to Good Muirburn Practice.* Edinburgh, H.M.S.O.

DEPARTMENT OF ENERGY, MINES AND RESOURCES, CANADA. 1986. Canada. Wetland Regions. *In: The National Atlas of Canada.* 5th ed. Ottawa, Canada Map Office.

DICKINSON, C.H. 1983. Micro-organisms in peatlands. *In: Mires: Swamp, Bog, Fen and Moor. General Studies*, ed. by A.J.P. Gore, 225–245. Amsterdam, Elsevier (Ecosystems of the World 4A).

DIERSSEN, K. 1982. *Die wichtigsten Pflanzengesellschaften der Moore NW-Europas. [The Major Plant Communities of North-west European Mires]*. Geneva, Conservatoire et Jardin Botaniques.

DRAKEFORD, T. 1979. Report of survey of the afforested spawning grounds of the Fleet catchment. Dumfries, Forestry Commission (unpublished report).

DRAKEFORD, T. 1982. Management of upland streams (an experimental fisheries management project on the afforested headwaters of the River Fleet, Kirkudbrightshire). Paper presented to Institute of Fisheries Management, 12th Annual Study Course, Durham.

DRURY, W.H., Jr. 1956. Bog flats and physiographic processes in the Upper Kuskokwim River region, Alaska. *Contributions from the Gray Herbarium of Harvard University*, No. 178.

DU RIETZ, G.E. 1954. Die Mineralbodenwasser-zeigergrenze als Grundlage einer natürlichen Zweigliederung der nord- und mitteleuropäischen Moore. *Vegetatio, 5/6*, 571–585.

DURNO, S.E. 1958. Pollen analysis of peat deposits in eastern Sutherland and Caithness. *Scottish Geographical Magazine, 74*, 127–135.

DUXBURY, J.M., & PEVERLY, J.H. 1978. Nitrogen and phosphorus losses from drained peat. *Journal of Environmental Quality, 7*, 566–580.

EDDY, A., WELCH, D., & RAWES, M. 1969. The vegetation of the Moor House National Nature Reserve in the Northern Pennines, England. *Vegetatio, 16*, 239–284.

EGGELSMANN, R. 1972. Physical effects of drainage in peat soils of the temperate zone and their forecasting. *In: Proceedings of the International Symposium on the Hydrology of Marsh-ridden Areas, Minsk*, 1–11.

EGGLISHAW, H., GARDINER, R., & FOSTER, J. 1986. Salmon catch decline and forestry in Scotland. *Scottish Geographical Magazine,102*, 57–61.

EIGNER, J., & SCHMATZLER, E. 1980. *Bedeutung, Schutz und Regeneration von Hochmooren.* Greven, Kilda-Verlag (Naturschutz aktuell No. 4).

ELLIS, M.M. 1936. Erosion silt as a factor in aquatic environments. *Ecology, 17*, 29–42.

EUROLA, S. 1962. Über die regionale Einteilung der südfinnischen Moore. [The regional classification of peatlands in south Finland]. *Annales Botanici Societatis Zoologicae Botanicae Fennicae Vanamo, 33*, 163–243.

EUROLA, S., HICKS, S., & KAAKINEN, E. 1984. Key to Finnish mire types. *In: European Mires*, ed. by P.D. Moore, 11–118. London, Academic Press.

EUROLA, S., & HOLAPPA, K. 1985. The Finnish mire type system. *Aquilo, Seria Botanica, 21*, 101–110.

FERGUSON, P., LEE, J.A., & BELL, J.N.B. 1978. Effects of sulphur pollutants on the growth of *Sphagnum* species. *Environmental Pollution, 16*, 151–162.

FITTER, A. 1978. *An Atlas of the Wild Flowers of Britain and Northern Europe.* London, Collins.

FLATBERG, K.I. 1984. A taxonomic revision of the *Sphagnum imbricatum* complex. *Kongelige Norske Videnskabers Selskabs Skrifter, 3*, 1–80.

FOSTER, G.N. 1987. Wetland Coleoptera in the Flow Country. Unpublished report to the Nature Conservancy Council.

FOSTER, G.N., & SPIRIT, M. 1986. *Oreodytes alpinus* new to Britain. *Balfour-Browne Club Newsletter*, No. 36, 1–2.

FOX, A.D. 1984. Aspects of the hydrology of Cors Fochno National Nature Reserve. PhD thesis, University College of Wales, Aberystwyth.

FRANCIS, I.S. 1987. The rates and processes of blanket peat erosion in Mid-Wales. PhD thesis, University College of Wales, Aberystwyth.

FRASER, G.K. 1948. *Peat deposits of Scotland. I. General account.* London, Department of Scientific and Industrial Research (Wartime Pamphlets of the Geological Survey No. 36).

FRY, G.L.A., & COOKE, A.S. 1984. *Acid deposition and its implications for nature conservation in Britain.* Peterborough, Nature Conservancy Council (Focus on Nature Conservation No. 7).

FUTTY, D.W., & TOWERS, W. 1982. *Soil Survey of Scotland. 3. Northern Scotland.* Aberdeen, Macaulay Institute for Soil Research.

GALVIN, L.F. 1976. Reclamation and drainage of peatland. *Farm and Food Research, 7*, 58–60.

GEIKIE, J. 1866. On the buried forests and peat mosses of Scotland, and the changes of climate which they indicate. *Royal Society of Edinburgh. Transactions, 24*, 363–384.

GIMINGHAM, C.H. 1984. Some mire systems in Japan. *Botanical Society of Edinburgh. Transactions, 44*, 169–176.

GODLEY, E. 1960. The botany of southern Chile in relation to New Zealand and the sub-Antarctic. *Royal Society. Proceedings, B, 152*, 457–475.

GODWIN, H. 1975. *The History of the British Flora.* 2nd ed. Cambridge, Cambridge University Press.

GODWIN, H. 1978. *Fenland: its ancient past and uncertain future.* Cambridge, Cambridge University Press.

GODWIN, H. 1981. *The Archives of the Peat Bog.* Cambridge, Cambridge University Press.

GODWIN, H., & CONWAY, V.M. 1939. The ecology of a raised bog near Tregaron, Cardiganshire. *Journal of Ecology, 27*, 313–363.

GOODE, D.A. 1970. Ecological studies on the Silver Flowe Nature Reserve. PhD thesis, University of Hull.

GOODE, D.A. 1973. The significance of physical hydrology in the morphological classification of mires. *In: Proceedings of the International Peat Society Symposium, Glasgow, 1973. Classification of Peat and Peatlands*, Paper 3.

GOODE, D.A., & FIELD, E.M. 1978. Notes on the vegetation of Shetland bogs. Nature Conservancy Council (unpublished report).

GOODE, D.A., & LINDSAY, R.A. 1979. The peatland vegetation of Lewis. *Royal Society of Edinburgh. Proceedings, 77B*, 279–293.

GOODE, D.A., & RATCLIFFE, D.A. 1977. Peatlands. *In: A Nature Conservation Review*, ed. by D.A. Ratcliffe, Vol. 1, 249–287; Vol. 2, 206–244. Cambridge, Cambridge University Press.

GOODWILLIE, R. 1980. *European Peatlands*. Strasbourg, Council of Europe (Nature and Environment Series, No. 19).

GOODWILLIE, R. 1987. Irish treasure. *Birds, 11*, 32–35.

GORE, A.J.P. 1983a. Introduction. *In: Mires: Swamp, Bog, Fen and Moor. General Studies*, ed. by A.J.P. Gore, 1–34. Amsterdam, Elsevier Scientific (Ecosystems of the World 4A).

GORE, A.J.P., ed. 1983b. *Mires: Swamp, Bog, Fen and Moor. Regional Studies*. Amsterdam, Elsevier Scientific (Ecosystems of the World 4B).

GORHAM, E. 1953a. A note on the acidity and base status of raised and blanket bogs. *Journal of Ecology, 41*, 153–156.

GORHAM, E. 1953b. Some early ideas concerning the nature, origin and development of peat lands. *Journal of Ecology, 41*, 257–274.

GORHAM, E. 1966. Some chemical aspects of wetland ecology. *In: Proceedings of the Twelfth Muskeg Research Conference, Ottawa*.

GORHAM, E., BAYLEY, S.E., & SCHINDLER, D.W. 1984. Ecological effects of acid deposition upon peatlands: a neglected field in 'acid-rain' research. *Canadian Journal of Fisheries and Aquatic Science, 41*, 1256–1268.

GRANLUND, E. 1932. De svenska högmossarnas geologie. [The geology of the Swedish *Hochmoore*]. *Sveriges Geologiska Undersökning. Afhandlingar och Uppsatser, 373*, 1–193.

GRANT, M.C., & LEWIS, W.M. 1982. Chemical loading rates from precipitation in the Colorado Rockies. *Tellus, 34*, 74–88.

GREEN, F.H.W. 1964. A map of annual average potential water deficit in the British Isles. *Journal of Applied Ecology, 1*, 151–158.

GREIG, D.A. 1975. Raised bogs in North-west Cumbria. Report on a vegetation survey of Glasson Moss, Bowness Common and Wedholme Flow, with notes on Drumburgh Moss. Nature Conservancy Council (unpublished report).

GROENENDAEL, J.M. van, HOCHSTENBACH, S.M.H., MANSFELD, M.J.M. van, & ROOZEN, A.J.M. 1975. *The Influence of the Sea and of Parent Material on Wetlands and Blanket Bog in West Connemara, Ireland*. Nijmegen, Catholic University.

GROSSE-BRAUCKMANN, G. 1962. Zur Moorgliederung und -ansprache. *Zeitschrift für Kulturtechnik, 3*, 6–29.

HARRIMAN, R. 1978. Nutrient leaching from fertilized forest watersheds in Scotland. *Journal of Applied Ecology, 15*, 933–942.

HARRIMAN, R., & MORRISON, B.R.S. 1982. Ecology of streams draining forested and non-forested catchments in an area of central Scotland subject to acid precipitation. *Hydrobiologia, 88*, 251–263.

HEAL, O.W., & SMITH, R.A.H. 1978. The Moor House programme. Introduction and site description. *In: Production Ecology of British Moors and Montane Grasslands*, ed. by O.W. Heal and D.F. Perkins, 3–16. Berlin, Springer-Verlag.

HILDREW, A.G., TOWNSEND, C.R., FRANCIS, J., & FINCH, K. 1984. Cellulitic decomposition in streams of contrasting pH and its relationship with invertebrate community structure. *Freshwater Biology, 14*, 323–328.

HILL, M.O. 1979. *TWINSPAN – a FORTAN Program for Arranging Multivariate Data in an Ordered Two-way Table by Classification of the Individuals and Attributes*. Cornell University, Ecology and Systematics.

HOBBS, N.B. 1986. Mire morphology and the properties and behaviour of some British and foreign peats. *Quarterly Journal of Engineering Geology, 19*, 7–80.

HOBBS, R.J., & GIMINGHAM, C.H. 1987. Vegetation, fire and herbivore interactions in heathland. *Advances in Ecological Research, 16*, 87–173.

HOLMES, N. 1983. *Typing British rivers according to their flora*. Peterborough, Nature Conservancy Council (Focus on Nature Conservation No. 4).

HORNUNG, M., & NEWSON, M.D. 1986. Upland afforestation influences on stream hydrology and chemistry. *Soil Use Management, 2*, 61–65.

HULME, P.D. 1980. The classification of Scottish peatlands. *Scottish Geographical Magazine, 96*, 46–50.

HULME, P.D. 1985. The peatland vegetation of the Isle of Lewis and Harris and the Shetland Islands, Scotland. *Aquilo, Seria Botanica, 21*, 81–88.

HULME, P.D. 1986. The origin and development of wet hollows and pools on Craigeazle mire, south-west Scotland. *International Peat Journal, 1*, 15–28.

HULME, P.D., & BLYTH, A.W. 1984. A classification of the peatland vegetation of the Isles of Lewis and Harris, Scotland. *In: Proceedings of the Seventh International Peat Congress, Dublin, 1984, 1*, 188–204.

HULME, P.D., & BLYTH, A.W. 1985. Observations on the erosion of blanket peat in Yell, Shetland. *Geografiska Annaler, 67A*, 119–122.

IGARASHI, Y., AKAZAWA, T., MATSUSHITA, K., & UMEDA, Y. 1984. Soil characteristics and geohistory on the Ishikari peat land, northern Japan. *In: Proceedings of the Seventh International Peat Congress, Dublin, 1984, 1*, 205–219.

INGRAM, H.A.P. 1967. Problems of hydrology and plant distribution in mires. *Journal of Ecology, 55*, 711–724.

INGRAM, H.A.P. 1982. Size and shape in raised mire ecosystems: a geophysical model. *Nature, 297*, 300–303.

INGRAM, H.A.P. 1983. Hydrology. *In: Mires: Swamp, Bog, Fen and Moor. General Studies*, ed. by A.J.P. Gore, 67–158. Amsterdam, Elsevier Scientific (Ecosystems of the World 4A).

INGRAM, H.A.P., & BRAGG, O.M. 1984. The diplotelmic mire: some hydrological consequences reviewed. *In: Proceedings of the Seventh International Peat Congress, Dublin, 1984, 1*, 220–234.

IVANOV, K.E. 1981. *Water Movement in Mirelands.* London, Academic Press.

JEFFERIES, T.A. 1915. Ecology of the purple heath grass (*Molinia caerulea*). *Journal of Ecology, 3*, 93–109.

JOHANSEN, J. 1975. Pollen diagrams from the Shetland and Faroe Islands. *New Phytologist, 75*, 369–387.

KATZ, N.Y. 1971. *Swamps of the Earth.* Moscow, Nauka.

KEATINGE, T.H., & DICKSON, J.H. 1979. Mid-Flandrian changes in the vegetation of mainland Orkney. *New Phytologist, 82*, 585–612.

KERSHAW, K.A. 1973. *Quantitative and Dynamic Plant Ecology.* London, Arnold.

KLING, G.W., & GRANT, M.C. 1984. Acid precipitation in the Colorado Front Range: an overview with time predictions for significant effects. *Arctic and Alpine Research, 16*, 321–329.

KOMAREK, E.V. 1971. Principles of fire ecology and fire management in relation to the Alaskan environment. *In: Fire in the Northern Environment*, ed. by C.W. Slaughter, R.J. Barney and G.M. Hansen, 3–22. Portland, Oregon, Pacific North West Forest and Range Experiment Station.

KORCHUNOV, S.S., KUSMIN, G.F., & IVANOV, K.E. 1980. Raised bog systems, their structure and influence on the environment. Bog protection. *In: Proceedings of the Sixth International Peat Congress, Duluth, Minnesota, 1980*, 55–58.

LEACH, S.J., & CORBETT, P. McM. 1987. A preliminary survey of raised bogs in Northern Ireland. *Glasra, 10*, 57–73.

LEE, J.A. 1981. Atmospheric pollution and the Peak District blanket bogs. *In: Peak District Moorland Erosion Study. Phase 1 Report*, ed. by J. Phillips, D. Yalden and J. Tallis, 104–109. Bakewell, Peak Park Joint Planning Board.

LEE, J.A., PRESS, M.C., WOODIN, S., & FERGUSON, P. 1986. Responses to acidic deposition in ombrotrophic mires. *In: Effects of Acidic Deposition on Forests, Wetlands and Agricultural Ecosystems*, ed. by T.C. Hutchinson and K. Meema, 549–560. Berlin, Springer-Verlag.

LEEKS, G.F.L., & ROBERTS, G. 1986. The effects of forestry on upland streams – with special reference to water quality and sediment transport. *In: Environmental Aspects of Plantation Forestry in Wales*, ed. by J.E.G. Good, 9–24. Cambridge, Institute of Terrestrial Ecology (ITE Symposium No. 22).

LEFEBVRE, G., LANGLOIS, P., LUPIEN, C., & LAVALLÉE, J. 1984. Laboratory testing on *in situ* behaviour of peat as embankment foundation. *Canadian Geotechnical Journal, 21*, 322–337.

LEWIS, F.J. 1905. The plant remains in the Scottish peat mosses. I. The Scottish Southern Uplands. *Royal Society of Edinburgh. Transactions, 41*, 699–723.

LEWIS, F.J. 1906. The plant remains in the Scottish peat mosses. II. The Scottish Highlands. *Royal Society of Edinburgh. Transactions, 45*, 335–360.

LEWIS, F.J. 1907. The plant remains in the Scottish peat mosses. III. The Scottish Highlands and the Shetland Islands. *Royal Society of Edinburgh. Transactions, 46*, 33–70.

LIKENS, G.E., BORMANN, F.H., JOHNSON, N.M., FISHER, D.W., & PIERCE, R.S. 1970. Effects of forest cutting and herbicide treatment on nutrient budgets in the Hubbard Brook watershed ecosystem. *Ecological Monographs, 40*, 23–47.

LINDSAY, R.A. 1977. Glasson Moss and the 1976 fire. Nature Conservancy Council (unpublished report).

LINDSAY, R.A., RIGGALL, J., & BIGNAL, E.M. 1983.

Ombrogenous mires in Islay and Mull. *Royal Society of Edinburgh. Proceedings, 83B*, 341–371.

LINDSAY, R.A., RIGGALL, J., & BURD, F. 1985. The use of small-scale surface patterns in the classification of British peatlands. *Aquilo, Seria Botanica, 21*, 69–79.

LYUBIMOVA, E.L. 1940. Nekotorye dannye o bolotakh zapadnago poberezh'ya Kamchatki. *In: Kamchatskii Sbornik I*, 157–225. Moscow, Nauka.

MACDONALD, J., WOOD, R.F., EDWARDS, M.V., & ALDHOUS, J.R., eds. 1957. *Exotic Forest Trees in Great Britain.* London, H.M.S.O. (Forestry Commission Bulletin No. 30).

MacLEAN, D.A., WOODLEY, S.J., WEBER, M.G., & WEIN, R.W. 1983. Fire and nutrient cycling. *In: The Role of Fire in Northern Circumpolar Ecosystems*, ed. by R.W. Wein and D.A. MacLean, 111–132. Chichester, Wiley.

McVEAN, D.N., & LOCKIE, J.D. 1969. *Ecology and Land Use in Upland Scotland.* Edinburgh, Edinburgh University Press.

McVEAN, D.N., & RATCLIFFE, D.A. 1962. *Plant Communities of the Scottish Highlands.* London, H.M.S.O. (Monographs of the Nature Conservancy No. 1).

MALCOLM, D.C., & CUTTLE, S.P. 1983. The application of fertilisers to drained peat. 1. Nutrient losses in drainage. *Forestry, 56*, 155–174.

MALMER, N. 1985. Remarks to the classification of mires and mire vegetation. Scandinavian arguments. *Aquilo, Seria Botanica, 21*, 9–17.

MALMER, N., & SJÖRS, H. 1955. Some determinations of elementary constituents in mire plants and peat. *Botaniska Notiser, 108*, 46–80.

MALTBY, E. 1980. The impact of severe fire on *Calluna* moorland in the North York Moors. *Bulletin d'Écologie, 11*, 683–708.

MARREN, P. 1986. The lethal harvest of crayfish plague. *New Scientist, 109*, 46–50.

MASING, V. 1984. New bog reserves in the Estonian S.S.R.: their scientific and economic significance. *In: Proceedings of the Seventh International Peat Congress, Dublin, 1984, 1*, 306–313.

MATTHEWS, J.R. 1937. Geographical relationships of the British flora. *Journal of Ecology, 25*, 1–90.

MATTHEWS, J.R. 1955. *Origin and Distribution of the British Flora.* London, Hutchinson.

MEADE, R. 1984. Ammonia-assimilating enzymes in bryophytes. *Physiologia Plantarum, 60*, 305–308.

METEOROLOGICAL OFFICE. 1952. *Climatological Atlas of the British Isles.* London, H.M.S.O.

MILLS, D.H. 1980. *The Management of Forest Streams.* London, H.M.S.O. (Forestry Commission Leaflet No. 78).

MOAR, N.T. 1969a. Two pollen diagrams from the Mainland, Orkney Islands. *New Phytologist, 68*, 201–208.

MOAR, N.T. 1969b. A radiocarbon-dated pollen diagram from north-west Scotland. *New Phytologist, 68*, 209–214.

MOEN, A. 1985. Classification of mires for conservation purposes in Norway. *Aquilo, Seria Botanica, 21*, 95–100.

MOORE, J.J. 1968. A classification of the bogs and wet heaths of Northern Europe. *In: Pflanzensoziologische Systematik*, ed. by R. Tüxen, 306–320. The Hague, Junk.

MOORE, P.D. 1968. Human influence upon vegetational history in north Cardiganshire. *Nature, 217*, 1006–1009.

MOORE, P.D. 1973a. The influence of prehistoric cultures upon the initiation and spread of blanket bog in upland Wales. *Nature, 241*, 350–353.

MOORE, P.D. 1973b. Objective classification of peats on the basis of their macrofossil content. *In: Proceedings of the International Peat Society Symposium, Glasgow, 1973. Classification of Peat and Peatlands*, Paper 15.

MOORE, P.D. 1977. Stratigraphy and pollen analysis of Claish Moss, north-west Scotland; significance for the origin of surface pools and forest history. *Journal of Ecology, 65*, 375–397.

MOORE, P.D. 1984. The classification of mires: an introduction. *In: European Mires*, ed. by P.D. Moore, 1–10. London, Academic Press.

MOORE, P.D., & BELLAMY, D.J. 1974. *Peatlands.* London, Elek Science.

MOORE, P.D., MERRYFIELD, D.L., & PRICE, M.D.R. 1984. The vegetation and development of blanket mires. *In: European Mires*, ed. by P.D. Moore, 203–232. London, Academic Press.

MOORE, P.D., & WILMOTT, A. [1979]. Prehistoric forest clearance and the development of peatlands in the uplands and lowlands of Britain. *In: Proceedings of the Fifth International Peat Congress, Poznán, Poland, 1976, 2*, 7–21.

MORRISON, B.R.S., & WELLS, D.E. 1981. The fate of Fenitrothion in a stream environment and its effect on the fauna following aerial spraying of a Scottish forest. *Science of the Total Environment, 19*, 223–252.

MOSS, C.E. 1913. *The Vegetation of the Peak District.*

Cambridge, Cambridge University Press.

MROSE, H. 1966. Measurements of pH and chemical analyses of rain-, snow- and fog-water. *Tellus, 18*, 266–270.

NATIONAL WATER COUNCIL. 1981. *River Quality: the 1980 survey and future outlook.* London, National Water Council.

NATURE CONSERVANCY COUNCIL. 1982. *Seventh report covering the period 1 April 1980–31 March 1981.* London.

NATURE CONSERVANCY COUNCIL. 1986. *Nature Conservation and Afforestation in Britain.* Peterborough.

NEILAND, B.J. 1971. The forest bog complex of south east Alaska. *Vegetatio, 22*, 1–64.

NEISHTADT, M.I. 1935. Yestestvennye obnazheniya torfa po zapnomy poberezhyu Kamchatki. *Izvestiia Gosudarstvennoe. Geograficheskoe Obshchestvo, 67*, 579–587.

NEISHTADT, M.I. 1936. Torfyanye bolota barbinskoi lesostepi. *Trudy Tsentral. Torf. Opytn Stants, 1*, 73–85.

NETHERSOLE-THOMPSON, D. & M. 1979. *Greenshanks.* Berkhamsted, T. and A.D. Poyser.

NEWBOLD, C., & PALMER, M.A. 1979. *Trophic adaptations of aquatic plants.* London, Nature Conservancy Council (CST Notes No. 18).

NEWSON, M.D. 1980. The erosion of drainage ditches and its effects on bed-load yields in mid-Wales. *Earth Surface Processes and Landforms, 5*, 275–290.

NEWSON, M.D. 1985. Forestry and water in the uplands of Britain: the background of hydrological research and options for harmonious land-use. *Quarterly Journal of Forestry, 79*, 113–120.

NIKONOV, M.N. 1955. Raionirovanie torfyanykh bolot v svyazi s ispol' zovoniem ikh v sel'skom khozyaistve. *Trudy Instituta Lesa, 31*, 49–63.

O'CONNELL, M., RYAN, J.B., & MacGOWRAN, B.A. 1984. Wetland communities in Ireland: a phytosociological review. *In: European Mires*, ed. by P.D. Moore, 303–358. London, Academic Press.

OGILVY, R.S.D. 1986. Whither forestry? The scene in AD 2025. *In: Trees and Wildlife in the Scottish Uplands*, ed. by D. Jenkins, 33–39. Abbots Ripton, Institute of Terrestrial Ecology (ITE Symposium No. 17).

ORMEROD, S.J., MAWLE, G.W., & EDWARDS, R.W. 1986. The influence of forest on aquatic fauna. *In: Environmental Aspects of Plantation Forestry in Wales*, ed. by J.E.G. Good, 37–49. Cambridge,

Institute of Terrestrial Ecology (ITE Symposium No. 22).

OSVALD, H. 1923. Die Vegetation des Hochmoores Komosse, Kap. 5. [The vegetation of the raised bogs of Komosse, Chapter 5]. *Svenska Växtsociologiska Sällskapets Handlingar, 1*, 265–310.

OSVALD, H. 1949. Notes on the vegetation of British and Irish mosses. *Acta Phytogeographica Suecica, 26*, 1–62.

PALMER, M.A., & NEWBOLD, C. 1983. *Wetland and riparian plants in Britain.* Peterborough, Nature Conservancy Council (Focus on Nature Conservation No. 1).

PARR, W. 1984. Consultation or confrontation? A review of forestry activities and developments on water catchment areas in south-west Scotland. Dumfries and Galloway Regional Council, Water and Sewage Department (unpublished paper presented to the Scientific Section of the Institution of Water Engineers and Scientists, 24 October 1984).

PEARS, N.V. 1975. Tree stumps in the Scottish hill peats. *Scottish Forestry, 29*, 255–259.

PEARSALL, W.H. 1950. *Mountains and Moorlands.* London, Collins (New Naturalist No. 11).

PEARSALL, W.H. 1956. Two blanket-bogs in Sutherland. *Journal of Ecology, 44*, 493–516.

PEARSON, M.C. 1954. The ecology and history of some peat bogs in west Northumberland with special reference to Muckle Moss. PhD thesis, University of Durham.

PEGLAR, S. 1979. A radiocarbon-dated pollen diagram from Loch of Winless, Caithness, north-east Scotland. *New Phytologist, 82*, 245–263.

PEIRSON, D.H., CAWSE, P.A., SALMON, L., & CAMBRAY, R.S. 1973. Trace elements in the atmospheric environment. *Nature, 241*, 252–256.

PENFORD, N. 1985. Islay peatlands: a survey and evaluation of selected sites. MSc thesis, University College London.

PENNINGTON, W. 1974. *The History of British Vegetation.* 2nd ed. London, English University Press.

PERRING, F.H., & WALTERS, S.M., eds. 1976. *Atlas of the British Flora.* 2nd ed. East Ardsley, Wakefield, EP Publishing, for Botanical Society of the British Isles.

PERRY, A.R. 1965. Distribution maps of bryophytes in Britain: *Sphagnum pulchrum* (Lindb. ex Braithw.) Warnst. *British Bryological Society. Transactions, 4*, 883.

PHILLIPS, J. 1981. Moor burning. *In: Peak District*

Moorland Erosion Study. Phase 1 Report, ed. by J. Phillips, D. Yalden and J. Tallis, 171–175. Bakewell, Peak Park Joint Planning Board.

PIERSMA, T., ed. 1986. Breeding waders in Europe: a review of population size estimates and a bibliography of information sources. *Wader Study Group Bulletin*, No. 48 (Supplement).

PISANO, E. 1983. The Magellanic Tundra Complex. *In: Mires: Swamp, Bog, Fen and Moor. Regional Studies*, ed. by A.J.P. Gore, 295–329. Amsterdam, Elsevier Scientific (Ecosystems of the World 4B).

PRESS, M.C., & LEE, J.A. 1982. Nitrate reductase activity of *Sphagnum* species in the south Pennines. *New Phytologist, 92*, 487–494.

PRESS, M., FERGUSON, P., & LEE, L. 1983. 200 years of acid rain. *Naturalist, 108*, 125–129.

PROCTOR, M.C.F., & RODWELL, J. 1986. National Vegetation Classification: Mires. 3 vols. University of Lancaster (unpublished draft).

PRUITT, W.O. 1978. *Boreal Ecology*. London, Edward Arnold.

PRUS-CHAKINISKI, T.M. 1962. Shrinkage of peatlands due to drainage operations. *Institution of Water Engineers. Journal, 16*, 436–448.

PRYTZ, K. 1932. *Der Kreislauf des Wassers*. Samfund, Copenhagen, Danmark Naturvidenskabelige.

PYATT, D.G. 1987. Afforestation of blanket peatland – soil effects. *Forestry and British Timber, 16*(3), 15, 17.

RATCLIFFE, D.A. 1964. Mires and bogs. *In: The Vegetation of Scotland*, ed. by J.H. Burnett, 426–478. Edinburgh, Oliver and Boyd.

RATCLIFFE, D.A. 1968. An ecological account of Atlantic bryophytes in the British Isles. *New Phytologist, 67*, 365–439.

RATCLIFFE, D.A. 1969. Distribution maps of bryophytes in Britain: *Pleurozia purpurea* Lindb. *British Bryological Society. Transactions, 5*, 833.

RATCLIFFE, D.A., ed. 1977. *A Nature Conservation Review*. 2 vols. Cambridge, Cambridge University Press.

RATCLIFFE, D.A. 1986a. Selection of important areas for wildlife conservation in Great Britain: the Nature Conservancy Council.s approach. *In: Wildlife Conservation Evaluation*, ed. by M.B. Usher, 135–159. London, Chapman and Hall.

RATCLIFFE, D.A. 1986b. The effects of afforestation on the wildlife of open habitats. *In: Trees and Wildlife in the Scottish Uplands*, ed. by D. Jenkins, 46–54. Abbots Ripton, Institute of Terrestrial Ecology (ITE Symposium No. 17).

RATCLIFFE, D.A., & WALKER, D. 1958. The Silver Flowe, Galloway, Scotland. *Journal of Ecology, 46*, 407–445.

RATCLIFFE, J.B., & HATTEY, R.P. 1982. Welsh Lowland Peatland Survey (Final report of the Welsh Wetland Survey). London, Nature Conservancy Council, Chief Scientist Team (unpublished report).

RAWES, M., & HOBBS, R. 1979. Management of semi-natural blanket bog in the northern Pennines. *Journal of Ecology, 67*, 789–807.

REED, T.M., & LANGSLOW, D.R. 1987. Habitat associations of breeding wading birds. *Acta Oecologica/Oecologia Generalis, 8*, 309–311.

REUSS, J.O., & JOHNSON, D.W. 1986. *Acid Deposition and the Acidification of Soils and Waters*. New York, Springer-Verlag (Ecological Studies, Vol. 59).

RICHARDS, W.N. 1984. Problems of water management and water quality arising from forestry activities. *In: Woodlands, Weather and Water*, ed. by D.L. Harding and J.F. Fawell, 67–85. London, Institute of Biology.

ROBERTS, M.E., & JAMES, D.B. 1972. Some effects of forest cover on nutrient cycling and river temperature. *In: Research Papers in Forest Meteorology*, ed. by J.A. Taylor, 100–108. Aberystwyth, Cambrian News.

ROBERTSON, R.A., & JOWSEY, P.C. 1968. Peat resources and development in the United Kingdom. *In: Proceedings of the Third International Peat Congress, Quebec, 1968*, ed. by C. Lafleur and J. Butler, 13–14.

ROBINSON, D. 1987. Investigations into the Aukhorn peat mounds, Keiss, Caithness: pollen, plant macrofossil and charcoal analysis. *New Phytologist, 106*, 185–200.

ROBINSON, M. 1980. *The effect of pre-afforestation drainage on the streamflow and water quality of a small upland catchment*. Wallingford, Institute of Hydrology (Report No. 73).

ROBINSON, M., & BLYTH, K. 1982. The effect of forestry drainage operations on upland sediment yields: a case study. *Earth Surface Processes and Landforms, 7*, 85–90.

ROIVAINEN, H. 1954. Studien über die Moore Feuerlands. [Studies on the bogs of Tierra del Fuego]. *Annales Botanici Societatis Zoologicae Botanicae Fennicae Vanamo, 28*, 1–205.

ROPER, P. undated. *Holidays in the Falkland Islands*. Stanley, Falkland Islands, Falkland Islands Tourism.

ROWE, J.S. 1983. Concepts of fire effects on plant individuals and species. *In: The Role of Fire in Northern Circumpolar Ecosystems*, ed. by

R.W. Wein and D.A. MacLean, 135–154. Chichester, Wiley.

ROYAL SOCIETY FOR THE PROTECTION OF BIRDS. 1985. *Forestry in the Flow Country – the Threat to Birds.* Sandy.

RUUHIJÄRVI, R. 1960. Über die regionale Einteilung der nordfinnischen Moore. *Annales Botanici Societatis Zoologicae Botanicae Fennicae Vanamo, 31*, 1–360.

RUUHIJÄRVI, R.E. 1983. The Finnish mire types and their regional distribution. *In: Mires: Swamps, Bog, Fen and Moor. Regional Studies*, ed. by A.J.P. Gore, 47–67. Amsterdam, Elsevier Scientific (Ecosystems of the World 4B).

RYAN, J.B., & CROSS, J.R. 1984. The conservation of peatlands in Ireland. *In: Proceedings of the Seventh International Peat Congress, Dublin, 1984, 1*, 388–406.

RYBNIČEK, K. 1985. A central European approach to the classification of mire vegetation. *Aquilo, Seria Botanica, 21*, 19–31.

RYDIN, H., & McDONALD, A.J.S. 1985. Tolerance of *Sphagnum* to water level. *Journal of Bryology, 13*, 571–578.

SAGE, B. 1986. *The Arctic and its Wildlife.* Beckenham, Croom Helm.

SCHUNKE, E. 1977. Zür Ökologie der Thufur Islands. *Berichte aus der Forschungsstelle Nedri As, Hveragerdi, 26.*

SCHWAAR, J. 1977. Humifizierungswechsel in terrainbedeckende Mooren von Gough Island, Südatlantik. *Telma, 7*, 77–90.

SCOTTISH WILDLIFE TRUST. 1987. *The Future of the Flows.* Edinburgh.

SERNANDER, R. 1908. On the evidence of Postglacial changes of climate furnished by the peat-mosses of northern Europe. *Geologiska Föreningens i Stockholm Förhandlingar, 30*, 467–478.

SERNANDER, R. 1910. Ausstellung zur Beleuchtung der Entwicklungsgeschichte der swedischen Torfmoore. *Congrès géologique international. Compte rendu de la XI session*, 203–211.

SHARROCK, J.T.R., ed. 1976. *The Atlas of Breeding Birds in Britain and Ireland.* Tring, British Trust for Ornithology/Irish Wildbird Conservancy.

SHIRT, D.B., ed. 1987. *British Red Data Books: 2. Insects.* Peterborough, Nature Conservancy Council.

SIMMONS, I.G. 1963. The blanket bog of Dartmoor. *Devonshire Association for the Advancement of Science, Literature and Art. Report and Transactions, 95*, 180–196.

SIMMONS, I.G., & CUNDILL, P.R. 1974. Late quaternary vegetational history of the North York Moors. I. Pollen analyses of blanket peats. *Journal of Biogeography, 1*, 159–169.

SJÖRS, H. 1948. Myrvegetation i Bergslagen. [Mire vegetation in Bergslagen, Sweden]. *Acta Phytogeographica Suecica, 21*, 1–299. [English summary: 277–299].

SJÖRS, H. 1950a. On the relation between vegetation and electrolytes in north Swedish mire waters. *Oikos, 2*, 241–258.

SJÖRS, H. 1950b. Regional studies in north Swedish mire vegetation. *Botaniska Notiser, 103*, 173–222.

SJÖRS, H. 1961. Surface patterns in boreal peatland. *Endeavour, 20*, 217–224.

SJÖRS, H. 1983. Mires of Sweden. *In: Mires: Swamp, Bog, Fen and Moor. Regional Studies*, ed. by A.J.P. Gore, 69–94. Amsterdam, Elsevier Scientific (Ecosystems of the World 4B).

SJÖRS, H. 1984. Peatlands and their development in southern Alaska. *In: Proceedings of the Seventh International Peat Congress, Dublin, 1984, 1*, 443–449.

SJÖRS, H. 1985a. A comparison between mires of southern Alaska and Fennoscandia. *Aquilo, Seria Botanica, 21*, 89–94.

SJÖRS, H. 1985b. On classification with respect to mires. *Aquilo, Seria Botanica, 21*, 117–119.

SKEFFINGTON, R.A., & ROBERTS, T.M. 1985. The effects of ozone and acid mist on Scots pine saplings. *Oecologia, 65*, 201–206.

SLATER, F.M., & AGNEW, A.D.Q. 1977. Observations on a peat bog's ability to withstand increasing public pressure. *Biological Conservation, 11*, 21–27.

SLATER, F.M., & SLATER, E.J. 1978. The changing status of *Sphagnum imbricatum* Hornsch. ex Russ. on Borth Bog, Wales. *Journal of Bryology, 10*, 155–161.

SMART, P.J. 1982. Stratigraphy of a site in the Munsary Dubh Lochs, Caithness, northern Scotland: development of the present pattern. *Journal of Ecology, 70*, 549–558.

SMART, P.J. 1983. The plant ecology of re-vegetated peat cuttings in ombrotrophic mires, with special reference to Thorne Moors, South Yorkshire. PhD thesis, University of Sheffield.

SMITH, A.G. 1970. The influence of mesolithic and neolithic man on British vegetation. *In: Studies in the Vegetational History of the British Isles*, ed. by D. Walker and R.G. West, 81–96. London, Cambridge University Press.

SMITH, A.J.E. 1978. *The Moss Flora of Britain and*

Ireland. Cambridge, Cambridge University Press.

SMITH, B.D. 1980. The effects of afforestation on the trout of a small stream in southern Scotland. *Fisheries Management, 11*, 39–58.

SMITH, L.T., ed. 1910. *The Itinerary of John Leland in or about the Years 1535–1543.* Vol. 5 (Part IX). London, G. Bell and Sons.

SPARLING, J.H. 1962. Occurrence of *Schoenus nigricans* L. in the blanket bogs of western Ireland and northwest Scotland. *Nature, 195*, 723–724.

SPARLING, J.H. 1967a. The occurrence of *Schoenus nigricans* L. in blanket bogs. I. Environmental conditions affecting the growth of *S. nigricans* in blanket bog. *Journal of Ecology, 55*, 1–13.

SPARLING, J.H. 1967b. The occurrence of *Schoenus nigricans* L. in blanket bogs. II. Experiments on the growth of *S. nigricans* under controlled conditions. *Journal of Ecology, 55*, 15–31.

SPARLING, J.H. 1968. Biological flora of the British Isles. *Schoenus nigricans* L. *Journal of Ecology, 56*, 883–899.

SPENCE, D.H.N. 1974. Subarctic debris and scrub vegetation of Shetland. *In: The Natural Environment of Shetland*, ed. by R. Goodier, 73–88. Edinburgh, Nature Conservancy Council.

SPIRIT, M.G., comp. [1987]. *Freshwater Invertebrates of Caithness.* Wick, Caithness and Sutherland District Councils Community Programmes Agency.

STACH *et al.* 1975. *Coal Petrology.* Berlin, Gebruder Borntraeger.

STEINER, G.M. 1984. *Österreichischer Moorschutzkatalog.* [*Austrian Mire Conservation Catalogue*]. Vienna, Verlag BMGU.

STEWART, A.J.A. 1980. *The environmental impacts of moor gripping.* London, Nature Conservancy Council (CST Report No. 296).

STEWART, A.J.A., & LANCE, A.N. 1983. Moor-draining: a review of impacts on land use. *Journal of Environmental Management, 17*, 81–99.

STONER, J.H., GEE, A.S., & WADE, K.R. 1984. The effects of acidification on the ecology of streams in the upper Tywi catchment in west Wales. *Environmental Pollution (Series A), 35*, 125–157.

STONER, J.H., & GEE, A.S. 1985. Effects of forestry on water quality and fish in Welsh rivers and lakes. *Institution of Water Engineers. Journal, 39*, 27–45.

STROUD, A.D., REED, T.M., PIENKOWSKI, M.W., & LINDSAY, R.A. 1987. *Birds, Bogs and Forestry.* Peterborough, Nature Conservancy Council.

SUCCOW, M. 1974. Vorschlag einer systematischen Neugliederung der mineralbodenwasser-beeinflussten wachsenden Moorvegetation Mitteleuropas unter Ausklammerung des Gebirgsraumes. *Feddes Repertorium, 85*, 57–113.

SUCCOW, M. 1980. Die Moortypen der DDR und ihre Bewertung für die Humuswirtschaft. *Zeitschrift für Angewandte Geologie, 26*, 193–203.

SUCCOW, M., & LANGE, E. 1984. The mire types of the German Democratic Republic. *In: European Mires*, ed. by P.D. Moore, 149–176. London, Academic Press.

TALLIS, J.H. 1964a. Studies on southern Pennine peats. I. The general pollen record. *Journal of Ecology, 52*, 323–331.

TALLIS, J.H. 1964b. Studies on southern Pennine peats. II. The pattern of erosion. *Journal of Ecology, 52*, 333–344.

TALLIS, J.H. 1964c. Studies on southern Pennine peats. III. The behaviour of *Sphagnum. Journal of Ecology, 52*, 345–353.

TALLIS, J.H. 1975. Tree remains in southern Pennine peats. *Nature, 256*, 482–484.

TALLIS, J.H. 1981. Causes of erosion, a working hypothesis. *In: Peak District Moorland Erosion Study. Phase 1 Report*, ed. by J. Phillips, D. Yalden and J. Tallis, 224–234. Bakewell, Peak Park Joint Planning Board.

TANSLEY, A.G. 1939. *The British Islands and their Vegetation.* London, Cambridge University Press.

TAYLOR, J.A. 1983. The peatlands of Great Britain and Ireland. *In: Mires: Swamp, Bog, Fen and Moor. Regional Studies*, ed. by A.J.P. Gore, 1–46. Amsterdam, Elsevier Scientific (Ecosystems of the World 4B).

THOMPSON, K. 1980. Peat and peatlands: structure, functioning and classification. *In: Soil Groups of New Zealand. Part 4. Organic Soils*, ed. by F.C.C.H. van der Elst and D.I. Kinloch, 7–16. New Zealand Society of Soil Science.

THOMPSON, K., & HAMILTON, A.C. 1983. Peatlands and swamps of the African continent. *In: Mires: Swamp, Bog, Fen and Moor. Regional Studies*, ed. by A.J.P. Gore, 331–373. Amsterdam, Elsevier Scientific (Ecosystems of the World 4B).

TOLONEN, K., PAIRANEN, J., & KURKI, M. 1982. Classification and some physical and chemical characteristics of peat soils. *In: Peatlands and their Utilization in Finland*, ed. by J. Laine, 29–41. Helsinki, Finnish Peatland Society.

TOLPA, S., JASNOWSKI, M., & DALCZYNSKI, A. 1967. System der genetischen Klassifizierung des Torfes Mitteleuropas. *Zeszyty Problemowe*

Postępow Nauk Rolniczych, 76, 9–99.

TOMLINSON, G.H., BROUZES, R.J.P., McLEAN, R.A.N., & KADLECEK, J. 1980. The role of clouds in atmospheric transport of mercury and other pollutants. *In: Ecological Impact of Acid Precipitation*, ed. by D. Drablos and A. Tollan, 134–137. Oslo, SNSF.

TROLL, C. 1944. Strukturboden, Solifluktion und Frostklimate der Erde. *Geologische Rundschau, 34*, 617–679.

TUBRIDY, M. 1984. *Creation and Management of a Heritage Zone at Clonmachnoise, Co. Offaly, Ireland.* Final Report (EEC Contract No. 6611/12). Dublin, Trinity College.

TUHKAMEN, S. 1987. The phytogeographical position of the Faeroe Islands and their ecoclimatic correspondences on other continents: problems associated with highly oceanic areas. *Annales Botanici Fennici, 24*, 111–135.

UNITED KINGDOM REVIEW GROUP ON ACID RAIN. 1987. *Acid Deposition in the United Kingdom 1981–1985.* Stevenage, Warren Spring Laboratory.

von POST, L., & GRANLUND, E. 1926. Södra Sveriges torvtillgångar. I. *Sveriges Geologiska Undersökning, C, 335*, 1–127.

WACE, N. 1960. The botany of the southern oceanic islands. *Royal Society. Proceedings, B, 152*, 475–491.

WACE, N. 1961. The vegetation of Gough Island. *Ecological Monographs, 31*, 337–367.

WALKER, D. 1961. Peat stratigraphy and bog regeneration. *Linnean Society of London. Proceedings, 172*, 29–33.

WALTERS, H., & LEITH, H. 1960. *Klimadiagramm-Weltatlas.* [*World Atlas of Climate Diagrams*]. Jena.

WARREN SPRING LABORATORY. 1987. *United Kingdom Acid Rain Monitoring. Results for 1986.* Stevenage.

WEIN, R.W. 1983. Fire behaviour and ecological effects in organic terrain. *In: The Role of Fire in Northern Circumpolar Ecosystems*, ed. by R.W. Wein and D.A. MacLean, 81–95. Chichester, Wiley.

WEIN, R.W., & MacLEAN, D.A., eds. 1983. *The Role of Fire in Northern Circumpolar Ecosystems.* Chichester, Wiley, on behalf of Scientific Committee on Problems of the Environment (SCOPE) of International Council of Scientific Unions (ICSU).

WELLS, D.E., & ZOLTAI, S. 1985. Canadian system of wetland classification and its application to circumboreal wetlands. *Aquilo, Seria Botanica, 21*, 45–52.

WELLS, S.M., PYLE, R.M., & COLLINS, N.M., eds.

1983. *The IUCN Invertebrate Red Data Book.* Gland, Switzerland, International Union for Conservation of Nature and Natural Resources.

WELSH WATER AUTHORITY. 1987. Afforestation in areas sensitive to acidification. Unpublished interim guidelines.

WHEELER, B.D. 1980a. Plant communities of rich-fen systems in England and Wales. I. Introduction – Tall sedge and reed communities. *Journal of Ecology, 68*, 365–395.

WHEELER, B.D. 1980b. Plant communities of rich-fen systems in England and Wales. II. Communities of calcareous mires. *Journal of Ecology, 68*, 405–420.

WHEELER, B.D. 1980c. Plant communities of rich-fen systems in England and Wales. III. Fen meadow, fen grassland and fen woodland communities, and contact communities. *Journal of Ecology, 68*, 761–788.

WHEELER, B.D. 1984. British fens – A review. *In: European Mires*, ed. by P.D. Moore, 237–281. London, Academic Press.

WICKMAN, F.E. 1951. The maximum height of raised bogs and a note on the motion of water in soligenous mires. *Geoligiska Föreningens i Stockholm Förhandlingar, 73*, 413–422.

WILLIAMS, C.T., DAVIS, B.N.K., MARRS, R.H., & OSBORN, D. 1987. *Impact of pesticide drift.* Huntingdon, Institute of Terrestrial Ecology, Monks Wood Experimental Station (contract report to NCC; ITE Project 1078).

WILSON, H., & WOMERSLEY, L. 1975. *Caithness County Structure Plan: Report of Survey.* Thurso, Caithness County Council.

WOIKE, M., & SCHMATZLER, E. 1980. *Moore. Bedeutung – Schutz – Regeneration.* Bonn, Deutscher Naturschutzring.

WOODIN, S.J. 1986. Ecophysiological effects of atmospheric nitrogen deposition on ombrotrophic *Sphagnum* species. PhD thesis, University of Manchester.

YALDEN, D. 1981. Sheep and moorland vegetation – a literature review. *In: Peak District Moorland Erosion Study. Phase 1 Report*, ed. by J. Phillips, D. Yalden and J. Tallis, 132–141. Bakewell, Peak Park Joint Planning Board.

YOUNG, M., & WILLIAMS, J. 1983. The status and conservation of the freshwater pearl mussel *Margaritifera margaritifera* (Linn.) in Great Britain. *Biological Conservation, 25*, 35–52.

ZOLTAI, S.C., & POLLETT, F.C. 1983. Wetlands in Canada: their classification, distribution and use. *In: Mires: Swamp, Bog, Fen and Moor. Regional Studies*, ed. by A.J.P. Gore, 245–268. Amsterdam, Elsevier Scientific (Ecosystems of the World 4B).